# AN INTRODUCTION

TO THE

# *PHILOSOPHY OF RELIGION.*

# AN INTRODUCTION

TO THE

# *PHILOSOPHY OF RELIGION.*

*JOHN CAIRD, D.D.*

GYAN

*Published by*

GYAN

Gyan Publishing House
5, Ansari Road
Daryaganj, New Delhi-110002
Phone: 011-47034999, 9811692060
E-mail: books@gyanbooks.com

*Distribution Network*
gyanbooks.com
India, USA, Canada, UK, Australia, France



ISBN: 978-81-212-8971-9 (PB)
First Published, 1880

2nd Impression 2023

*Printed at:* Gyan Press, Delhi.



**AN INTRODUCTION TO THE *PHILOSOPHY OF RELIGION***

AUTHOR: JOHN CAIRD

# AN INTRODUCTION TO

# THE PHILOSOPHY OF RELIGION

Being the Croall Lecture for 1878-79.

# AN INTRODUCTION

TO THE

# PHILOSOPHY OF RELIGION.

BY

JOHN CAIRD, D.D.,

PRINCIPAL AND VICE-CHANCELLOR OF THE UNIVERSITY OF GLASGOW,
AND ONE OF HER MAJESTY'S CHAPLAINS FOR SCOTLAND.

*Negligentia mihi videtur, si postquam confirmati sumus in fide, non studemus quod credimus intelligere.*—ANSELM.

GLASGOW:
JAMES MACLEHOSE, ST. VINCENT STREET,
Publisher to the University.
1880.

# PREFATORY NOTE.

The substance of this book was delivered in Edinburgh as the "Croall Lecture" for 1878-9. The author has not, however, deemed it necessary to retain in the following pages the form of lectures—a form which he has found to give rise to arbitrary divisions and interruptions of the continuity of thought.

In addition to the works referred to in the footnotes, the author desires to express his obligations to the following books:—Baur's *Christliche Gnosis* and *Dogmengeschichte*; Pfleiderer's *Die Religion* and *Religionsphilosophie*; Vera's Preliminary Dissertations to the French Translation of Hegel's *Philosophie der Religion*; Vatke's *Die Menschliche Freiheit*; Wallace's *Logic of Hegel*; Bradley's *Ethical Studies*; Muir's *Sanskrit Texts*; Prof. Max Müller's *Introduction to the Science of Religion* and other works; and, above all, Hegel's *Philosophie der Religion*, a work to which he has been more largely indebted than to any other book.

University of Glasgow,
*April*, 1880.

# CONTENTS.

## PRELIMINARY REMARKS.



## CHAPTER I.

### OBJECTIONS TO THE SCIENTIFIC TREATMENT OF RELIGION: FIRST OBJECTION, FROM THE RELATIVE CHARACTER OF HUMAN KNOWLEDGE.



## CHAPTER II.

### SECOND OBJECTION, FROM THE IMMEDIATE OR INTUITIVE NATURE OF RELIGIOUS KNOWLEDGE.

## CHAPTER VI.

### THE RELIGIOUS CONSCIOUSNESS.



## CHAPTER VII.

### INADEQUACY OF RELIGIOUS KNOWLEDGE IN THE UNSCIENTIFIC FORM.



## CHAPTER VIII.

### TRANSITION TO SPECULATIVE IDEA OF RELIGION.

# INTRODUCTION TO

# THE PHILOSOPHY OF RELIGION.

## PRELIMINARY.

A PHILOSOPHY of Religion starts with the presupposition that religion and religious ideas can be taken out of the domain of feeling or practical experience and made objects of scientific reflection. It implies that, whilst religion and philosophy have the same objects, the attitude of the human spirit towards these objects is, in each case, different. In the one they are present to it in an immediate way as objects of devotion or spiritual enjoyment; they come before it at most only in the form of outward fact or of figurative representation. In the other, they become the objects of reflection or intellectual apprehension, and are finally elevated to the form of pure or speculative thought. Feeling, indeed, in all cases, involves a kind of knowledge; the objects of emotion, whether moral or aesthetic or religious, must be grasped by the subject of them with an implicit intelligence, apart from which, its relation to them would be no deeper than that of blind instinct or animal impulse. But the knowledge which is involved in feeling, is as yet, only implicit or virtual knowledge; it must become something more and higher before it truly deserves the name. And that something higher philosophy claims as its prerogative to elicit. In philosophy we pass out of the sphere of immediacy, in which the mind is still, in a sense, one with its object, in which subject and object are dissolved in an atmosphere of intuitive emotion. Abandoning the blessedness of simple faith, we enter into that colder yet loftier region in which reason opposes itself to its object, breaks up the natural harmony wherein no contradiction of thought has yet betrayed itself, and advances to the search after a deeper and indissoluble unity. Nor, in asserting this as its prerogative, does philosophy admit of any limits to the range of its activity. Whatever is real is rational, and with all that is rational philosophy claims to deal. It does not confine itself to finite things, or content itself with observing and classifying physical phenomena, or with empirical generalisations as to the nature and life of man. Its vocation is to trace the presence and the organic movement or process of reason in nature, in the human mind, in all social institutions, in the history of nations, and in the progressive advancement of the world. In other words, so far from resting in what is finite and relative, the peculiar domain of philosophy is absolute truth. It offers to thought an escape from the narrow limits of our own individuality, even of our own nationality and age, and an insight into that which is universally and objectively true. In all provinces of investigation it seeks as its peculiar employment to penetrate beneath the surface show of things, beneath empirical appearances and accidents, and to find the ultimate meaning and essence. Its aim is to discover, not what seems, but what is, and why it is; to bind together objects and events in the links of necessary thought, and to find their last ground and reason in that which comprehends and transcends all—the nature of God Himself.

According to this view, then, there is no province of human experience, there is nothing in the whole realm of reality, which lies beyond the domain of philosophy, or to which philosophical investigation does not extend. Religion, so far from forming an exception to the all-embracing sphere of philosophy, is rather just that province which lies nearest to it, for, in one point of view, religion and philosophy have common objects and a common content, and in the explanation of religion philosophy may be said to be at the same time explaining itself.

But can this high claim of philosophy be justified? Before we yield ourselves up to its guidance, must not philosophy be asked to prove that there is nothing presumptuous in this assertion of its universal authority? Before we admit the pretensions of reason to treat thus of all things in heaven and earth, to regard nothing as too high or sacred to be subjected to its inquiries, must we not, as a preliminary condition, ask it to give us satisfactory proof of its capacity to deal with them? Without a prior criticism of the organ of knowledge, can we tell whether in any given case it may not be entering on forbidden ground?

It may be answered, in general, that the only way in which philosophy *can* prove its rights is by philosophising. The capacity or incapacity of reason to deal with any object or class of objects cannot be determined by a preliminary inquiry, for this, if for no other reason, that the inquiry could only be conducted by the faculty which is impugned. If the incapacity is asserted on external authority, it is only reason itself that can judge of that authority and pronounce on its claims. If the incapacity is attempted to be proved on rational grounds, the examination of these grounds, again, must be conducted by reason itself. In either case a second preliminary inquiry would be needed to discover whether the capacity to conduct the first is not precluded by the limits of human reason. You cannot, in short, enter on a criticism of the instrument of thought without taking for granted, at least, its adequacy for the work of self-criticism. But this presupposition is really the abandonment of the whole question at issue. For not only might it be said that the criticism of mind and its capacities is itself the most difficult and subtle task to which thought can be set, and that the instrument which is presumed to be capable of that task needs no further proof of its capacity for any other; but it must be added that the examination of mind, regarded as an instrument or organ of thought, cannot really be dissociated from the work of thought itself. To examine thought is at the same time to examine the things it thinks. To follow out that examination fully is simply to enter on the whole range of philosophical research, and to investigate the capacity of thought to deal with any class of objects is to furnish the most complete justification of its claims, viz., by thinking them.

Whilst, however, the foregoing considerations may be offered as a general answer to the demand for a proof of the competency of reason to deal with any province of truth prior to its actual entrance on the work of investigation, there are various special grounds on which its competency in the particular province of religion has been questioned. A scientific treatment of religious ideas, a philosophy of God and divine things, is, according to one school of thinkers, precluded by the very nature of human knowledge, which, as essentially relative and finite, can never attain to the cognisance of that which is infinite and absolute. By others, it has been maintained with more or less precision of thought, that, though human intelligence is not precluded by its necessary conditions from all access to the sphere of infinite or absolute realities, yet the only knowledge which is here possible to it is intuitive and immediate, not ratiocinative. The organ of religious knowledge, it is held, is not reason, but simply feeling or faith, or immediate and unreasoning apprehension: with finite objects and relations it is the province of the human understanding to deal, but religious truth, because of its very loftiness and grandeur, escapes the grasp of logic, is not reducible to definite notions or doctrines, or capable of being elaborated into a reasoned system or body of truth. Lastly—to name no other class of objections—the claim of philosophy to deal with religious knowledge has been resisted on the ground that religious truth differs from all other kinds of truth in this, that it has been authoritatively revealed, and an authoritative revelation implies the incompetence of human reason either to discover or to criticise its content. It is obvious that if any of these views is tenable—if religious truth is either altogether beyond the scope of human intelligence, or attainable only by intuition and not by rational insight, or, lastly, forms the content of a fixed supernatural revelation — the construction of a Philosophy of Religion, in any right sense of the words, is an impossible task. It is necessary, therefore, before proceeding further, to examine in detail the objections which thus meet us on the threshold of our undertaking.

# CHAPTER I.

## EXAMINATION OF OBJECTIONS TO THE SCIENTIFIC TREATMENT OF RELIGION:—THE RELATIVITY OF HUMAN KNOWLEDGE.

BETWIXT that knowledge which can properly be termed science, and religion a distinction in recent times has been drawn by certain acute thinkers which, if valid, would be fatal to the claim of theology or of a philosophy of a religion to be ranked among the sciences. Science, it is said, deals with nature, religion with the supernatural. But can we know anything of the supernatural, or anything, at most, beyond the bare fact that it is? Is the supernatural accessible to human intelligence in such wise that you can build up, by the rigorous processes and methods with which in our physical investigations we work, a science that can claim co-ordinate rank with astronomy, or chemistry, or biology? The answer which has been given is, No! we deny the possibility of a science of the supernatural. The fact and importance of the religious sentiment we admit. All history and our own experience tell us that there are irrepressible instincts which point to something above the domain of nature—to a realm of mystery which transcends the finite and phenomenal world. When we have done our best in the field of human knowledge, in the observation and generalisation of facts and phenomena, we know that there lies beyond, a vast, unsearchable region out of which all phenomena spring, and we recognise in this the proper sphere of the religious sentiment, of those feelings of reverence, awe, submission which are awakened in every rightly constituted mind in the presence of the unknown and inscrutable. But when you try to go further than this—to find in this region available data of knowledge,—both experience and reason pronounce the attempt to be futile. And when theologians or philosophers present us with a series of definitions, notions, detailed propositions and dogmas with reference to this world of mystery, in which the existence, personality, and interior nature of the Absolute, and its relations to the finite world, are laid down with a show of systematic precision, and we are asked to accept this pseudo-science as entitled to rank as knowledge beside the sciences of observation and experience, we cannot admit the claim. "Natural theology," says one eminent scientific authority, "is a science falsely so called. . . . It seeks to weigh the infinite in the balance of the finite. . . . . It is to the scientific man a delusion, to the religious man a snare." "If," writes another, "religion and science are to be reconciled, the basis of reconciliation must be this deepest, widest, and most certain of all facts—that the power the universe manifests to us is utterly inscrutable."[1] "We not only learn by the frustration of all our efforts that the reality underlying appearance is totally and for ever inconceivable by us; but we also learn why from the very nature of our intelligence it must be so."[2] "The office of theology," a third writer declares, "is now generally recognised as distinct from that of science. . . . It confesses its inability to furnish knowledge with any available data. It restricts itself to the region of faith, and leaves to philosophy and science the region of inquiry."[3]

Now, there is much in this view of the distinctive provinces of science and religion which we may, without giving up anything worth contending for, be ready to admit. If it means merely that the science of religion is not of the same order, dealing with the same class of objects, and reaching its results by the same method, as the physical sciences, in other words, that it is not an inductive science, this may readily be conceded. For it means no more than this, that the objects of religious know-

[1] Herbert Spencer's *First Principles*, p. 46. [2] *Ibid.*, p. 98.
[3] Lewes' *Hist. of Phil.*, i., p. 17.

ledge cannot be perceived by the senses, or generalised out of the facts and phenomena which sense perceives. It means that God cannot be seen or touched or handled, and that by no mere generalisation from the finite could you ever reach the infinite. But if the implied assertion be that human knowledge is absolutely limited to things finite and phenomenal, that thought cannot transcend the objects which exist in space and time, and take cognisance of that which eye hath not seen, nor ear heard, nor imagination in its highest constructive efforts can conceive, and that theology and speculative philosophy, in so far as they pretend to the possession of such knowledge, are fictitious and spurious sciences, this is a view which cannot, without a surrender of the most cherished convictions, be accepted. It may be that the labour of countless thinkers in this province of inquiry has all been labour in vain, that the intellectual instincts which age after age have attracted the highest minds to it, have been mere illusion, and that the results they seem to have reached are altogether deceptive and worthless; but if this be so, the very extent and persistency of the delusion demand the most careful scrutiny of the arguments of those who claim to have exposed it.

The view to which I have now referred—the limitation of science to things finite, and the impossibility of any such science as theology or philosophy of religion—is one which, held perhaps in a vague and uncritical way by many, has received its fullest and ablest exposition in the writings of Mr. Herbert Spencer; and to his treatment of the subject, resuming as it does, the arguments of previous writers, and re-stating them with much freshness of thought and fertility of illustration, I shall in what follows, confine myself. His thesis is, that the provinces of Science and Religion are distinguished from each other as the known from the unknown and unknowable. Science deals with ascertained phenomena, their order and relations, and comprehends all knowledge that is definite and positive. But positive knowledge does not and cannot embrace the whole possibilities of existence. Every addition to the gradually increasing sphere of science does but bring it into wider contact with the sphere of nescience, with the unknown and unknowable background in which lies the origin and explanation of all things, the unascertained something which phenomena imply but do not reveal. Now this dark impenetrable background beyond experience is the province of religion. But the attitude of mind which alone is possible with respect to this, is, not intelligence, but simply silent reverence for the unknowable; and this Mr. Spencer maintains is the common essence of all religions, and that which gives to religion the widest and purest sphere of action. The more completely our notion of the unknown reality is purified from earthly analogies, from anthropomorphic conceptions and images—the more, in short, we approximate to the state of simple awe before the altar of the Unknown and Unknowable, the nearer do we come to the perfect ideal of religion.

The grounds on which this thesis is maintained are twofold. Human intelligence can be proved to be incapable of any absolute knowledge (1) empirically, by pointing out that every attempt to press our knowledge beyond certain limits, every ultimate conception, religious or scientific which we try to frame, gives rise to "alternative impossibilities of thought": (2) rationally, by an examination of the nature of human intelligence, which issues in a demonstration of the relativity of all human knowledge. The empirical or inductive proof, however, when closely examined, turns on the same principle with, and is resolvable into, the deductive. I shall therefore treat mainly of the latter.

Mr. Spencer here adopts and carries to its logical results that doctrine of the relativity of human knowledge which, derived as it is supposed, from Kant, has been reproduced in this country with special application to theology, by Sir W. Hamilton and Mr. Mansel. It is, in substance, this: that inasmuch as to think is to 'condition,' to think or know the 'unconditioned,' or the infinite and absolute, would be simply to think the unthinkable. 'Infinite' and 'Absolute' are merely terms expressive of the negation of the conditions under which thought is possible. Take the first of these terms: The very nature of thought implies distinction and therefore limitation. A thing can only be thought by being distinguished from other things, defined as possessing what others lack, lacking what others possess. But the Infinite cannot be thus limited, and is therefore unthinkable. "A consciousness of the Infinite necessarily involves a self-contradiction; for it implies the recognition by limitation and difference of that which can only be given as unlimited and indifferent." Take the other term, the Absolute, and the same incompetency of thought will be seen to apply to it: for thought is possible only as the relation of the thing thought of to the thinker, and an object of thought can only be known or enter into consciousness in relation to the thinking subject. All human knowledge therefore is necessarily relative. Things in themselves, or the Absolute, or God as He is in Himself, we can never know. "The conception of the Absolute thus implies at the same time the presence and absence of the relation by which thought is constituted." A science of nature, of man, of all that this finite world contains, we may have; but a science of God and things divine is nothing less than a contradiction in terms.

With this proof of the inherent incapacity of human intelligence to know the Absolute, Mr.

Spencer, however, with what consistency we shall see in the sequel, attempts to combine the assertion that we are constrained to believe in the existence of the Absolute, and that we can, in a vague manner, not amounting to positive thought, have a certain 'consciousness' of it. "Though the Absolute," he says, "cannot in any manner or degree be known in the strict sense of knowing, yet we find that its positive existence is a necessary datum of consciousness, and that so long as consciousness continues, we cannot for an instant rid it of this datum."[1] "Reality, though not capable of being made a thought, properly so called, because not capable of being brought within limits, nevertheless remains as a consciousness that is *positive*, is not rendered negative by the negation of limits."[2]

On the foregoing argument I offer the following observations:—

1. The two elements of the theory are irreconcilable. It is impossible to hold at once that human intelligence is limited to the finite, and that it is cognisant of an existence beyond the finite; or, otherwise expressed, that all knowledge is relative, and yet that we know the *existence* of the Absolute.

It is indeed easy to understand the genesis of this theory—the logical necessity which forced the mind of its author to the combination of two elements which, when closely examined, are seen to be contra-

[1] *First Principles*, p. 29. [2] *Essays*, vol. iii., p. 273.

dictory. The assertion that man's knowledge is limited to the finite and relative would have no meaning save by a tacit reference to an infinite and absolute object to which his knowledge does not extend. When we say that a thing is only a phenomenon or appearance, a quality or attribute, we of course imply that there is something which is not mere appearance but reality, not a mere quality but a substance, with whose deeper nature we place the former in contrast. In order to pronounce that we know only phenomena we must needs be aware that there is something other than phenomena, we must know at least of the existence of things in themselves, realities lying behind phenomena, from the knowledge of which, in the full sense of the word, our intelligence is debarred. If we knew no other than finite and phenomenal existences, then we should never know or be able to characterise them *as* finite and phenomenal. To pronounce, in short, that our knowledge is, in any sense, limited, we must have access to some standard to which that limited knowledge is referred, we must be aware, at least, of the existence of a something beyond the limit, which is to our intelligence inaccessible.

But whilst the two elements—consciousness of the limits of human intelligence, and consciousness of that which transcends those limits—are correlative and inseparable, it is impossible, save by a *tour de force*, for a theorist who holds that human knowledge can never transcend the finite, to bring these two elements together. If we start with the assertion that thought is by its necessary conditions subjective and finite, or, on the other hand, that the Absolute is only another name for that which is out of relation to thought, we cannot, save by an act of violence, drag in a consciousness, in any sense, of the Absolute in order to meet the exigencies of our theory. We cannot, in other words, deny all consciousness of the Absolute in order to maintain that human knowledge is limited, and in the same breath assert a consciousness of the Absolute in order to justify our cognisance of that limitation. In so far as the lower animals are devoid of reason, they are unconscious of their irrationality, and it is only *we*, in virtue of our rational, intelligent nature, who can discern their lack of it. So, it might be possible for another and higher intelligence, an observer of human nature possessed of absolute knowledge, to pronounce that man's knowledge is purely relative, that there is a region of realities from which human thought is shut out, but it is not possible for one and the same consciousness to be purely relative and conscious of its relativity. Grant the fundamental assumption of the theorist, and it follows that humanity is not only hopelessly ignorant of reality, but also absolutely unconscious of its ignorance.[1]

2. The proper conclusion from the doctrine of

[1] *V.* note *infra*, p. 32.

relativity as held by Mr. Spencer and kindred writers, is, not that the Absolute is unknowable, but that no such being exists, or, what comes to the same thing, that the assertion of its existence is meaningless. It is true that neither in the speculations of Mr. Spencer nor in those of the school from which he derives his doctrine that human knowledge is only relative and finite, is that doctrine set forth as subversive of religion, or as depriving religion of any place or function in the spiritual life of man. On the contrary, the avowed aim of Sir W. Hamilton and his theological interpreter, Mr. Mansel, was, by demonstrating the natural and essential weakness of human intelligence, to lend new and exclusive authority to a supernatural revelation, and to supersede reason by faith, as the sole organ of religious knowledge. In Mr. Spencer the doctrine of relativity, though carried out to the evaporation of all definite conceptions of God and divine things, leaves still a field for the exercise of the religious aspirations in the region of "the unknown and unknowable," and in the belief in the existence of an Absolute whose nature is for ever incomprehensible.

But the doctrine of relativity common to both classes of theorists leaves no room even for that shadowy and ineffable object of reverence which is Mr. Spencer's substitute for God, much less for the communication by supernatural interposition of that knowledge of spiritual realities for which human intelligence is essentially incompetent. For, as to the latter view, it is to be remarked that if the disability ascribed to human intelligence were merely that which, according to the theological doctrine of depravity, affects the human spirit as in a fallen, diseased, abnormal condition, in that case it is quite conceivable that a supernatural agency might restore the capacity of receiving and apprehending the knowledge of God. But the disability or incapacity in question is not of the nature of a remediable weakness affecting human intelligence, it is a disability which belongs to human intelligence as such. If thought is, by its very nature, imprisoned in the relative, supernatural aid can no more communicate to it a knowledge of the Absolute, than it can convey ideas of colour to a man born blind. Not even a revelation from heaven can introduce into the finite mind a kind of knowledge which, without ceasing to be finite, it cannot attain. If again, with Mr. Spencer, we reduce the content of religious thought to a bare consciousness of the *existence* of the unknowable Absolute, it is obvious that his fundamental theory of intelligence is destructive even of this evanescent residuum of religious knowledge. If relativity is the necessary and inalienable condition of thought, it must apply to the thought of Being or existence as much as to any other. If nothing absolute can enter into consciousness, but the very act of thinking a thing reduces it to the relative, that which we think of as *existence* is not absolute, but only relative or subjective existence. The being we ascribe in thought to the Absolute is not absolute being, but being in relation to consciousness. It is impossible, with reference to this notion, to transcend that subjectivity which pertains to *all* notions, or by thinking to reach, in the case of being, that reality which is beyond all phenomenal thought. But then this is equivalent to saying that we cannot predicate reality even of the existence of the Absolute, or that we do not and cannot know that the Absolute exists. That which stands for God in this theory, the unknowable Absolute, is simply the negation of thought, that from which every predicate, even that of being, falls away. It is in other words the non-existent, the negation of thought, and therefore of being also, in any sense in which we can use the expression.

3. The principle on which, in this theory, the unknowableness of the Absolute rests, is, when closely examined, nothing more than a false abstraction. It first creates or conjures up a fictitious logical entity, and then charges consciousness with imbecility because of its inability to think that fiction. The theorist begins by conceiving of an absolute reality, unconditioned, unqualified, existing in and for itself independently of any mind to know it; and then

he proceeds to conceive of that object, thus presumed to be outside of thought, as causing or awakening certain impressions or ideas in the knowing subject. The latter—the reality as it is in or for the subjective consciousness—is, therefore, something different from the former, the thought of the thing from the thing in itself. It has lost its absoluteness by descending into thought, it has become coloured or conditioned by the consciousness that contemplates it. Inasmuch, therefore, as in consciousness, the object is not the pure independent object, but only the object as it is for a subject, in itself it must remain for ever unknown.

But is not the notion which constitutes the basis or starting point of this demonstration a purely illusory one, and does not the demonstration consist in first creating a fictitious and impossible object, and then pronouncing the mind's incapacity to think it an inherent disability? What is the Absolute behind thought which the theorist first sets himself to conceive, and what is that modification or degradation from reality which it undergoes by entering into thought? Is there any reality, or is it possible for intelligence so to escape from itself as to imagine or conceive of such a thing as a reality which is not a thinkable, intelligible reality —a reality which has not its inseparable correlate in an intelligence that thinks it? When we examine the relation of thought to reality, of subject to object, of knowing to being, we shall find that the unity expressed by these correlatives is one which is absolutely indissoluble, and that though by an effort of abstraction we can distinguish, yet we can never divide or isolate, the one from the other. We can distinguish the centre of a circle from the circumference, the north from the south pole of a magnet, the one end of a stick from the other; but by no effort of abstraction can we, in any of these cases, think one of the correlatives as an object existing by itself in absolute isolation from the other—conceive, *i.e.*, of a centre existing in pure individuality without relation to a circumference, of a north pole which has in it no implication of a south, of a stick with only one end. Nor is it any limitation or disability of finite intelligence which makes this feat an impossible one, but simply its incapacity to give independent reality to an abstraction. In like manner, the endeavour to conceive of an absolute being or reality existing apart by itself and having no relation to thought is the quest after a chimera. The words 'objectivity,' 'object,' carry with them as their inseparable correlatives 'subjectivity,' 'subject,' and to ask us to conceive of an object which is out of relation to a subject, is to ask us to conceive of that which is given only *in* relation as existing *out of* relation—of that which has no meaning save in and for consciousness, as existing outside of consciousness. To be incapable of performing such a feat is no more a proof of the limitation of intelligence than to be incapable of conceiving a half which is out of all relation to another half, or an outside which carries with it no implication of an inside. It is only by a fictitious abstraction that we suppose ourselves to transcend the unity of knowing and being, and to conceive or imagine a being which exists absolutely, apart from all knowing, or which is absolutely unknowable. What remains when we segregate being from knowing, reality from thought, is not an unknowable something, but utter non-entity.

The illusory notion of a reality existing beyond consciousness is perhaps due in some measure to the obvious truth that there *are* innumerable realities which exist beyond the knowledge or consciousness of the individual. The affirmation that all reality is relative to thought is by the unreflecting mind confused with the obviously absurd assertion that the world exists only as we think it, that it is our poor thought that creates and uncreates the world. But it is one thing to say that no reality exists prior to my individual thought of it, and another thing to say that thought or intelligence is presupposed in all objective reality. To deny the former assertion is only to maintain that the existence of the individual is contingent and limited in time, and that its knowledge is partial; but to deny the latter is to subvert the fundamental basis of all knowledge and to reduce the intelligible world to chaos. Nothing can have any reality for us save as it is capable of entering into thought or is, in itself, thinkable reality; but the thought which is in nature and in man, in all things and beings, is not a thought which we create but which we find in them, not a system of relations which our minds can make or unmake, but which we discern or discover —a rationality which is independent of us but to which our reason responds. All science starts with the tacit presupposition that nature is intelligible, that there is reason or thought in things; and its progress is only the ever-advancing discovery of laws, of rational relations, of a coherent, self-consistent system, in the objects and events of the material world. The history of science is the history of mind or intelligence finding itself in nature. And the same principle applies to the higher investigations which deal with man and the social and moral relations of the spiritual world. Here, too, the presupposition which constitutes the stimulus and the final cause of inquiry is that the world of mind is an intelligible world, that thought or reason will find itself—elicit the hidden presence of rational relations, of an objective reason—in the facts and events it contemplates. Nor when we rise above nature and man, above the whole finite world to that out of which all its phenomena spring, can the universal presupposition fail us. If reason is irresistibly impelled to seek, above and beyond the manifold and changeful phenomena of the world of time and sense, a permanent unity, an infinite and absolute reality that is ever manifesting and realising itself in 'all thinking things, all objects of all thought,' it cannot here, any more than at any previous stage (if it seem to do so, it is only by being untrue to itself) take up the self-contradictory and suicidal attitude of seeking by thought an object which has no relation to thought, and of discovering the final explanation of all rational relations in the irrational, the basis of all things and beings in that which is for intelligence a blank non-entity. On the contrary, we shall see more fully in the sequel that that which is at once the presupposition and the final goal of thought is not and cannot be an Absolute which is simply the negation of thought, but rather that which comprehends all finite things and thoughts only because it is itself the Unity of Thought and Being. We shall see, too, how, so far from suffering any diminution of reality by becoming relative to finite thought, this is an Absolute whose very nature it is to realise itself in the thought or self-consciousness of finite intelligence; and on the other hand how finite mind or intelligence, so far from meeting here the dark impassable limit to its activity, finds in this Absolute the highest and fullest realisation of its own freedom and life.

4. The worship of the Unknowable is really an impossible attitude of mind. The feelings of awe, reverence, humility, which are supposed to be called forth by the contemplation of that which lies beyond the limits of consciousness, are not legitimately due to such an object.

At first sight it looks like a kind of intellectual paradox, that men whose whole life is a life of thought should select as the supreme object of reverence that which is the negation of thought—that those who are distinguished for the genuine and enlightened zeal with which they devote themselves to the service of truth should suppose themselves capable of revering a divinity which is neither more nor less than the apotheosis of ignorance. But perhaps it is not difficult, on close inspection, to detect the source of this misdirected homage. The emotions called forth by the mysterious and inscrutable have a certain superficial resemblance to religious feeling. It is where science and definite thought end that imagination finds scope for its peculiar activity, and in its negative attitude towards the finite it may easily mistake the indefinite for the infinite. There is a sense in which all intense feeling transcends the limits of logic, and is capable of a richness and fulness of content which baffle definition and outstrip the compass of the hard and fixed categories of the understanding. Our most exalted spiritual experiences are those which are least capable of being expressed by precise scientific formulæ, and when we attempt to express them, the language we use insensibly takes a negative form. "In such access of mind—" are the words in which a well-known writer describes that sense of the ineffable which characterises the moments of rapt poetic feeling,—

> In such access of mind, in such high hour
> Of visitation from the living God,
> Thought was not; in enjoyment it expired.
> Rapt into still communion that transcends
> The imperfect offices of prayer and praise,
> His mind was a thanksgiving to the Power
> That made him; it was blessedness and love.

And similarly, religious inspiration can only record its sense of the surpassing glory and splendour of unseen and eternal realities by describing them as things which eye hath *not* seen, nor ear heard, and which have *not* entered into the heart of man; or again when it would tell of the strange ecstasy of which, in communion with God, the devout spirit is sometimes conscious, it can only describe its experience as a "peace that passeth understanding," a "joy unspeakable and full of glory."

If therefore there is an aspect of the religious consciousness in which its attitude towards the finite seems to be a purely negative one, and the object of its aspirations can be determined only by saying that it is that which the finite *is not*, it is easy to see how, by stopping short at this point of view, a plausible basis is found for the theory of religion which regards the object of it as that of which no more can be said than that it transcends definite thought—that it is that which surpasses finite apprehension, the unknown and unknowable.

But whilst, as we shall attempt to show in the sequel, the logic of religion does contain a purely negative movement, and in the process by which thought rises to the knowledge of God, the first step may be said to be the negation of the finite; in other words, whilst it is in the perception of the vanity and nothingness of earthly and finite things, the profound sense of the evanescence and unreality of the world and the things of the world, that the beginning of all religion lies, yet this negative attitude, so far from being final, has its whole value as a step or stage towards a higher goal. From the negative infinite which is the mere negation of the finite, the vague indefinite in which thought wanders away without aim or end, the religious consciousness is constrained, as we shall see, by an inward impulse which is a necessity at once of feeling and of reason, to rise to that higher and truer Infinite which realises and reveals itself in nature and man, in all the inexhaustible riches of finite thought and being. But without anticipating the speculative analysis of the religious consciousness, it is easy to see, even at this stage of our inquiry, that no such emotions as those to which this theory lays claim can be called forth by a purely negative object. Religion, by its very nature, contains, and must ever contain, an element of mystery; but a religion *all* mystery is an absurd and impossible notion. Finite intelligence cannot be the measure of the infinite. The realm of truth is inexhaustible, and the highest human intelligence at its furthest point of progress in spiritual knowledge, must still see stretching away before it the region of the unknown, the unfathomable depths of that Being before whom the befitting attitude must ever be that of humility, of reverence, of awe and aspiration. But it is obvious that these emotions owe their existence and their strength to the fact that their object is contemplated as something more than the unknown, and that we must conceive of that in Him which lies beyond our knowledge, as, though unknown, *not* unknowable. In order to awaken humility and awe, or indeed to awaken any emotion whatever, the object must be something more than the blank negation of thought. It is because we conceive of the unknown not as "a mystery absolutely and for ever beyond our comprehension," but as containing more of what is admirable to us than we can grasp, because our intelligence is confronted by an object which is immeasurably above it in its own line, that there is awakened within us a sense of our own littleness in contrast with its greatness. In the presence even of finite excellence—of human genius and learning—we may be conscious of feelings of deep humility and silent respectful admiration ; and this, too, may be reverence for the unknown. But that which makes this reverence a possible and a wholesome feeling is that it is reverence, not for a mere blank inscrutability, but for what I can think of as an intelligence essentially the same with my own, though far excelling mine in its range and power: and the salutary humility which possesses me in the presence of such minds arises from the fact that I know and can appreciate the thing they are, and that I see in it that which dwarfs my own petty attainments. In like manner, the grandeur which surrounds the thought of the Absolute, the infinite Reality beyond the finite, can only arise from this, not that it is something utterly inconceivable and unthinkable, but that it is for thought or self-consciousness the realisation of its highest ideal of spiritual excellence. The homage rendered to it is that which is felt for a Being "in whom are hid all the treasures of wisdom and knowledge," all the inexhaustible wealth of that boundless realm of truth in which thought finds ever increasing stimulus to aspiration, ever growing food for wonder and delight. Far removed is this reverence from the mere dumb wonder of ignorance or the grovelling awe of the supernatural which, as it is exhibited in the fetish-worshipper, is the nearest approximation to the religion of the unknowable. Instead of ignorant wonder we have here intelligent admiration, instead of blind submission, trust and sympathy and love, instead of the paralysis of thought before a portentous and insoluble enigma, the ennobling and ever renewed impulse to thought which arises from the assurance that the illimitable realm of truth is open to us, that "God is light and in Him is no darkness at all," and that for the human spirit it will be life eternal to know God.

## Note to page 18.

In order to meet the obvious difficulty above indicated Mr. Spencer has propounded a curious theory, by which he supposes himself to have demonstrated the possibility at once of denying the conceivability of the Absolute, and yet of having a certain undefined consciousness of its *existence.* "What," he asks, "must we say concerning that which transcends knowledge? Are we to rest wholly in the consciousness of phenomena? Is the result of inquiry to exclude utterly from our minds everything but the relative, or must we also believe in something beyond the relative?" Repudiating the logical conclusion to which, unquestionably, the reasonings of Hamilton and Mansel lead, that "as the Absolute and Infinite are merely names indicating, not an object of thought or consciousness at all, but the mere absence of the conditions under which thought is possible," and that as "reason cannot warrant us in affirming the positive existence of what is cognisable only as a negation, we cannot rationally affirm the existence of anything beyond phenomena"—he attempts to point out a qualification to the arguments of these writers, which saves us from a scepticism so complete. In the first place, he bids us "observe that every one of the arguments by which the relativity of our knowledge is demonstrated distinctly postulates the positive existence of something beyond the relative. To say that we cannot know the Absolute is, by implication, to affirm that there *is* an Absolute," and this "proves that the Absolute has been present to the mind, not as a nothing, but as a something."[1] To which the obvious answer is, No doubt it does, no doubt our conception of the finite and relative as such does imply a knowledge of the infinite and absolute; but then, the legitimate inference is, not that a belief in the existence of the Absolute is consistent with Mr. Spencer's theory, but that the theory is wrong because it precludes such a belief. A theory which asserts that our knowledge is, by the necessary conditions of all knowledge, wholly of the finite and relative,

[1] *First Principles*, p. 89.

and that the Infinite and Absolute are therefore outside of all possible thought, cannot, by any such expedient as Mr. Spencer's, escape from the illogical affirmation of a finite which has in thought no correlative Infinite, a relative which has in thought no correlative Absolute. If to think the finite and relative imply the power to think the Infinite and Absolute, both elements must be present in thought with the same reality, and our knowledge of the one must be as true and real as that of the other. There cannot be a real knowledge of the one and only a sham knowledge of the other. Knowledge of correlatives must, in all cases, be of the same kind.

But whilst we cannot have a real knowledge of the Absolute, we may, it is said, have "an indefinite consciousness of it," "a positive, though vague, consciousness of that which transcends distinct consciousness." Mr. Spencer's proof of this rests on a distinction of the Matter from the Form of our knowledge. In the case of such antithetical notions as Limited and Unlimited, Relative and Non-relative, he maintains that, though in thinking the Unlimited and Non-relative we abstract or abolish the limits or conditions which constitute the Form, we still leave behind the Matter or "raw material" of the notion. Impossible, therefore, though it is "to give to this consciousness any qualitative or quantitative expression whatever, it is not less certain that it remains with us as a positive indestructible element of thought."[1]

To this it may be answered :—

1. That to represent the Infinite or Absolute as Matter without Form, does not render it in any way "a consciousness that is positive," or give it the reality which is here ascribed to it. From the fact that we can distinguish in thought the elements or moments of a notion, it does not follow, as we have already seen, that we can ascribe to each of these elements an absolute or independent existence. You can think or be conscious of a limited, conditioned object, of matter having a definite form : does it follow that, the limits, conditions, form, being withdrawn, you can have a consciousness of something that has no limits, no conditions, of a matter that has no form whatever ? To imagine that you can is simply to mistake distinction for divided or separate existence, to confound abstractions with realities. Mr. Spencer first, in order to maintain that the Absolute is inconceivable, defines it as that which has no relation to thought ; and then, in order not to annihilate it altogether, drags it back half over the boundary of the thinkable. But he cannot thus play fast and loose with the object of thought. It must be either thinkable or unthinkable—wholly incogitable and therefore

[1] *First Principles*, p. 91.

a sheer blank or non-entity, or capable of becoming, as truly as the finite, a real and positive, though indeed inexhaustible, object of thought.

2. Partly, perhaps, the explanation of Mr. Spencer's idea that we can have a vague consciousness of that which is not an object of definite thought, lies in the confusion of the *unimaginable* with the *unthinkable*. To prove, on the one hand, that the Infinite is unthinkable, he adduces an illustration of a thing which we cannot imagine or definitely picture to the mind. We can think or form a clear conception of one inch, but not of the millions of miles that separate us from the sun, still less of boundless extension. On the other hand, to prove that the Infinite does not altogether escape our consciousness, he points out that that which imagination cannot conceive or picture to itself, thought may yet in some measure apprehend. Space, however vast, even infinite extension, is so far defined to thought that we can distinguish it from force or duration. But the answer is that the thought which is here contrasted with imagination is *not* vague or indistinct, but as distinct and apprehensible as any object of consciousness can be. We can think, in the sense of understanding what we mean, what is contained in the conception of ninety-two millions of miles, as clearly as in that of one mile, and the relation of the one to the other is perfectly definite; and the same

might be shown of the notion of extension itself. If, therefore, there is anything in the illustration, what it goes to prove is, not that the finite and relative are clearly thinkable, and that of the Infinite and Absolute we have only a "vague consciousness"; but that in the unity of thought, Infinite is as clear and positive an element of consciousness as finite, Absolute as relative.

3. It is true that when we think away all conditions, limits, definite qualities of objects, something may still be said to be left, but that something is not what Mr. Spencer designates "the raw material of definite thought which remains after the definiteness which thinking gives to it has been destroyed, something which persists in us as the body of a thought to which we can give no shape," and which he identifies with the Infinite or Absolute, the reality behind all appearances. Abstract from your notion of a thing all specific determinations, all that by which you distinguish it from other things, and there is indeed a something left which constitutes the last abstraction of thought, viz., the pure unmingled abstraction of Being. But this empty identity, this logical abstraction, is not a thing of which we have only a dim, undefined consciousness, a "reality which is not capable of being made a thought properly so called." We cannot, indeed, think of it, or into it, more than it is, or grasp it with the

fulness of thought wherewith we think more concrete objects. But take it for what it is, and we know it as thoroughly as any other object, we know all about it that there is to be known. Also, it must be added, that it is a strange perversion of thought which takes this *caput mortuum*, this logical phantom, and gives it the place of the highest reality, the object of profoundest veneration, in bowing down to which science and religion are to find their ultimate reconciliation. For, in so doing, we are simply turning away from all the concrete wealth of the world of thought and being, and deifying the barest, thinnest abstraction of logic. It is not too much to say that almost any object of reverence would be more worthy than this, and that in nature-worship, animal worship, even the lowest fetishism, there is a higher cultus than in the blind veneration of the philosophic Absolute.

## CHAPTER II.

### OBJECTIONS TO THE SCIENTIFIC TREATMENT OF RELIGION, CONTINUED:—THE IMMEDIATE OR INTUITIVE CHARACTER OF RELIGIOUS KNOWLEDGE.

THE foregoing objection to the scientific treatment of religion and religious ideas is based, as we have seen, on the principle that thought is essentially subjective and finite, and therefore incapable, unless it transcend itself, of attaining to the knowledge of that which is infinite and absolute. But not less does religion escape the grasp of philosophy when its objects, though no longer represented as absolutely incognisable, are held to be cognisable only by an organ other than reason or self-conscious intelligence. This is the doctrine maintained, under various modifications, by those who assert that our knowledge of God and divine truth is *intuitive* or *immediate*. Sometimes this doctrine meets us as the principle of a philosophical school, sometimes in the more indefinite form of popular teaching. In the former case it is the expression of a tendency familiar to the student of philosophy under the form of theories of 'Innate Ideas,' 'Philosophy of Common Sense,' 'Primary Beliefs,' 'Fundamental Principles of Cognition,' 'Intuitional Morality,' etc. In the latter, it expresses, sometimes the recoil of pious feeling from the apparent coldness and hardness of science and systematic thought, and the felt inadequacy of logical forms to embody the emotions and experiences of the religious life; sometimes the reaction of the spiritual nature from the doubts which reason seems to cast on its holiest convictions, and the instinctive clinging of faith to beliefs from which the logic of the understanding seems to be bearing it away. In all such cases alike the tendency is to seek an escape from the criticism of reason by denying its jurisdiction. Finite truth, it is felt, can be apprehended by the understanding, but the organ of communication with God and divine things is one which transcends the methods and processes of logic, brings the consciousness into immediate converse with its objects, and conveys to us an inexplicable yet absolute assurance of their reality. Not by arguments, inductive or deductive, do we attain to a belief in the existence and character of God, not in the formal definitions and dogmas of theology can we find the adequate expression of our spiritual convictions. We believe in God because we know Him, though we can neither prove nor define Him. We feel and realise spiritual truth, though in terms and propositions we cannot express it.

In some points of view this revolt of faith against reason in the province of religious belief is by no means indefensible. Though its aim is to silence reason, it is not in itself altogether irrational. I shall endeavour, therefore, in the first place, to examine a little more fully some of the sources to which this tendency to rest in intuitive and immediate knowledge may be traced; and, in the second place, to show the inadequacy of intuition or immediate knowledge as a basis of certitude in religion.

I. In general, the theory of intuition, or the assertion of a knowledge above reason, may be traced to the reaction of the religious nature from the seeming incertitude, narrowness, and inadequacy of rational thought. The attempt to prove, or find argumentative grounds for, our religious ideas, seems often to be the abandonment of a higher, in the search for a lower, kind of certitude. In the attitude of devotion, in simple faith and communion with God, the spiritual mind seems to be in immediate converse with its objects, and to have the same assurance of their reality which the ordinary consciousness has of the reality of the external world. The certainty of that which it knows is bound up with the certainty which it has of itself. It seems to know God and divine things, not by the intermediation of any process of proof, but because in its own consciousness there is a revelation of their presence which is beyond the reach of doubt. It does not ask how it comes to know God, or how it is possible for the individual mind to transcend its own limitations and attain to a knowledge of objective realities? It does not ask how it can verify their existence or justify its own conceptions of them? They are *there*, and the sense of their reality comes to it with a force of conviction which it feels no need to define or defend.

It is a grievous descent from this exalted attitude of intuitive and uncritical certitude when the critical and questioning intellect comes in to separate between consciousness and its object, and to place us in the position of external observers and reasoners. The questioning of the understanding disturbs the intensive serenity of simple faith, and that which it seeks to substitute in the form of rational knowledge is, in many ways, unsatisfactory to the religious mind. For, in the first place, reflection or ratiocination takes away the mind from the divine realities themselves, and instead of God, gives us only arguments, notions, and propositions about Him. In the second place, these notions and propositions, inasmuch as they are necessarily abstractions, rend the fair and seamless unity of truth, break up the living reality into isolated fragments, and since these, however numerous or precise, are at the end only partial and incomplete, they can never take the place of the living unity, or restore to thought that which it had lost. The understanding works by fixed categories which represent only separate aspects of truth. What it produces, therefore, is a number of fixed abstractions standing in hard and fast distinction from each other; and the one thing which it is incapable of reproducing is that which is the most important of all—the living link which bound them together and made them one. Moreover, inasmuch as finite analysis, carried ever so far, cannot exhaust that which has in it an infinite content, the results attained by reason must ever fall short of that which is implicitly given in faith. Intuition takes in at a glance what scientific definitions, however numerous, cannot embrace. We may conceive it possible for scientific analysis to exhaust the contents of a *finite* object, and then to reconstruct them into a rational unity. It is not absolutely inconceivable that human knowledge should one day be able to construct a system of the whole finite world, and so restore for thought that satisfaction which the ordinary consciousness possesses in outward perception. But an exhaustive analysis and ideal reconstruction of the nature of God, a philosophical theory which would recreate for reason the immediate satisfaction of faith, is an impossibility.

The pure in heart may know God, but the critical understanding can never comprehend Him. Lastly, it may be said, philosophy, in contrast with intuition, labours under this fatal defect, that the attempt to prove God is virtually to put something above Him. A revelation of a higher nature to a lower, of an infinite to a finite, we may conceive, but not a finite nature proving, or arguing down to, an infinite. To derive our knowledge of God mediately from any principle or ground of argument is really to make that principle, and the consciousness that can grasp it, higher than God. God's existence is the reason of itself and of all finite things, but to attempt to prove Him is to try to find in the finite the reason of the infinite; it is to make God finite by discovering the necessity of His being in something outside of itself.

The conclusion, then, to which these various objections seem to point is that, not reason, but intuition or faith, is the legitimate organ of spiritual knowledge. The human mind, in seeking after a philosophy of God and things divine, is setting out on a vain and impossible quest. Its true wisdom is to abandon the attempt, and to fall back on that primary, uncritical certitude and implicit fulness of knowledge which, in our immediate spiritual experience, we already possess.

Now, waiving for the moment the criticism of the pretensions of intuition as the organ of religious knowledge, let us examine what force there is in the foregoing objections to the endeavour after a mediated, that is, a rational or philosophic knowledge in the province of religion.

1. It may be suggested that these objections are based, in some measure at least, on a misapprehension of the function of reason in religion, in other words, of the end aimed at by a philosophy of religion. The contrast between intuition and reason in their relation to spiritual emotion—between the intensive satisfaction of the mind in the attitude of communion with God and the spiritual coldness and unrest of its rationalising activity—would be relevant only if reason aimed at a directly religious result. But philosophy does not pretend to make men pious. It presupposes religion, but makes no claim to produce it. It no more aspires to create piety than ethics to create morality or æsthetics to create art. Philosophy, it is true, would have no power to deal with religion, if religion were not implicitly rational. In religion as in all other spheres of human activity—in morality, in art, in the social and political relations of life, in the history of nations and of the world—there is present that underlying element of thought or reason which is the distinctive characteristic of man. But in all these provinces of human experience that element may, and at first must, be present without our thinking about it. We act before we reflect and

philosophise about our actions. We enter into the relations of life, we create institutions; silently and spontaneously the rational force that is in us gives birth and development to the social organisms of the family, the community, the state; and only later do we reach the point of intellectual progress where thought turns back to reflect on the significance of its own creations and read into them their rational meaning. And in all these cases, if we contrast the attitude of immediate and spontaneous experience with the attitude of reflective thought, the former may well appear to be clothed with an interest, a vivacity, a flow and fulness of life, which are lacking to the latter. In like manner the religious nature expresses itself in experiences which lift man above the things of time and sense, and in which the spirit rises into aspiration, reverence, communion with the invisible and eternal, long before it is impelled by its intellectual instincts to deal with religion as an object of thought. And when it enters on this latter work, its attitude is, in one point of view, a lower and less attractive one. It is impossible to enjoy at one and the same moment the blessedness of devotion and the colder satisfaction of reflex thought. We cannot have at once that which belongs to the thought of God and that which belongs to thinking about our thought of Him. But this difference between the two kinds of knowledge, or rather the two stages through which knowledge passes, cannot in religion, any more than elsewhere, be urged in proof of the inferiority of the stage of reflection. Religion and theology, intuition and speculation, immediate and mediate or philosophic thought, are not rivals, and their value is not to be tested by the same criterion.

2. It is no valid objection to rational or scientific thought in religion that it is narrower and more abstract than intuition, or, in other words, that faith embraces a wider and richer content than the explanations of reason can overtake. In the pursuit of its own high ends, science must begin by sacrificing the spontaneous unity and harmony of immediate perception. Science is, no doubt, the search for unity; but the unity it seeks in nature, in the human mind, in all thinking things and all objects of thought, is a deeper one than that which meets the common eye. The highest and richest kind of unity—that after which reason seeks—is not superficial sameness, not that outward and empirical wholeness or harmony which impresses itself on the senses or is given unsought to feeling or immediate consciousness. It is the unity of principle beneath variety of phenomena, the unity which is discerned when opposing elements have been reconciled, and differences embraced and harmonised—in other

words, the unity of thought which has broken up the immediate, external unity into contradictions, and re-united them in the grasp of reason. Now, it is this last which is the unity that science seeks, and to the search for which, in all departments of human experience, our intellectual instincts prompt. But the process by which it can be reached is obviously one, the first step of which implies an antagonistic attitude to its point of departure. Analysis, division, abstraction, are the instruments with which science must begin its work. It must break up the fair and rounded wholeness of immediate experience, it must take part from part, member from member, narrow and concentrate its attention on a single element or limited group of phenomena, broken off from its relation to the whole. It must, in short, deal with abstractions and be content to give up that concrete unity which the world possesses for ordinary thought. But it is only to the unreflecting mind that science has an aspect of crabbedness and narrowness. Nor, indeed, outside of the domain of religion do we hear science complained of as hard and cold, as substituting technical dogmas and freezing abstractions for the realities of nature and life. The botanist's herbarium, the collection of classified specimens of vegetable or animal life in a museum, have lost, indeed, the spontaneous beauty of nature, of delicately moulded form and ever varying freedom of movement. The science of optics dissolves the prismatic splendours on which the untaught eye gazes with wonder and delight, and occupies itself with the consideration only of laws of reflexion and refraction, &c. In the strain which charms the untutored ear science thinks only of numerical relations of sounds, regulated periods and intervals, laws of harmony and the like. In all these cases it substitutes for the inartificial simplicity which we intuitively recognise in nature what might be regarded as repulsive abstractions, bare and rigid formulæ, artificial classifications from which the life, the harmony, the unity that charmed us are gone But the sacrifice is one which the commonest intelligence condones, as a necessary step in that progress by which we are to substitute for the rude unities of popular observation, the real and profounder unities of thought—of identity of principle under diversities of form, of relation, order, organic development, beneath seeming disorder and aimless contingency and change. Nor is it felt to be a valid charge against science that its results are only partial—that scientific analysis falls far short of exhausting that fulness of content which is given to ordinary consciousness in the immediate aspect of the world. Nature, in its concrete richness and vastness, ever transcends the puny efforts of human investigation, and the combined results of all the sciences, though they, each in its own province, help to restore the secret unities of phenomena, leave us far short of the final synthesis by which thought, treading in the wake of the creative intelligence, might reconstruct the reasoned unity of the world. Nevertheless, partial and incomplete though its work be, we feel that it is not vain or valueless. Though the vast context be still undeciphered, it is something to have infused the lucidity of thought into a single page of the inexhaustible volume. Why then, when we turn to that province where scientific insight, the attainment of real and rational knowledge, would seem to possess the highest value and interest for the spirit of man, should thought be arrested because of its seeming ruggedness; and impression, feeling, instinctive and uncritical knowledge, be exalted to the place of honour? A narrow, logical dogmatism may be justly chargeable with the intrusion of finite methods into the sphere of infinite truth; and the formulas, the arid distinctions and dogmas of scholastic theology may produce results from which religious feeling turns away with a not unjustifiable impatience. But for the barrenness of spurious science true philosophy is not responsible. And if, in its endeavour after intellectual satisfaction in religion—in the attempt to get beyond subjective impressions, arbitrary notions, changeful opinions, and to reach the firm ground of objective and eternal truth—the first results of philosophy should present to the ordinary mind a hard and forbidding aspect, this is no more than, from the very conditions of philosophy or philosophical knowledge, we might naturally expect.

3. Finally it has been alleged, as we have said, that any other than an immediate or intuitive knowledge of God is self-contradictory, as implying that we can prove or attain to the knowledge of God by something that is higher than God, or at any rate, by something that is regarded as having an independent truth or reality. We can conceive, it is said, a higher nature revealing itself to a lower, we can conceive an immediate revelation of God to or in the finite consciousness; but a mediate or reasoned knowledge, that is, a knowledge which concludes to God by the mediation of some other idea or object, is impossible. The full answer to this objection implies considerations which can only be given in the sequel; but meantime it may be indicated, first, that whatever force it contains tells as much against immediate, as against mediated or rational knowledge of God. For any intuitive or immediate knowledge of God that does not ignore all distinction between the knower and the known, between the finite consciousness and its infinite object, and so reduce the two natures to bare sameness or identity, must involve the notion objected to, viz., that of something conceived of as different from,

and even in a sense, outside of God. Any kind of knowledge, immediate or mediate, implies, at the very least, a conscious relation between the knower and the being or object known, otherwise there could be no more knowledge than of one part of a stone by another. The theory of immediate knowledge therefore implies the positing of a finite, conceived of as distinguished from, and opposed to the Infinite; and as in order to the attainment of a relation between two terms, there must be a third term by which they are mediated, it follows that immediate knowledge must virtually include a process of thought; that is, it must include all that is objected to in mediated or rational knowledge. But, secondly, whilst the objection to a knowledge of God attained deductively, by any process of logical proof, is, in one point of view, a valid one, inasmuch as God is just the Being who cannot be deduced, who exists in and for Himself, and contains within Himself the reason of His own existence, yet this objection would no longer hold against a rational or mediate knowledge of God in which the proof or process of mediation is, when closely viewed, one *which is contained within His own nature.* Now, as will be shown hereafter, religion is simply the return of the finite consciousness into union with the infinite, the reconciliation of the human spirit with the Divine;

and a philosophy of religion is, not the thoughts or reasonings of a finite observer as to the being and nature of God and our relations to Him, but simply a conscious development of the process which is given implicitly in religion and in religious feelings and acts—the process, viz., by which the finite spirit loses or abnegates its finitude and self-sufficiency, and finds its truer self in the life and being of God. God is not proved or known by anything foreign to His own being. He reveals Himself in thought and to it. All true thought of God is itself divine thought—thought, that is, which is not arbitrary and accidental, but in which the individual mind surrenders its narrow individualism and enters into the region of universal and absolute truth. If, therefore, rational or speculative knowledge is, in one point of view, man's knowledge of God, it is in another God's knowledge of Himself.

II. Having thus reviewed some of the reasons which lead many to have recourse to intuition in preference to rational or systematic thought as the organ of religious knowledge, we may now briefly examine the validity of intuition or immediate knowledge as a basis of certitude in religion.

Intuition or immediate instinctive sentiment, it is maintained, is the ultimate basis of certitude. For the highest certainty is that which the mind possesses when in immediate converse with its objects. The conviction we reach by arguments and reasonings can never exceed or even equal in strength and vivacity that which we feel when, in the form of immediate fact, the thing is before us—that certainty, *e.g.*, which, in immediate perception, we seem to have of the existence and reality of the external world. When the existence of God is only the conclusion of a process of reasoning, when spiritual ideas are attained by elaborate deductions and embodied in logical definitions and dogmas, the method of knowledge is one which is liable to error even in the hands of the trained and scientific reasoner; and to him, alike with those who are least capable of weighing the force of scientific evidence, truth so reached fails to convey that full and irresistible sense of reality which the pious spirit feels in immediate converse with things divine. That which I know immediately and intuitively transcends in certitude all other knowledge, for the certainty of it is bound up with the mind's certainty of itself. I can no more doubt what I thus know than I can doubt my own existence.

Now on this view it is to be remarked—

1. That if the assertion that our knowledge in religion is immediate and intuitive means simply that here, as elsewhere, truth is its own witness, and that only that can claim the character of truth or reality which appeals to, and finds a response in, the human consciousness—this is not a principle

which philosophy has any interest to dispute. To say that whatever is asserted to be true must be recognisable by the mind as true, and that there is no higher court of appeal, no authority outside of thought, by which truth can be mediated to thought—this, so far from implying the exclusion of philosophy from religion or any other department of knowledge, is rather the very fundamental principle on which all philosophy may be said to rest. The aphorism of Des Cartes (*Cogito ergo sum*), with which modern philosophy begins, is, rightly viewed, only the expression of this principle. For what this aphorism means is, that all reality is reality for consciousness, that no existence has any meaning save in relation to consciousness, and therefore that all other certitude must ultimately rest on the certitude which consciousness has of itself. It is possible to doubt everything else save this ultimate relation of reality to thought. If I try to doubt this, in the very act of doubting I presuppose it, for the doubt itself is an emphatic assertion of the reality of thought. Whatever, therefore, has reality must be capable of approving itself to consciousness, and an immediate, intuitive certainty is the first form, for many the only form, in which this approval expresses itself.

2. But whilst all this may be conceded, the concession does not by any means imply that intuition or immediate knowledge is to be regarded,

in opposition to philosophy or speculative thought, as the criterion of truth in religion. Though the intuitive witness of the spirit *may* implicitly contain the highest evidence of truth, it does not by any means always or necessarily contain it. To assert the unity of thought and reality, or to make thought the criterion of truth, does not mean that any thought or sentiment or notion which I find in my mind, and of which I can give no further explanation or reason, must be regarded as absolute truth. But it is this last assertion which, presented in forms more or less disguised, is really the fundamental position of the intuitional school. In all my knowledge, intellectual, moral, religious, there is of course much that is deductive, that rests on prior reasonings, judgments, notions ; but—it is argued—when I trace back my beliefs or convictions in any case to their foundation, I must needs find some ultimate basis beyond reasoning. . The chain of proof—to change the figure—is not suspended in the air. What ultimately I arrive at is certain primary beliefs or presuppositions, of which I can give no further justification, no reason or explanation. There are, and must be, beyond all derivative knowledge, certain underived ideas as to what is true or right or beautiful or divine; and without dissolving knowledge into universal scepticism, I must accept these as their own authentication.

Plausible, however, as this view seems to be,

it is open to these obvious objections:—(1) That immediate conviction is no proof that we *have* reached the primary or underivative element of knowledge, and (2) that even if we had reached it, the certainty of immediate conviction is purely empirical. To take for granted that notions or beliefs which present themselves to the common mind spontaneously and without any conscious process of reflection, are to be accepted as ultimate and underived, and therefore as absolutely true, would obviously be a very hap-hazard procedure. For very little consideration is needed to see that many notions or beliefs which occur to the mind with an air of spontaneity and self-evidence are the result of a process of thought more or less complicated; and, again, that, so far from being incapable of question or verification, such notions are not seldom nothing more than unwarrantable popular assumptions. By a process of arbitrary association, combinations of ideas may unconsciously be formed of which the result assumes to the mind the aspect of an ultimate and insoluble necessity of thought; and almost any intense feeling or inveterate belief, of which the origin is not remembered, or which has been silently imbibed from the intellectual atmosphere in which our minds have grown up, becomes apparently its own evidence, and supersedes all further need of rational proof. It is obvious, therefore, that a feeling of conviction which can be artificially produced cannot be adduced as evidence that, in any given case, we have reached a primary element of thought. But (2) even if such a primary underived element of knowledge could be reached, immediate consciousness of it would not of itself constitute a sure and absolute ground of certitude. Immediate knowledge, as being merely empirical and subjective, cannot be accepted as its own guarantee. We cannot legitimately rear a universal and absolute structure on a basis which is particular and accidental, or conclude from a fact of experience to the existence of objective and necessary truth. But the fact that I feel in a particular way, or find in my mind a notion or impression of which I cannot get rid, is simply an empirical fact, a thing which happens, and nothing more. It cannot be assumed without further reason that my moral and spiritual intuitions are, even for me, a revelation of infallible truth; and for the diversified and contradictory beliefs of different minds the appeal to intuition would be alike valid. When I assert that I have an intuition or ultimate sentiment of what is beautiful or morally right, or that certain religious ideas are true, because my consciousness intuitively and immediately responds to them, it is quite a valid answer on the part of any one who differs from me, that he has no such intuitions, or that his intuitions certify to something altogether different from the ideas and doctrines patronised by mine. It is true, indeed, that the upholders of intuitional morality and religion are wont to claim for their ideas the sanction, not of the individual mind only, but of the common sense or consciousness of mankind. But if this claim could in any case be made good, the infallibility of notions universally, or all but universally, received is not a thing beyond dispute. The members of a community or society at the same stage of intellectual or spiritual progress will necessarily coincide in their general elementary beliefs, and a time has been when the whole world accepted, on the apparently irrefragable testimony of sense, facts, and ideas, which the progress of knowledge has proved to be futile. But, in point of fact, there are no moral and spiritual ideas or none beyond the barest abstractions, to which any such universal consent can be ascribed. On the most fundamental questions of morality and religion, on the question of what is right and wrong, on the question of the existence and nature of God, it is impossible to point to any two successive ages or periods of human culture and civilisation, in which precisely the same beliefs have prevailed; or, again, to any one age of the world in which the fundamental notions entertained on these subjects by all peoples and societies, however different their national genius or intellectual and spiritual atmosphere, were precisely coincident. It is, for instance, only by thinning down the idea of God to an abstraction which would embrace under a common head the rudest fetishism and the spiritual theism of Christianity that a *consensus gentium* can be alleged on behalf of the fundamental idea of religion. But of what worth as a criterion of certitude is an intuition which leaves out of the idea of God to which it certifies all that can interest the intelligence or elevate the character of the worshipper, and assures him only of a bare *caput mortuum* devoid of all spiritual significance? If, however, the appeal to universal intuition is so modified as to embrace only the more developed and cultivated ages and races, whilst the opinions of all others are set aside as irrelevant and erroneous, then the answer is, that that which distinguishes between true and false, irrelevant and significant intuitions, cannot be mere intuition, but must be some higher principle. The standard by which the admissibility of different organs of immediate knowledge is judged must be, not immediate knowledge itself, but those principles of thought, education, moral and spiritual culture, by which the more advanced nations and times are distinguished from the less advanced. That, in short, to which we appeal as the ultimate arbiter in religious truth is not subjective notions and impressions, which are variable as the influences of temperament, tradition, association, to which the minds of men are subjected; but it is the objective authority of reason itself, which, in its universality, its absoluteness, its self-consistency, alone has the right to dominate all individual thought and the power to give irrefragable assurance of its own deliverances.

In conclusion, it may be remarked that much of the zeal with which the intuitional theory is advocated is doubtless to be ascribed to this, that it is regarded by many as the only alternative from sensationalistic or empirical theories. If we cannot consent to hold that the only real element of knowledge is that which is furnished by the senses, and that the whole content of thought, including our highest moral and spiritual ideas, is an artificial result manufactured out of sensations by arbitrary association, then it is supposed we must secure for these ideas the authority of original and infallible intuitions. If hedonistic moralists would explain away our ideas of right and duty as only a factitious product of association, morality must be saved by claiming for it an independent authority in conscience, which is God's voice speaking directly and immediately within the breast. If theism finds no certain basis in arguments which would deduce the infinite from the finite, and cannot on that ground meet the assaults of philosophical scepticism, then we must claim for our theological convictions an authority which rises above the arguments and objections of human logic, to grasp at once and with ineffable assurance the truth in which we rest.

But the choice of alternatives thus presented is by no means exhaustive. Denying that our moral and religious ideas are a mere product of association, we are not therefore driven to the theory that they have their source in inexplicable intuitions. This indeed would be tantamount to the admission that for our highest convictions we must be content to give either a bad reason or no reason at all. There is another, and a truer theory of human knowledge according to which, as we shall have occasion hereafter to show, it is possible to give to our moral and religious ideas an independent authority, without reducing them to the level of blind and irrational prejudices. Even over what have been deemed our primary beliefs it is possible to extend the domain of reason without depriving them, in one point of view, of their primary and fundamental character; it is possible to explain them rationally without explaining them away. For the highest explanation and justification is given to any idea or element of thought when it is shown to be a necessary moment of the universal system, a member of that organic unity of thought, no part of which is or can be, isolated or independent, or related to any other accidentally or arbitrarily, but wherein each idea has a place or function involved in its own nature and in its necessary relations to all other ideas and to the whole. Nor does this mean that the proof of any idea or belief is its place in a process of syllogistic deduction. We may admit that there are notions, ideas, beliefs, which cannot be deduced syllogistically, which the logic of the understanding cannot justify, and yet maintain that by a profounder logic, which enters into the genesis and traces the secret rhythm and evolution of thought, they can be shown to rise out of, and be affiliated to, other ideas, and to form constituent elements in that living process of which all truth consists. And as the life of any member of a living organism may be said to be proved by this, that it is an essential part of the system, that it is at once means and end, implying and implied in all the rest; so, of any moral and spiritual idea it is the only and all-sufficient justification—that which lends to it the highest necessity—that it can be shown to be a necessary moment of that organic whole, that eternal order and system, of which universal truth consists, and which is only another name for Him who is at once the beginning and the end, the source and consummation of all thought and being.

## CHAPTER III.

### OBJECTIONS TO THE SCIENTIFIC TREATMENT OF RELIGION, CONTINUED:—RELIGIOUS KNOWLEDGE GIVEN IN A POSITIVE REVELATION.

IF immediate is opposed to mediate or scientific knowledge, not less, it would seem, is that knowledge which is positive or given on authority to that which is apprehended in its grounds or principles by the activity of thought. Are not the ideas of revelation and science reciprocally exclusive? Is not philosophy excluded from the province of religious truth in so far as the latter is communicated to us in a positive, authoritative revelation? If there is a department of human knowledge which is fenced off from all question or criticism, if there are certain propositions or doctrines with respect to which the only legitimate attitude of reason is that of absolute passivity, of unconditional submission to external authority, have we not here obviously a privileged territory into which philosophy may not enter? In all with which philosophy deals reason must find itself. Facts which remain arbitrary and isolated, ideas which rest on no objective ground save that of testimony or tradition, propositions and formulas which do not justify themselves to thought—with these philosophy can have nothing to do. Does not, then, the content of a supernatural, authoritative revelation lie, by the very nature of the thing, outside of that domain of which reason can take cognisance?

Now, undoubtedly the notion of revelation, nay, rightly understood, of a supernatural revelation is presupposed in the notion of religion, or forms the inseparable correlate of it. There can be no elevation of the finite spirit into communion with the infinite which does not imply divine acts or a divine process of self-revelation. Neither thought nor the aspirations of the religious nature can be satisfied with the rationalistic notion of a merely subjective religion—of opinions and beliefs wrought out by the purely spontaneous activity of the human mind, and implying nothing more on the divine side than is involved in the original creation of man's rational nature. A God who does not reveal Himself ceases to be God; and religious feeling, craving after a living relation to its object, refuses to be satisfied with a mere initial or potential revelation of the mind and will of God—with a God who speaks once for all, and then through the whole course of history ceases to reveal Himself.

But whilst revelation is the necessary presupposition of religion, the idea of revelation is not necessarily exclusive of the activity of reason. Instead of thwarting or quelling or limiting thought, it may be so conceived of as to be in harmony with the free play and development of thought. It is not necessary to think of revelation as a source of knowledge which is either contrary to reason or above reason—which either revolts human intelligence or reduces it to absolute passivity, or leaves it no other function than the formal one of grammatical construction and logical interpretation and arrangement. On the contrary, it would not be difficult to show that the true idea of revelation, that which is most honouring to God, is at the same time that which is most ennobling to man—the idea, that is, of a revelation which addresses itself, not to the ear or the logical understanding only, but to the whole spiritual nature, which does not constrain us mechanically to receive the truth, but enables us to know it, which does not tell us merely what God would have us believe, but raises us into conscious intelligent sympathy with His mind and will. What, however, we are here concerned to show is, simply, that any conception of revelation which excludes the activity of human reason in the province of religion is untenable.

1. The cleft between reason and revelation may

be supposed to be absolute, so that what revelation asserts reason denies, and *vice versa;* in which case, of course, all speculation and philosophy in the province of religion are at an end. But no such absolute dualism between reason and revelation has ever been maintained, save as a rhetorical exaggeration on the part of religious writers, or as a form of covert cynicism—a sarcastic device for the insinuation of doubts which could not be openly expressed. The paradox expressed in the well-known phrases, *Quo absurdius eo verius,* and *Credo quia impossibile,* could never embody the conviction of any sane mind save with the tacit reservation that the absurdity or impossibility asserted was only relative, and that there is an absolute standard by which truth and possibility can be measured. There may be men of taste so depraved that their admiration might be taken as an infallible sign of ugliness, their disgust as a test of beauty. In like manner, the mistrust of Church teachers in man's unregenerate reason may have expressed itself in the paradoxical form that a dogma is the more probable the more absurd and irrational it seems to be, and that when an article of faith appears to fallen reason absolutely contradictory and impossible, we may conclude it to be certainly true. But even here the paradoxical rejection implies the real recognition of reason as the ultimate standard. We are to conclude a thing to be true *because* it seems absurd, and to believe it *because* it seems impossible. What, however, in such cases we are really called to believe is not itself the absurd or impossible, but a truth which we are capable of thinking, and apart from our knowledge of which the words 'absurd' and 'impossible' would have no meaning. If, in religion or anywhere else, the absurd could be true, or the impossible real, then the above-quoted sayings would be tautological. They would be simply the assertion that religion is, of all things, the most absurd and impossible. Sceptical writers, again, such as Bayle and Gibbon, assuming a tone of deference for the doctrines of religion, have sometimes conceded that, though contradictory and irrational, these doctrines might nevertheless be true, inasmuch as the organ of religious belief is not reason but faith. 'This Church dogma, this article of the creed, this doctrine of our holy faith, seems to reason's eye, not only incomprehensible, but altogether self-contradictory and incredible; but that is because it does not really belong to the province of reason; it comes to us certified, not by the carnal understanding, but by a higher authority, which it would be impious to question.' Perhaps, too, this is an attitude of mind into which, consciously or unconsciously, not a few sincerely religious men have a tendency to fall. There may be doctrines claiming the sanction of revelation which yet seem to them glaringly inconsistent with the fundamental principles of justice and equity, or, again, which appear to be belied by the undoubted results of philosophic thought or of scientific research. But instead of attempting an adjustment in thought of the apparently conflicting deliverances of reason and revelation, they try to allay their disquietude and to silence their doubts by the device of treating reason and revelation as entirely independent authorities. They will let science and philosophy go their own way and work out their results by their own principles and methods; but whatever those results may be, the pious mind will not let its faith be shaken in those doctrines which seem to rest on the authority of a divine revelation.

It is obvious, however, that this way of settling the relations of religion and science is an impossible one. The human spirit is not a thing divided against itself so that faith and reason can subsist side by side in the same mind, each asserting as absolute principles which are contradicted by the other. If it were so, then either there must be a higher umpire than both to decide between them, or thought and knowledge are reduced to chaos. For, in the first place, we must have rational grounds for the acceptance of a supernatural revelation. It must verify its right to teach authoritatively. Reason must be competent to judge, if not of the content, at least of the credentials, of revelation. But an authority proving by reason its right to teach irrationally is an impossible conception. The authority which appeals to reason in proof of its rights commits itself, so to speak, to be essentially rational. To prove to reason a right to set reason at defiance is self-contradictory, inasmuch as the proof itself must be one of the things to which that right extends. To try to convince me that I ought to distrust my natural reason and believe things that revolt it, involves the same practical paralogism as the attempt to prove to an insane man that he is insane. In the second place, reason itself lies nearer to us than any external authority, and no other or outward evidence can be sufficient to overturn its testimony. An appeal to the senses or the imagination can only, at most, be presumptive and provisional—an indication that truth *may* be present, though we do not see it, but never in any case a proof that it *is* present, still less that it is present where we see only incoherence and contradiction. Even a miracle, which is possible only as a breach of an order that is not absolute, could never be accepted as proof of a breach of an order which *is* absolute. There can be no such thing as a moral or metaphysical miracle, and certainly a physical wonder could not prove its existence. The attempt therefore to maintain an unreal equilibrium between faith and reason—between a reverence which accepts, and an intelligence which rejects, the same things—can only issue in one of two results, practical unbelief or the violent suppression of doubt. No adjustment of the difference can be satisfactory save an adjustment *in thought*. Either the doctrines of positive religion must be shown to be in harmony with reason, or, at least, reason must be silent as to their truth or falsehood. Thought must, with intelligent insight, pronounce for them; or it must be shown why, from their very nature, thought can pronounce neither for nor against them.

2. It is then virtually a contradiction in terms to say that a revelation of what is contrary to reason should be received as true. But the content of a revelation, it may be said, though not contrary to reason, may be above reason. And in point of fact this last is the notion which, since the time of Leibnitz, has been the favourite apologetic device of ecclesiastical writers. Nothing can be accepted as revealed which contradicts reason, yet revelation may communicate to us what transcends reason. A revelation may contain divine mysteries—doctrines which surpass the compass of human intelligence, but which, as not being inconsistent with other known truth, may be accepted on sufficient authority. Finite reason could not discover these doctrines, nor even, when discovered, can it comprehend them; but it does not contradict them; and if they are announced on satisfactory evidence of their authority, it may and ought to believe

in them. As not contrary to reason, human intelligence may receive them; as above reason, it cannot philosophise about them. Let us briefly examine this distinction between what is contrary to reason and what is above reason as applied to the content of our religious belief.

1. The ideas or doctrines to which this distinction is applied are above reason. By this what is meant is not that they are essentially irrational, but that they are above the grasp of *finite* reason. With a higher reason than ours, with infinite wisdom, they are perfectly accordant. This can only mean that reason is divided into a higher and lower which are to be distinguished quantitatively, but which, qualitatively considered, are one and the same. That this is so is obvious, not only from the impossibility of thought conceiving of a kind of thought outside of or essentially different from itself, but also from the concession that if the doctrines in question could be shown to be *contrary* to human reason, they must be rejected; since, otherwise, if there were two kinds of reason, inconsistency with the one would be no sufficient ground for rejecting what might be coherent with the other. Is, then, this notion of a quantitative division of that reason or thought which is in itself essentially one, at all tenable? Where or how is the line of division to be drawn? How shall I know that any given doctrine belongs to the prohibited

domain? Is it only by experience of its insolubleness? or is there an absolute definable limit which finite reason cannot cross? If the former,—if the proof of any revealed doctrine being above reason is merely that the endeavour to penetrate with spiritual insight into it has hitherto proved vain, this would be equivalent to the assertion that all yet unsolved problems are insoluble, or that nothing which has once baffled human reason can ever yield to persistent inquiry, or, in short, that, unlike every other kind of knowledge, religious knowledge is unprogressive. If, on the other hand, the limit is alleged to be an absolute one, which yet thought can define, or, at least, which it is capable of discerning; then to this assertion there is the fatal objection which has been already urged with reference to the doctrine of the relativity of human knowledge, viz., that the capacity to posit an absolute limit to thought implies that thought has already virtually transcended that limit.[1]

2. What is above reason, in the sense implied in the alleged distinction, is really what is contrary to reason. We know of no other reason than one, and what can never be brought into coherence with that reason is to us equivalent to the absurd or self-contradictory. Of what is in itself knowable, though beyond our present knowledge, we can pronounce that it is not contrary to reason.

[1] *V. supra*, p. 16 ff.

But we cannot say the same of that which is above reason in the sense of absolutely transcending human intelligence, of that which can never be construed by human thought. What lies beyond reason in this sense is simply the irrational or nonsensical. If it does not appear to contradict reason, it is only because a proposition, the terms of which are absolutely unintelligible, cannot be said to be false. To make it an argument in favour of any doctrines that they are not contrary to reason, they must belong to the province of that reason to which they are not opposed. To be not contrary to *our* reason proves nothing for doctrines which, by supposition, belong to a different order of reason, and which may, for aught we know, be contrary to that.

3. The revelation of a mystery, in the sense of a doctrine altogether transcendent, relating to things outside the sphere of finite thought, is self-contradictory. A partial knowledge may be conveyed to us of things that are in themselves within the compass of human thought. Ideas which we are as yet incapable of grasping in their highest form may reach our minds in a form which, though less adequate, is still essentially true. But no revelation from heaven can disclose to us what is absolutely supra-rational, or even so much concerning it as to enable us in any real sense to believe in it. According to the notion of a revelation of things above reason, we are to know so much about the

mysteries of religion as to make it possible to believe them, whilst yet we are absolutely incapable of rationally apprehending them. But any such combination of knowledge and ignorance, if we examine what we mean, will be seen to be contradictory and impossible.

The revelation of a mystery, if by that we do not mean merely the revelation of the fact that there is much in the universe which we do not know, must be the revelation of something which can be construed by the mind, which is conveyed to it in terms of human thought, which can be expressed in coherent propositions. Now it is quite possible, no doubt, to construct any number of propositions concerning things absolutely unknown so as not, on the face of them, to involve contradictions. If the symbols $x$, $y$, $z$ represent unknown objects, it does not contradict reason to predicate any number of relations between them—to say, *e.g.*, that $x + y = z$, or that $3x = y$, etc. The doctrine of the Trinity is no such unintelligible combination of symbols, but a doctrine which may be shown to be the central truth not only of Christian faith, but of Christian philosophy. But if it related to objects altogether transcendent, such as, in the view of some theologians, are the objects represented by the terms 'Person' and 'Substance,' there would be nothing contrary to reason, nor therefore unbelievable, in the assertion that in the Godhead there are three Persons in one Substance. Or again, if the term 'Procession,' as applied to the interior nature of the Godhead, expresses a relation absolutely incomprehensible, reason can have no difficulty on the score of non-contradictoriness in accepting the proposition either that the Third Person proceeds from the First, or that He proceeds from the First and Second together. Not only may all this and much more be received on the authority of supernatural revelation, but it may be received on, or without, any authority whatever. For when we examine what such propositions mean, they resolve themselves into this, that any relations may be expressed between unknown symbols without self-contradiction, or still more simply, into the proposition that the unintelligible is not self-contradictory.

It may be said that this is not an adequate account of what is contained in the revelation of a mystery. For a doctrine may express known relations between unknown objects. Though, for instance, we do not and cannot comprehend the realities represented by such terms as Person and Substance, we do know what is meant by the words 'unity,' 'plurality,' and the like. What therefore, in this view of it, the doctrine of the Trinity conveys to us is the information that of the unknown elements of the divine essence we can predicate the intelligible ideas at once of unity and trinity, or of a trinity which is consistent with unity. But, waiving other considerations, the utmost which such a revelation—the revelation, viz., that of a nature which we do not and cannot know, plurality can be predicated in a sense not inconsistent with unity—conveys to us, is that the nature of God is not self-contradictory. Surely, however, this is neither a doctrine above reason, nor even one which, by its own unaided light, reason is incapable of discerning.

Finally, it may be held that, though relating to objects above the sphere of human reason, a revelation may yet communicate to us a measure of knowledge concerning them through finite types and analogies. It may therefore contain truth that is comprehensible with respect to realities which in themselves, are incomprehensible. We may receive and derive spiritual benefit from a revelation which conveys to us figures of things in the heavens, though the things themselves are to us inaccessible.

And, no doubt, this account of the function of revelation is, to a certain extent, true. There is a kind of knowledge of divine things which, in a practical sense, is far more valuable than philosophic knowledge, and which is accessible to minds that are incapable of and never aspire to the latter. And to all minds knowledge, whether it ever reach the philosophic form or no, must first come couched in the forms of feeling, of immediate perception, of representations which are not absolute truth, but truth strained through finite images and materialised conceptions. But of all such representations, unless they are purely illusory, it must hold good that, implicitly and in undeveloped form, they contain rational thought, and therefore thought which human intelligence may ultimately free from its sensuous veil. The simplest sensuous intuition of the outward world, the half-imaginative generalisations which compose the knowledge of ordinary minds, are far short of speculative insight, but they are prophetic of it. They are true so far as they go; but they are so only because a truth underlies them which in a purer form the philosophic mind can grasp. And, in like manner, eternal things may be disclosed to us under finite forms and representations; but between the earthly figure and the heavenly reality there must be a real relation. If a representation is a true representation, it must belong to the same order with the thing represented. The relation between them is a thinkable relation and one which, though immature individual intelligence may not apprehend it, thought or intelligence in general is capable of apprehending. Nothing that is absolutely inscrutable to reason can be made known to faith. It is only because the content of a revelation is implicitly rational that it can possess any self-evidencing power, or exert any moral influence over the human spirit.

But if the contents of revelation be no longer regarded as above reason, then human reason not only may seek, but ought to seek, all the light which reverent and thoughtful investigation can throw on them. It may endeavour to verify them, to disengage them from what is accidental, to develope their organic unity, to trace their connection with the other elements of its knowledge, to give them, in short, that form of knowledge which we designate philosophic thought.

## CHAPTER IV.

### THE NECESSITY OF RELIGION.

IN all religious experience there are involved feelings and acts which are possible only to spiritual and intelligent beings, which are grounded in certain necessary relations of the human spirit to the Divine, and which, therefore, do not arise accidentally, but in unconscious obedience to the hidden logic of a spiritual process. Now, it is the work of philosophy to unfold these relations, and to trace out the steps of that process by which the finite spirit transcends its own finitude and rises into communion with the things unseen and eternal—to show, in other words, how it is necessary to mind, as mind, to relate itself to God, and to determine that idea of God which its religious experience involves. It is in performing this work that philosophy shows the necessity of religion.

The phrase 'necessity of religion' does not, it need scarcely be said, imply anything so obviously untrue as that every individual man must needs be religious. To show that religion is necessary for man as man, we are not required to show that no human being has existed who has not felt that necessity. We speak of the necessity of religion as we speak of the necessity of morality or law or science or philosophy. It is possible to maintain that morality is based on principles which are not arbitrary but which rise out of the very essence of reason, and in the recognition and realisation of which every rational being finds the fulfilment of its own nature, whilst at the same time we admit, as we cannot help admitting, not only that many individual men are vicious, but that there are individuals and even races at so low a point of human progress as to have scarcely any, or only the most rudimentary, notions of right. It is possible, again, to hold that there is a science of Æsthetics, capable of being logically evolved from necessary principles, without at the same time ignoring the fact that there are multitudes of human beings in whom the sense of beauty is either dormant or depraved. So also, it may be possible to show that religion has in it the highest necessity—a necessity involved in the very nature of reason, and therefore of all rational beings as such, though in the development of the individual there may be an element of contingency or arbitrariness, which makes it possible for him to fall short of his true nature and destiny.

Nor, again, in maintaining the necessity of religion are we required to show that the religious ideas of all men or of all races and ages have been coincident; or, conversely, that that only is necessary in religion in which all men and ages have concurred. Universal truths are not truths about which all men agree. The universal element in religion is not reached by leaving out from the various positive religions the special characteristics which distinguish them from each other, and retaining only those ideas or beliefs which are found to be common to all. For, not only would such a process—a process by which, for instance, that only in Christianity would be held to belong to the essence of religion which it has in common not only with the great historical religions, but with the lowest fetishism or idol-worship—reduce religion to a vague sentiment or abstraction of the most meagre and indefinite character, but it would take no account of that in the highest religion which constitutes its most valuable element. It is not that which is common to barbarism and civilisation which is most truly human, but precisely that in which civilisation differs from barbarism. As in the case of the individual, so in that of the race, there are many ideas which are essentially true, which yet are capable of being grasped by the human intelligence only at a certain stage of its intellectual progress. It is therefore conceivable that there may be in a religion ideas or doctrines which are essentially and absolutely true, whilst yet, in the actual experience of the world, the knowledge of them may have come at a late period of history, and even then only to a limited section of the race. Moreover, it is obvious that wherever we are obliged to introduce the notion of growth or development—wherever that which we contemplate is a thing which reaches its perfection, not by the accretion or accumulation of like materials, but by gradual evolution, from the germ or embryo to the perfect organism—there the true idea of the thing cannot be got by finding out what is common to the lowest and highest, and to every intermediate stage of its existence. To leave out of view the bud or flower or fruit, or to consider only what is common to these with the seed and stalk or stem, would not help us to the essential idea of the plant. If, therefore, in the religious history of the world we can discover any indications of a progressive development, it is not by leaving out of view what is peculiar to Christianity—those ideas or doctrines which constitute its special glory and excellence, and taking account only of that which it has in common with the earliest and rudest nature-worship, that the essential idea of religion is to be extricated. If we accept the notion of an organic development in religion, there is indeed a kind of necessity which is predicable of the lowest as well as of the highest religions of the world. The former contains something which cannot be left out of the perfect idea of religion, something which is its necessary presupposition; and the highest religion, while it transcends, at the same time must take up and comprehend all that is true and valuable in the lowest. But, if this be so, so far from the universal truth in religion being that which is common to all religions, there is not a single idea in the highest or perfect religion which remains what it was in those which preceded it. In all organic development the perfect organism, while it comprehends and absorbs, at the same time annuls and transmutes all that pertained to the earlier and imperfect stages of its life. Manhood presupposes, but does not retain, physically or mentally, the characteristic qualities of youth or childhood or infancy. That which really is common to all the stages of human life is therefore not to be reached inductively, but by grasping that idea which gives to all its successive forms and aspects the character of one organic whole. In like manner, a merely empirical consideration of the various religions of the world, or even of their historic succession and relations, however important as supplying the materials for a 'science of religions,' does not in itself constitute such a science, or give us that which is really universal in religion. To reach that, we must be able to go beyond the mere historical forms and to see beneath them the idea which is ever advancing to its fuller realisation—which, at each successive stage of its progress, loses nothing but leaves nothing unchanged, and fulfils the past only by transmuting the past. The perfect or absolute form of the idea, so far from giving us that which is common to all other forms, will thus retain in it unchanged not a single element which belonged to them. While it explains the latent significance of all that was true in the imperfect religions, it will transcend, and by transcending, annul or destroy them.

To show the necessity of religion then is to show that the religious relation—the transcendence of all that is finite and relative and the elevation of the finite spirit into communion with an Infinite and Absolute Spirit—is a thing which is involved in the very nature of man. Already we have discussed the theory of Nescience, and have attempted to prove that the alleged impossibility of a knowledge of God was based on that hard opposition of the finite and infinite, the relative and absolute, which belongs to an imperfect metaphysic. What, on the other hand, we have now to show, is not only that the finite mind may, but that it must rise to the knowledge of God. Not only is thought not precluded by its own conditions from the knowledge of God, but there is a sense in which it may be maintained that thought could not be thought without that knowledge, latent or explicit. So far from finding in the finite the only sphere of knowledge and regarding a knowledge of the Infinite as only illusion and error, we may, on the contrary, assert that finite knowledge, as finite, is illusory and false, and that all true knowledge contains in it an absolute or infinite element, apart from which the whole complex of finite knowledge and experience would be reduced to chaos.

When, however, we attempt to examine the grounds on which the necessity of religion is maintained, and the steps of the process by which we are led to it, we are met by a theory, which, if true, would preclude all such attempts. If the world can be explained in terms of matter and of material sequences and laws, if the whole system of things, life and intelligence included, can be reduced to mechanical force and its transmutations, there is not only no need for, but no possibility of, that higher explanation which is involved in the idea of God and of the relations of the human spirit to Him. What, as we shall see, the phrase 'necessity of religion' implies is that in the nature of man as an intelligent self-conscious being there is that which forces him to rise above what is material and finite and to find rest nowhere short of an Infinite, all-comprehending

Mind. What, on the contrary, the theory in question implies is that there is no call for any such explanation, inasmuch as the phenomena of the natural, and also, with high probability, those of the spiritual world, admit of explanation without it, and on principles which are more simple as well as more scientific.

The idea of the necessity of religion has often been obscured by the false issue on which the arguments of controversialists have turned. Attempted refutations of Materialism and Positivism have proved ineffective, because the Theist has tacitly accepted as his own the untenable position ascribed to him by his opponents. The real weakness of the Materialist does not lie where the Theist often thinks to find it, nor his own strength in that which he labours to maintain. When the former tries in various ways to explain the world in terms of matter and material sequences or laws—to reduce the whole system of things, life and intelligence included, to molecular changes and mechanical force, and so to eliminate God from the world—the necessity for that explanation which religion involves is pitched too low when it is represented as the necessity for an 'Almighty Creator' or an 'All-wise Designer and Governor of the World.' Against such a conception it may, as we shall see more fully hereafter, be justly objected that it is essentially dualistic. Not only is the God who is conceived of as an external Creator or Contriver reduced to something finite, but the link between Him and the world is made a purely arbitrary one, and the world itself is left without any real unity. You cannot begin with the existence of matter or a material world, and then pass by a leap to the existence of a spiritual, intelligent Being conceived of as its external Cause or Contriver. Betwixt two things thus heterogeneous the category of causation establishes no necessary bond. Nor again, can you give real or systematic unity to the world by any theory of it which requires repeated interpositions of a purely arbitrary power. If our conception of the world is such as to require the interposition of a fresh creative act in order to account for organic and vital phenomena, and for each new group or species of organisms, and again for the existence of intelligent, conscious beings; and if, finally, to account for the innumerable relations between these various orders of existence and especially those in which we discover the connection of means and end, we must have recourse to the notion of a perpetual series of new supernatural acts,—if this be our conception of the world, and of the way in which it calls for a God to explain it, there would be some ground for the assertion that it is essentially a dualistic conception, and that it fails to give any rational or systematic unity to the world. For system there cannot be where we have a succession of isolated elements with the gaps or interstices filled up by an arbitrary factor, or the perpetual recurrence of inextricable knots, with a *deus ex machinâ* brought in to cut them.

Over this explanation of the world, the simplicity of the materialistic theory gives it many advantages. Viewed generally, it is a theory which attempts to give unity, coherence, and completeness to our conception of the universe by regarding all its phenomena as ultimately resolvable into the dynamical action of atoms or particles of matter. When we have determined the nature of these atoms and the laws of their motions, we shall, it is supposed, have before us the secret of the whole knowable world. Physical science has now ascertained that the phenomena with which it deals are only different modifications of a common energy. Heat, light, electricity, magnetism, are but different modes of motion produced under different conditions, and they are all either directly or indirectly convertible into each other. And as motion itself can only be conceived of as the effect or expression of force, all physical phenomena are ultimately resolvable into manifestations of force. Further, it is the obvious tendency of modern investigation to resolve chemical into mechanical problems, that is, into questions of molecular physics. When we advance a little higher, we find, indeed, that science has not yet been able to trace the production of vital phenomena in the plant and animal to the operation of known physical or chemical laws. But when it is considered that phenomena so different as those of light, heat, electricity, &c., are proved to be but various modifications of a common energy, each of which is the exact quantitative equivalent of that from which it has been transformed; and further, that the so-called vital energies of plants and animals are dependent on the chemical interactions of the food they consume and the air they breathe, and that therefore there is no energy in organised substance which has not formerly existed in the form of chemical or physical energy; and, finally, when we perceive that, according to the latest biological speculations, protoplasm, the ultimate basis of life, is simply a combination of chemical elements, acting and reacting on each other, and is found to be, as to form, function, and substantial composition, identical in all organisms from the lowest to the highest,— the result, it is maintained, to which we are led by the strongest presumptive proof, is that life is simply transformed physical or chemical energy, and is therefore ultimately resolvable into molecular force. Lastly, though it is admitted that there is still an unbridged gulf between organisation and thought, yet when we reflect on the close and inseparable relation that subsists between the various mental activities of conscious beings and the physical organisation with which they are connected; when we consider that of the thoughts and emotions which in endless multiplicity and variety constitute our conscious life, there is not a single one which is not correlated to some physical change or modification in the brain matter of the thinker, may it not be said that the conclusion to which scientific investigation points is that thought itself is but a function of matter, or the highest expression of the same molecular force which has its earliest expression in the phenomena of inorganic nature? "I can discover," are the well-known words of one of the most eminent of modern biologists, "no logical halting-place between the admission that such is the case (*i.e.*, that 'the vital actions of a fungus or a foraminifer are the properties of their protoplasm and the direct result of the nature of the matter of which they are composed'), and the further concession that all vital action may, with equal propriety, be said to be the result of the molecular forces of the protoplasm which displays it. And if so, it must be true, in the same sense and to the same extent, that the thoughts to which I am now giving utterance, and your thoughts regarding them, are the expression of molecular changes in that matter of life which is the source of our other vital phenomena."[1] "Is there not a temptation," is the language of a kindred

[1] Huxley's *Lay Sermons*, p. 138.

scientific authority, "to close to some extent with Lucretius when he affirms that 'nature is seen to do all things spontaneously of herself, without the meddling of the Gods!' or with Bruno when he declares that matter is not 'that mere empty capacity which philosophers have pictured her, but the universal mother who brings forth all things as the fruit of her own womb?' Believing as I do in the continuity of nature, I cannot stop abruptly where our microscopes cease to be of use. By an intellectual necessity I cross the boundary of the experimental evidence, and discern in that matter which we, in our ignorance of its latent powers, and notwithstanding our professed reverence for its Creator, have hitherto covered with opprobrium, the promise and potency of all terrestrial life."[1] What, then, is claimed for this theory is, that it gives us a view of the world and of all the various orders of being contained in it, which is simple and self-consistent, which represents all phenomena as the expression of certain known principles or laws, and furnishes us with an explanation of them which is independent of any arbitrary factor. It does not require or admit of any supernatural interposition either at the beginning or at any subsequent stage of the process for which it professes to account. It is a theory, therefore, which is absolutely exclusive of that explanation of the world on which religion is held to rest—of the

[1] Tyndall's *British Association Address*, p. 55.

idea of God, and of that conscious relation to Him in which religion consists.

Now, I do not believe that the argument of the materialist can be adequately met, or the necessity of religion maintained, by having recourse to the notion of an anthropomorphic Creator or Designer. An external and arbitrary omnipotence solves indeed all difficulties, but it solves them only too easily; and even when we add to omnipotence the intelligence and wisdom which moulds the materials it has created out of nothing into ingenious relations and adaptations to preconceived ends, the conception of God thus suggested, apart from other objections, is one which falls far short of that infinite all-embracing intelligence after which our religious aspirations crave.

There is, however, another point of view from which at once the weakness of the materialistic, and the necessity of the religious conception of the world may, as I think, be conclusively shown;—the former, inasmuch as it may be demonstrated that the basis from which materialism starts, and on which it seeks to construct the world, is no real basis, but one which is reached only by a false abstraction; the latter, because it may be shown that, when we begin at the real beginning—when thought starts where alone it legitimately can start—it is forced onwards, from step to step, by an irresistible inward necessity, and cannot stop short till it has found its goal in the sphere of universal and absolute truth, or in that

Infinite Mind which is at once the beginning and the end, the source and the final explanation of all thought and being.

Following the train of thought thus suggested, I shall now endeavour to show, in the first place, what is that inherent weakness which vitiates the materialistic point of view, and renders it impossible to rest in materialism as an adequate explanation of the world; and, secondly, what is the necessity of thought which forces us onward to the absolute point of view of religion.

## I.

The inadequacy of all materialistic theories of the world may be said to be twofold: (1) Professing to exclude mind, or ultimately to reduce it to a function of matter, they really presuppose or tacitly assume it at the outset; (2) The principle which they employ as the master-key to all the phenomena of the world—that of force or mechanical causality—is applicable only to inorganic nature, is inapplicable to organic or vital phenomena, and utterly breaks down as an explanation of consciousness or intelligence.

1. The tendency, as we have seen, of modern materialistic speculation is to reduce mind to a mode, mental activity to a function, of matter. The principle of the convertibility of force is, it is with more or less explicitness suggested, applicable to

the phenomena of consciousness and thought, in common with those of material nature. As mechanical force is transformable into chemical, and the latter may be shown in any given case to be the exact equivalent of the former, so, in like manner, vital force is but transformed chemical or mechanical force; and, finally, we reach only another stage of the process when we find vital energy converted into sensation, volition, and the other phenomena of consciousness.

Now, waiving for the moment other objections, the fundamental fallacy which all such representations involve is, that they tacitly presuppose, and must needs presuppose, at the beginning, what they profess to reach at the end. You cannot get to mind as an ultimate product of matter, for in the very attempt to do so you have already begun with mind. The earliest step of any such inquiry involves categories of thought, and it is in terms of thought that the very problem you are investigating can be so much as stated. You cannot start in your investigations with bare, self-identical, objective facts, stript of every ideal element or contribution from thought. The least and lowest fact of outward observation is not an independent entity—fact minus mind, and out of which mind may, somehow or other, be seen to emerge; but it is fact or object as it appears to an observing mind, in the medium of thought, having mind or thought as an inseparable factor of it. Whether there be such a thing as an absolute world outside of thought, whether there be such things as matter and material atoms existing in themselves before any mind begins to perceive or think about them, is not the question before us. If it were possible to conceive of such atoms, at any rate you, before you begin to make anything of them, must think them; and you can never, by thinking about atoms, prove that there is no such thing as thought other than as an ultimate product of atoms. Before you could reach thought or mind as a last result, you must needs eliminate it from the data of the problem with which you start; and that you can never do, any more than you can stand on your own shoulders or outstrip your own shadow.

The vicious circle which materialism involves is traceable to a common illusion to which all minds are subject, of which many educated minds cannot wholly disabuse themselves, and which it is the function of philosophy to correct. The ordinary and unreflecting observer seems to himself to be confronted by a world of realities existing in themselves, just as he perceives them, and of which he is simply the passive spectator. All he knows of these outward realities,—their solidity, extension, figure, number, weight, measure, their permanent identity, their likenesses and differences, nay, their varied colours, sounds, tastes, &c.,

—are to him objective facts, existing in nature just such as they are reflected in the mirror of his own consciousness. The more cultured observer has, of course, got beyond any such blind sensationalism, admitting, as he does and must admit, that something at least of what ordinary thought ascribes to nature and external objects, exists only relatively to the sensibility of the observer. But he, too, not seldom, in a more elaborate though still unconscious way, is betrayed into the same error of transferring to the phenomenal world, or to outward experience, what is due to, and presupposes, the originating power of thought. He will look at the actual world as it is before him. He will accept nothing that is not given by observation and experience. Nothing for him shall have any further import or validity than it can be shown to have from the most careful observation of nature. He will simply record, at most classify and generalise, her facts and phenomena, and have nothing to do with empty abstractions and subjective fictions. Yet here too there is often the same illusion to which I have referred. The empiricist or materialist, while supposing himself to be dealing with hard material facts and experiences, is found employing such abstractions as *force, law, matter*, as if they were on the same level with sensuous things, and treating them in his investigations and reasonings as real entities, immediately given, apart from the activity of thought to which they truly belong. Or again, while contemning all that is supersensible, he is continually using, and cannot advance a single step without using—though often in a hap-hazard and uncritical manner—such categories as *unity*, *multiplicity*, *identity*, *difference*, *cause*, *effect*, *substance*, *properties*, &c., which are pure metaphysical forms, unconsciously adopted, without warrant or justification, from that realm of ideas which he ignores or denies. The empiricist, in short, is, and cannot help being, an unconscious metaphysician, the materialist an unconscious spiritualist.

To illustrate this briefly:—All our knowledge of nature, let it be conceded, is derived from experience. But experience involves something that is not given in sensation, and without which experience itself could not exist. It is by our organs of sense that we converse with nature. The utmost, however, which, by their means, we can attain is simply isolated and transient sensations. But isolated sensations are not knowledge. If this were all, our consciousness would be but the stage athwart which flitted an endless series of fugitive impressions—transient, unrelated, incoherent, chasing and obliterating each other, incapable of being arrested so as to be compared or combined, incapable not merely of being built up into a solid framework of science, but of constituting the smallest object of real knowledge. No repetition or reproduction could make these dumb phantoms articulate; for there would be nothing to give them the capacity of self-identification, the power of reporting or explaining their own recurrence. We must have the presence of some unifying, concentrating power amidst the flux of impressions, in order to reclaim them from chaos, to identify, relate, compare, co-ordinate them into coherent objects of knowledge. And this constant amidst the variable, this unifying power, is, and can only be, that spiritual self, that self-conscious Ego, which is not given by sense, which is not in this or that sensation but common to all sensations, to which they are each and all referred, and which locks them together in the unity of thought. In one word, to constitute the reality of the outward world—to make possible the minimum of knowledge, nay, the very existence for us of molecules and atoms—you must needs presuppose that thought or thinking self, which some would persuade us is to be educed or evolved from them.

The originating power of thought is thus implied or presupposed in order to gain even that point of departure for science which is involved in the existence of outward things, since no relations are predicable save of objects that have each a definite identity. It is only a wider expression of the same principle when we connect things together in an ordered system by the notion of *Cause and Effect*. The particular sciences are only a deliberate and systematic following out of the process by which, at the outset of experience, thought correlates isolated sensations. That notion of Force or Physical Causality, from which the materialist would construct the world independently of mind, is itself a creation or category of mind, and instead of looking for thought or mental energy as the final product into which force is convertible, we must regard force as itself something which exists only for thought. It is true that what the empiricist understands by Causality is nothing more than the regular co-existences and successions of phenomena which sensible experience gives, and that he regards any bond of necessity between them as a mere subjective fiction or metaphysical illusion. But, that causality is not an illusive notion superimposed on experience, is proved by the fact that no experience, and especially no scientific or systematic experience, would be possible without it. The notion or belief in the uniformity of nature, on which all science rests, is not built up by experience, but is presumed in every single act of scientific observation. For in the endeavour to account for any change, we imply that it is a change in an order which is, by supposition, constant, and it is only on that presupposition that there is any need to account for it. Alteration that is not referred to what does *not* alter is the alteration of nothing. That there are sequences which are not arbitrary but invariable—linked together by a bond of absolute necessity—is a foregone presumption in every investigation or experiment by which we seek to discover and register the conditions under which phenomenal change takes place. In other words, science, in order to its very existence, rests on an idea, not indeed brought to or superimposed on nature, but perceived in nature, yet which mere sensible experience could never give us—the idea, namely, of necessary causation. And so we recur again to the principle that you cannot evolve thought out of the forces or material energies of nature, seeing that in order to any knowledge of these, nay, to the very existence of these—if the word existence is to have any meaning for us—thought is already presupposed. All materialistic explanations involve the vicious circle, that matter which is the object of thought is that which produces thought. To make thought a function of matter is thus, simply, to make thought a function of itself.

2. The second vice involved in materialistic theories is, as I have said, that of attempting to make mechanical causation the master principle by which all the phenomena of the world, from those of inorganic nature up to conscious intelligence, are explained. Chemical relations are, it is suggested, only a special form of molecular physical relations,

vital relations are simply specially conditioned chemical or molecular relations; and, though the proof is yet wanting, it will one day be the triumph of scientific investigation to find in sensation, feeling, volition, in all the phenomena of mind, that which is only a function of material organisation, and therefore only a new manifestation of the universal, all-dominating agency of mechanical force.

But is this principle, when we closely examine it, thus capable of universal application? Can we extract from it any intelligible explanation, not only of organisation, but of life and thought? In the first place, are the phenomena of organisation adequately explained by the action, under any conceivable conditions, of mechanical and chemical forces? When we pass from the relations of inorganic to those of organised existences, is there no demand for any new and higher conception in order to the apprehension of the latter? Now, without pretending to deal with the question from the point of view of the scientific investigator—nay, even conceding to him that a time may come when the evolution of life from inorganic substances, apart from the influence of pre-existing life, shall be no longer a conjecture—I think it may be shown that there is here a gap, a solution of continuity, which it is impossible by the help of the supposed master-principle of force to bridge over.

From the purely scientific point of view, in opposition to physical theories of life, biological writers have called attention to such facts as these:—that no single instance has as yet been adduced of the production of life from purely chemical constituents; that therefore *generatio æquivoca*, or, the evolution of life independently of the influence of preceding life, is still an unsupported hypothesis; and that protoplasm, the supposed physical basis of life, cannot be placed on the level of mere chemical compounds. The protoplasm which can be analysed, and of which the chemical constitution is known, is not living but dead protoplasm, whilst that protoplasm which can be designated living, though containing similar elements with that which is not living, manifests qualities or functions that are totally new, and which, therefore, cannot be ascribed to its merely chemical or physical composition. If a substance manifests, at one time, qualities which are purely mechanical or chemical, and at another time, such qualities as the capacity of building itself up into an organised structure, and such functions as those of assimilation and reproduction, the legitimate inference, it is argued, is that, in the latter case, the new phenomena are due to the presence of a new factor, which was not present in the phenomena we designate mechanical or chemical.

But leaving such considerations to those who

are competent to deal with them, there is, I think, another point of view from which the inadequacy of the theory in question may be shown. Conceding that there is a sense in which matter may be said to contain in it the potentiality of life, and even that, as above said, under certain conditions of inorganic matter or certain modes of the activity of inorganic forces, life may begin to manifest its presence, it still remains as impossible as ever to embrace organic under a common category with inorganic nature, or to apply the principle of mechanical causation to the phenomena of life. For, when we reach life, whatever the antecedent physical conditions of its evolution may be, the phenomena before us demand a new and higher conception to grasp them. Here the thought or intelligence that is present in nature, and without which the world would be unintelligible and science an impossibility, breaks forth into a new and higher expression of itself, reveals itself in a phenomenal form which it needs a new principle of intelligence to interpret. In the simplest forms of life, and more palpably in the more highly developed organisms, there meets us that which compels the mind to pass from the conception of force or efficient causation to the altogether more complex conception of self-causation or self-development—of a cause which dominates and co-ordinates other causes and bends them towards the attainment of a common end.

In other words, the highest idea which inorganic nature or the sphere of physical causation reveals is that of force—of a unity which appears successively under different forms; what the inorganic world or the sphere of life reveals is not the idea of a unity which passes away in one form to reappear in another, but of a unity which perpetually goes out into differences and returns upon itself, or, in more formal language, a unity which maintains itself by continuous self-differentiation and integration. Now, what we have here to insist on is, that, whether the phenomena of organisation be empirically the consequent of inorganic phenomena or no, they can be understood only by the aid of a new and higher category. In them we have intelligence disclosing itself in a richer movement, and therefore demanding a higher activity of our intelligence to grasp it. What more, then, let us for a moment inquire, does this richer movement or expression of thought involve? It involves, I answer—not to dwell on other points—at least these three ideas:—

(*a*) The idea of system or systematic unity;

(*b*) The idea of a systematic unity which is immanent or self-sustained; and

(*c*) The idea (perfectly manifested, indeed, only in the yet higher stage of thought or intelligence) of a unity which exists not merely for you, the observer, but also for the organism itself.

(*a*) In all organisms there is involved the new conception of *systematic unity.* With certain apparent exceptions, the unities of the inorganic world — those unities which are produced by mechanical and chemical forces—are either mere unities of aggregation, in which the parts are related to each other only externally, and the whole is indifferent to the parts; or unities in which the whole is produced by the annulling of the individual existence of the parts or elements of which it is composed. The parts of a stone are only repetitions of each other; they exist, so to speak, outside of each other, and are only accidentally combined in a mass which is held together by external or mechanical force. If any part is struck off, the diminished mass remains a unity as complete as the original whole. But a living organism is not a mere aggregation of independent parts, but a systematised unity of members, each of which has its individual place and function. If any one member be severed from such a system, both the whole and the lopped-off member cease to be unities and become fragments; they descend into the lower stage where there is no unity but that of mechanical aggregation. The totality here is something more than the sum of its parts; there are infused into the parts the invisible elements of order, proportion, diversity of form, distribution of function according to a general idea or end. And so, if you break up the organic structure into isolated parts, that which constituted the essential existence of the organism is gone.

But (*b*) in organic structures we find not only the idea of system, but also the idea of system which is *self-developed*—in other words, not only of a unity of diversified parts or elements correlated by one principle, but of a unity which is due to the self-activity of that principle. We can conceive in mere inorganic matter a systematic order imposed from without and maintained simply by the action of inorganic forces. Every human construction, such as a house or a piece of mechanism, is an order of this kind, for it is the arrangement of many dissimilar parts for the realisation of a common idea or plan. But in all such constructions, the idea or plan is something foreign to the nature of the separate parts or materials by means of which it is realised; and, in order to produce it, these parts must surrender or be deprived of their individual existence and value. The stones, the wood, the lime, which compose the house have nothing in themselves which makes it necessary that they should be combined in the house; the iron, steel, brass, and other materials of the watch or steam-engine, have not anything in their own nature which is unfulfilled until they come together in the skilfully-planned machine. There is, indeed, thought in them—the thought which even mechanical force involves—but the further thought that has combined them into a common artificial unity, is not in them, but imposed on them arbitrarily and, so far as their own essential nature goes, accidentally and externally. Instead of fulfilling their own nature in producing that end, they are *used up* to produce it. In a complex living organism it is quite otherwise. Here we come upon the conception of a unity in which the idea or end is not arbitrarily imposed from without, on certain independent materials, but is the result of an internal spontaneity or self-activity, working out diversities of member, form, function, from its own inherent self-producing energy, and, at the same time, in the very act of differentiating, re-integrating its diversities into the common unity. Here, also, instead of the end being outward and accidental to the means, it is their own immanent end; instead of the parts being used up for the production of the end, we have a membered totality in the production and maintenance of which the parts have their own natural fulfilment or realisation. In mechanical phenomena, the force which we conceive of as cause loses itself in the effect: the motion that is in the impinging ball passes away from it into that on which it impinges; motion that produces heat ceases to exist in its original form, &c. In chemical compounds, again, though we find different elements united according to the laws of affinity, yet in the neutral product we have a unity or totality in which the elements or extremes cease to possess any distinct individuality, the properties which constituted that individuality having vanished in the result they have gone to produce. But in an organic structure the relation of the members to the whole can no longer be conceived under the category of physical causation. For here we have a cause which does not pass away into, but lives and maintains itself *in*, its effects; and, on the other hand, we have effects which reflect themselves back on the cause, and in their very existence produce and perpetuate it. Every member or organ lives, maintains itself, has its own worth and development in the energy it gives forth; it is for ever giving up itself, only for ever to receive itself—losing itself to save itself. Instead of ceasing to possess what it gives away, it would be marred or cease to be, if its giving away were interrupted or arrested. We have here, in short, cause which is its own cause, which is at once cause and effect. Or—to state what is the point we have really reached—we have here an object of thought to which the conception of physical causality is inapplicable and for the interpretation of which it is altogether inadequate. We have reached a class of phenomena which demand a new conception or category to embrace them; or, stated otherwise, we find here that thought which is in Nature, which, indeed, Nature *is*, and which alone makes science or a knowledge of nature possible, rising to a new stage in the process of its self-revelation, flashing out upon us, so to speak, a new and deeper expression of its presence and power.

The third element in the conception of life which transcends the category of force will be better understood when we pass, finally, from the phenomena of life and organisation to those of thought and self-consciousness. If even organisation cannot be conceived as the expression of molecular changes or embraced under the category of force, it is obviously impossible that thought or intelligence can be embraced under it. "Thought," it has been confidently asserted, "is as much a function of matter as motion is." "I believe," writes Mr. Huxley,[1] "that we shall arrive at a mechanical equivalent of consciousness, just as we have arrived at a mechanical equivalent of heat:" and again, "Even those manifestations of intelligence and feeling which we rightly name the higher faculties, are not excluded from this classification" (*i.e.*, of phenomena resolvable into muscular contraction), "inasmuch as, to every one but the subject of them, they are known only as transitory changes in the relative positions of parts of the body." "As surely," again he writes, "as every future grows out of the past and present, so will the physiology of the future gradually extend

[1] *Macmillan's Magazine*, vol. xxii., p. 78.

the realm of matter and law until it is co-extensive with knowledge, with feeling, and with action."[1] It is indeed conceded by this eminent writer, and others of kindred tendencies, that there lies between physical and mental phenomena, between "muscular contractions" and "irritations of nervous tissue"—the molecular changes of organised matter which are the physical antecedents of thought—and the feelings, ideas, volitions which are their result, an impassable gulf. "How it is," says Mr. Huxley, "that anything so remarkable as a state of consciousness comes about as the result of irritating nervous tissue, is just as unaccountable as the appearance of the Djin when Aladdin rubbed his lamp in the story." "The passage," says Mr. Tyndall, "from the physics of the brain to the corresponding facts of consciousness is unthinkable." But if we reflect for a moment on the two propositions, first, that mind or mental activity is a mode or function of matter—that our feelings, ideas, volitions are the results of molecular changes in our physical organisation; and secondly, that, nevertheless, the connection between the two is absolutely unthinkable, I think we shall see that the inconceivability in the latter case is simply the result of the impossible problem involved in the former. If you first lay down the principle that heterogeneous and incommensurable

[1] *Lay Sermons*, p. 142.

classes of phenomena are to be embraced under a category applicable only to one of them, you need not wonder if, afterwards, you can discover no connecting link between them. If you resolve that the relations of mind and matter are to be brought under a category applicable only to material sequences, what can you expect but that the inadequate category should furnish no explanation of these relations? In truth, the alleged mystery of the connection of matter and mind is both less and greater than is by these writers supposed. It is less; for if material phenomena can be observed and known by the mind, there can be no absolute and impassable gulf between the two. If it is a mental movement, a process of thought, by which we have any cognisance of molecular changes in the brain, or by which such changes have for us any meaning or existence, then it is obvious that the latter cannot be absolutely foreign to, or separated by a hard impassable barrier from, the former. The gulf between the two is not "intellectually impassable," seeing that, in knowing or taking cognisance of material phenomena, the intellect actually passes it. On the other hand, the mystery of the connection of matter and mind is greater than the theory of these eminent physiologists represents, inasmuch as it is a connection which physical causation is altogether inadequate to explain. As in the transition from the inorganic to the organic world, so now when we pass from all the phenomena that belong to unconscious nature to the realm of consciousness or intelligence, we reach a point where our previous data can no longer suffice for the apprehension and explanation of the new elements that present themselves. We may fumble at the lock with the old categories, but we need another key to fit the wards before the door to the realm of consciousness will open to us. And the reason is not difficult to see. Partially, in the phenomena of life, but much more in those of consciousness or thinking intelligence, we have a result which it is impossible to co-ordinate with their physical antecedents. Material things have an existence which is purely objective; they exist, so to speak, not for themselves, but for us who observe them. But in feeling or sensation in the lower animals, and, much more completely, in thought or consciousness in man, we have a kind of existence which is subjective as well as objective, we have objects which exist, not for an outward observer only, but also for themselves. In the inorganic world we have existences—atoms, aggregates of matter, compounds,—the parts of which are outside of each other. In the organic world, but most of all in the realm of consciousness, we have a kind of externality which is at the same time internal, which is grasped by, and, so to speak, dissolved into itself. In the case of an animal organism the demand is made on thought to conceive not merely a totality of parts gathered up into the unity of a single life, but a unity which in sensaton and feeling realises, and in a sense becomes aware of itself. In a mind, again, which feels and thinks and wills, we are forced to think, not only a multiplicity of differences which, as in organism, though constituting a self-centred unity, have still nevertheless an external, spatial existence, an outwardness which neither life nor feeling can dissolve; but we have also the absolutely new and higher result of a multiplicity of differences which are wholly retracted out of a spatial outwardness. Here the faintest residuum of self-externality disappears and is dissolved into the perfect unity of self-consciousness. In self-consciousness we reach a point where the notion of force or the category of causation has lost all relevancy, for here we pass into a region where there are no longer any things divisible into parts, any objects existing outside of each other and so capable of being outwardly related as causes and effects. The indivisible unity of self-consciousness or of the self-conscious ego, transcends all differences, both external and internal. No *external* force can be the cause of thought, for every such force or agent exists in relation to thought, and the effect to be produced is already pre-supposed in the cause that is supposed to produce it. Nor, *internally*, can you conceive of one part of consciousness as the cause or force which gives rise to another, for in every part of consciousness the whole is present; in all the phenomena of mind, the ego or self is the universal and constant factor. You may attempt, as has often been done, to apply material analogies to mental phenomena—as when moral action is represented as the result of the force of motives acting on the will. But the analysis here is a purely fallacious one. It is only by an imaginative abstraction that one bit of mind or one 'faculty' of consciousness is thus, as if by a spatial division, separated from another. The mind that is to be acted on in volition is already present in the motives that are supposed to act on it. It is the mind that is moved which constitutes or gives their constraining power to the motives that are conceived to move it. In no single moment of its experience can thought be entirely passive, for the activity to which it yields is an activity which thought itself creates and constitutes, an activity, the form of which thought itself has already determined.

The objections we have now urged seem to be fatal to that false simplicity which materialism attempts to give to the world by reducing all things to expressions of force. To find unity, system, connection, continuity, in all things, is indeed the true and proper aim of science. But it is in vain that we attempt to realise it by seeking the explanation of a highly complicated system in its lowest and meagrest factor. The true explanation is to be found rather by reversing the order, by seeking the key to the beginning in the end, not to the end in the beginning. It may still be true that "in matter we have the promise and the potency of all terrestrial life," but it is in the sense in which it is also true that in the first prelusive note we have the promise and the potency of the whole symphony, in the first faint touch impressed on the canvas by the hand of genius the promise and the potency of the magnificent and finished work of art. In every great work of thought, the ideal in all its completeness governs the whole process; and there is not, from the very outset, one arbitrary stroke, one note or touch, that is not instinct with the power of the whole, and prophetic of its fulfilment. So, if we are ever to get at the true explanation of the world, it will doubtless be one according to which there will be no irrational gap or breach of systematic continuity between one order of existences or one class of forces and another, but the transition from the inorganic to the organic, from lower to higher forms of life, and, last of all, from all inferior orders of being to the self-conscious mind that thinks them, will be seen to be that of intelligible sequence and evolution—in other words, of a succession of elements so rigidly concatenated that the very lowest and least shall be in determinate relation to, and contain in it the prophecy and foreshadowing of, the last and highest, and the highest shall involve in it the lowest as its necessary presupposition. But if so, if we are in one sense to find in the lower the explanation of the higher, it will not be in the lower as lower, or in any qualities that specially pertain to it, but because the power of the higher is already working in it. If vegetable or animal life shall ever be shown to be evolved from inorganic matter, it will be only because inorganic matter contains in it something more than that which we designate inorganic—viz., that latent capacity of self-development which becomes explicit in the plant or animal. If thought can in any sense be said to be evolved from organisation, it can only be because the animal organisation contains in it implicitly something more than animal, higher than organic relations, viz., the germ of that perfect return upon itself, which mind in its self-consciousness for the first time explicitly reveals; and so, if you insist on seeing in matter the cause of mind, it is because you have already conceived of matter as more than matter, as containing in it virtually all that mind is. But a materialism which starts from a matter which is virtually mental or spiritual, ceases to be materialism in anything but the name. What it really means is, not that matter conceived of as something independent is the cause of mind, or that thought is only material force transformed; but that mind in the germ is that from which mind springs, that intelligence has its origin in that which is implicitly intelligent. But this is a view of the world which spiritualises matter rather than materialises mind : for in the whole realm of being down to the lowest existence in outward nature, it leaves nothing absolutely foreign and heterogeneous to thought, nothing which, either actually or virtually, thought cannot claim as its own.

## II.

Having now attempted to show in what respects the materialistic conception of the world is inadequate, we shall now endeavour to show what is that inward or rational necessity which forces the mind to rise to the point of view of Religion, in other words, which constitutes what we have called the *Necessity of Religion.*

We have seen that a theory which makes mind the final result or last development of nature is untenable, inasmuch as consciousness, which this theory represents as last, is also first. It cannot be resolved into anything that does not already involve itself, it is the presupposition and all-embracing element of that material world from which it is supposed to be evolved.

But when we have reached this point, we still seem to be far short of our professed aim. The disproof of the materialistic reduction of all things to the expression of mechanical force does not furnish any proof of God or any justification of the religious attitude of mind. Priority of thought or mind does not seem to prove the priority of Infinite or Absolute Mind, or to involve the necessity of that relation of the finite mind to it which religion implies. To prove the necessity of religion, it must be shown that that elevation of the human spirit above the finite, that upward movement of mind, which is involved in religion, is contained in the very nature of mind, is necessary to mind as mind. In the preceding section we have traced a certain progressive movement of thought according to which we are compelled, in our knowledge of the world, to proceed from lower to higher categories, embracing its phenomena under relations of ever deepening unity, as we advance from the mere co-existence of material objects in space, to their connection by mechanical force, then to their deeper reciprocal relationship under the notion of organic, self-differentiating, self-integrating unity, until we reach the highest finite unity, that of thought or self-consciousness in man. Can it be shown that not even at this point is the upward impulse arrested, but that by a like necessity we are driven beyond the finite, to find the ultimate rest of thought no where short of that which is Infinite and Absolute? To have shown that thought is the *prius* of all things is not enough, unless we can further show that the thought of which we thus speak is not individual or finite thought, but that the mind is impelled onwards by its own inward dialectic until it finds its goal in a thought which is universal and absolute—a thought or intelligence on which all finite thought and being rest. This is the task which is involved in the attempt to prove the necessity of religion.

1. In the very notion of a spiritual, self-conscious being there is already involved what may be called a virtual or potential infinitude. The first breath of spiritual life is indeed, in one sense, the realisation of this capacity, but in another sense, it is only the beginning of a realisation which is itself incapable of limitation. We are rational and spiritual beings only in virtue of the fact that we have in us the power to transcend the bounds of our narrow individuality, and to find ourselves in that which seems to lie beyond us. As contrasted with Nature and with other and lower orders of being, it is the prerogative of mind to be in virtual possession of a kind of infinitude; and its true life may be said to consist in the ceaseless endeavour to render that actually, which is from the beginning virtually, its own. Both Nature and man are finite; but when we consider the import of the terms 'finite' and 'infinite,' it is obvious that the finitude which belongs to the latter is very different from the hard and fast limitation which must be ascribed to the former. The finitude of material Nature is that of things which, by their very conception, are reciprocally exclusive, each individual existence lying outside of all others in

space, absolutely bounded by them, and capable only of being externally related to them. But the finitude which pertains to a spiritual, self-conscious being is the finitude of a nature which is limited only by that which is essentially one with itself, and which finds or realises itself in all by which it is limited. The individuality of Nature is an individuality which asserts itself against all that is without. The individuality of Mind is an individuality which is ever discovering in what is without—in all things and beings external to it—the means of its own progressive development. At first sight man seems to be bounded on all sides by a world of beings external to him, by forces which impose upon him conditions which he cannot escape, by laws which he cannot control or modify. Not only materially and physically is he subject to the same limitations which affect every other part of material Nature, but even in his inner and spiritual being he seems to be equally bounded. The very awakening of the consciousness of self is at the same time the awakening of the consciousness of a world without, to which, it would seem, the mind's relation is a purely passive and receptive one—a world which is continually pouring in upon it through the channel of sensation, experiences, and influences which it can neither make nor unmake, and which constitute the sole materials and the absolute limit of its knowledge.

When, however, we look more closely into the spiritual nature of man, we discern in it a peculiarity which distinguishes it from the finitude of Nature, and which is the silent prophecy or presentiment of that infinitude to which it aspires. For a spiritual nature is one to which, as above said, it essentially belongs to find or realise itself in that which lies beyond itself. Every atom of matter lies outside of every other. Even organised substances have parts outside of parts—parts characterised by an externality or reciprocal exclusiveness which not even feeling or sensation in the animal can wholly overcome; and beyond the individual animal nature there is a whole world of existences which are to it absolutely impenetrable. But it is the characteristic of a spiritual, intelligent being, that it is not and cannot be shut up in its own individuality, that it shares in the life of the world without, in the life of Nature and of all other spiritual beings, so that it is its growing participation in *their* life that constitutes the measure and the value of its own. Thus, when we examine more closely into the origin and nature of human knowledge, we find it impossible to rest in that representation of it which conceives of a world in absolute separation from us—of matter without as something essentially different from mind, and of the latter as only passively receiving impressions from the former. So far from that, our knowledge of Nature is really the breaking down of every barrier between mind and that which is objective or external to mind, and the discovery in all the objects and events of the outward world of a being and life that is essentially akin to our own. What, for instance, science finds in Nature is not something foreign to mind, but that which, as essentially rational, is a discovery to mind of its own latent wealth. It is not only a revelation of the world to the observing mind, but of the observing mind to itself. We not only see the mirror of Nature, but we see ourselves in it. Those unities which we call laws of nature and by which its individual objects are linked together in order, system, coherent relations, are nothing foreign to mind: they are things of thought, rational relations, discoveries to the intelligence that grasps them of the treasures of a realm which is its own, and in which it is free to expatiate. And when we turn from the realm of Nature to that of spirit, still less does thought find here a foreign element, an alien matter which limits its freedom or resists its progress. On the contrary, if we find ourselves in Nature, still more profoundly do our social relations become to us a revelation of ourselves, 'another which is not another,' a means of realising the latent wealth of our own spiritual being. Of all that is meant by such words as love, sympathy, affection, trust, of all the treasure of moral ideas which are contained in our relations to the family, the community, the state, we should never, if isolated in our own individuality, become the conscious possessors. Considered from a merely individualistic point of view, the social institutions amidst which we live are, every one of them, limits to our freedom. But considered from a higher point of view, it is just here, most of all, that there is provided an escape from the narrowness and poverty of the individual life, and the possibility of a life which is other and larger than our own, and yet which is most truly our own. For, to be ourselves, we must be more than ourselves. What we call love is, in truth, the finding of our own life in the life of another, the losing of our individual selves to gain a larger self. And as the scope of our sympathy widens till it embraces the more complex life of the family, the nation, the race, at each successive step we are simply expanding the range of our own spiritual life, escaping farther and farther from the finitude of the individual self, and approximating more and more to a life which is unlimited and universal. It is true that this process is never a completed one. In the intellectual and spiritual life the limits of our natural finitude are broken down, but even there the limit is one which ever re-appears. Our finitude, if it has not the fixed limitation of Nature, yet ever returns upon us in the sense of a limit that is continually removed only to be continually replaced. There is ever a boundless world beyond, which though a possible, is never for us an actual possession. The perfect unity of the ideal and the actual, of the universal and the individual life, is never reached by us, it is a goal that ever vanishes as we pursue it. We never are, but are ever only becoming, that which it is possible for us to be. We never enter into full possession of that which, as spiritual beings, is our rightful inheritance. And yet, in another point of view, we already possess and enjoy it; in the very fact that we can feel and know it to *be* our ideal inheritance, there is to us a revelation of the Infinite and of our essential relation to it. For it is to be considered that the distinction between knowing and being, between the ideal and the actual, between aspiration and experience, is one which is made by thought, and which therefore thought can transcend—nay, in the very act of making it, has already transcended. We cannot express the full meaning of our spiritual life unless by speaking of ourselves in one moment as striving after that, of which, in another moment, we can speak of ourselves as already in possession. Whether in our intellectual or our moral life, to distinguish between our actual selves and the object or end after which we aspire, is possible only because we are implicitly conscious of a relation to that object or end: and in the very distinction is presupposed the identity that is beyond the distinction. That we are capable of a perpetual progress in knowledge and goodness, and yet that every actual attainment leaves us with an ideal that is still unsatisfied; that we are conscious that our knowledge is limited, whilst yet we can set in thought no absolute limit to our knowledge, that we are conscious of our moral defects and, nevertheless, can feel that there is no point of moral advancement beyond which we may not aspire;—in this boundless possibility of advancement, combined with a latent standard of excellence which throws contempt on our highest actual attainments, we have that in our nature, as conscious spiritual beings, which constitutes what we have termed a potential infinitude. In other words, when we examine into the real significance of the rational and spiritual nature and life of man, we find that it involves what is virtually the consciousness of God and of our essential relation to Him.

2. The same idea may be regarded from a somewhat different point of view by recurring to the principle that the knowledge of a limit implies a virtual, and, in some sense, an actual transcendence of it. We can only, it may be maintained, be conscious of imperfection because we have within us, latent or explicit, a standard of absolute perfection by which we measure ourselves. It is our implicit or virtual knowledge of God, the relation of our nature as spiritual beings to Him, which alone gives reality to our partial knowledge, and

makes us aware that it *is* partial. It may indeed be said that no such conclusion is involved in the principle to which we have referred. Nothing so vast, it may be urged, as the knowledge of an Infinite Being is needed in order to awaken in us a sense of our finitude. The consciousness of our own imperfection may arise in us from something far less than the presence in our minds of the idea of absolute perfection as the standard of self-criticism. All that is required to produce it is simply the consciousness of that which is in any measure greater than ourselves—the consciousness, at each stage of our progress, that *something* lies beyond us. The sense of obstructed effort is sufficient to teach me the limitation of my own power, and all that is needed for that is that the obstruction be only a shade more powerful than myself. The conception of my own imperfect knowledge is forced on me by the presence of any intelligence relatively greater, however imperfect in itself. Not, therefore, a knowledge of the Infinite, but a knowledge of any thing or being that is less limited than myself, is, it would seem, all that is needed to bring home to me the sense of my own finitude.

But to this it must be answered that the standard to which, in the consciousness of our imperfection, we implicitly appeal cannot be itself a finite one, inasmuch as it is not applicable only to one or more stages of human attainment, but to all stages alike. It is a standard which, however far I advance, or can conceive myself to advance, would still reveal to me my finitude. It is an ideal for the finite as finite, and one, therefore, which must itself transcend the finite. All knowledge, even the most elementary, rests on the tacit assumption of an absolute criterion of knowledge—the assumption that we have as the basis of our consciousness a final standard of truth, an ideal of what is knowable, an ultimate ground of certitude which is the measure of all individual opinion, and which itself cannot be questioned without self-contradiction. I do not ultimately measure my knowledge or become aware of its limited and imperfect character by comparison with any other man's knowledge, for that also may be erroneous and imperfect, and to no finite or fallible authority can I render that submission which is due to absolute truth. But the secret or implicit conviction on which all knowledge rests, and to which all individual opinions and beliefs are referred, is that absolute truth *is*, or, in other words, that though my thought may err, there is an absolute thought or intelligence which it is impossible to doubt. That this is so, that the secret ground on which all finite intelligence rests is the consciousness of an Absolute Intelligence, or of an Intelligence in which absolute trust is to be reposed, will be obvious when we consider that our very doubts and uncertainties imply the consciousness of an absolute standard to which our doubts are referred. To extend our doubts to this is impossible, or possible only by the subversion of all consciousness, including the doubt itself. Absolute scepticism is suicidal, for it at least asserts its own truth, that is, it asserts as a truth that there is no such thing as truth; in other words, it implies a negation of the very standard to which it brings particular beliefs, and by which it condemns them. No assertion, no single experience or act of consciousness, is possible save as presupposing an ultimate intelligence which is the measure and the ground of all finite thought. Even in maintaining that the human mind is incapable of absolute knowledge the sceptic presupposes in his own mind an ideal of absolute knowledge in comparison with which human knowledge is pronounced defective. The very denial of an absolute intelligence in us could have no meaning but for a tacit appeal to its presence. An implicit knowledge of God, in this sense, is proved by the very attempt to deny it.

The same thing may be otherwise expressed by saying that all human knowledge, when we examine closely into its nature, will be seen to rest on or involve the pre-supposition of the unity of knowing and being, or of a unity which embraces all thought and existence. The ultimate basis of consciousness is not the consciousness of self, for the individual's consciousness of self would have no meaning if it did not rest on a more universal consciousness which lies beneath it. The consciousness of self is given only in relation to the consciousness of that which is not self. We cannot separate, in any act of thought, the two factors or elements—the object perceived or thought of, and the subject or mind which thinks it. We may distinguish, but we cannot divide these two, or for a moment conceive an object or thing in itself apart from a thinking subject, or again the latter in abstraction from objects thought of. Subject and object are correlatives as indivisible as the notions of outward and inward, motion and rest, parent and child, &c. But the very fact that the two elements are inseparably related proves and rests on the consciousness that there is a unity which lies beyond the distinction. In relating my individual self to an outward object, I at the same time necessarily presume that the two, I and the object, are not only distinguishable as terms in the relation, but that there is a wider unity in which they are both alike embraced. In other words, the distinction between self and not-self, between the individual mind and the world of outward objects, is a distinction which thought, by the very fact that it can make it, shows that it can transcend, and has already virtually transcended. The consciousness which apprehends both self and its object cannot be confined only to *one side* of the contrast. When we think, we rise above our individual existence as limited by the outward world, to an existence which is not so limited, which comprehends both all individual selves and the world. We do not think, that is, as individual beings, but as passing over to and sharing in a universal thought or reason. Were we shut up in our own individuality, our life would be that only of the animal, or that to which the animals are supposed to be confined—a thing of isolated sensations, without any consciousness either of a permanent self or object, or of a universality beyond and comprehending both. But it is our prerogative as spiritual beings, that we can rise above the feeling of the moment, above all that is isolated and individual. We can make our own individual selves objects of thought quite as much as other individual selves. We can enter into a sphere of thought which has no relation to our individual selves. We can think of a time when we did not exist, we can think away our own and other individual existence, but we cannot think away thought or conceive of *its* non-existence. If we try to annul all existence, to think that nothing exists, the nothing is still a thinkable nothing, a nothing that is for thought, or that implies a thought or consciousness behind it. Thus all our conscious life as individuals, rests on or implies a consciousness that is universal. We cannot think, save on the pre-supposition of a thought or consciousness which is the unity of thought and being, or on which all individual thought and existence rest.[1]

We have seen then that the nature of man as a spiritual being involves these two things: (1) the capacity of transcending his own individuality, of finding or realising himself in that which lies beyond him and seems to limit him; (2) the latent or implicit consciousness of the absolute unity of thought and being, or of an absolute self-consciousness on which all finite knowledge and existence rest. In these two principles—the first of which implies the never-ending impulse to transcend ourselves; the second of which points to a Universal or Absolute Mind as that in which the effort to transcend ourselves finds its ultimate explanation, we discern, deep laid in man's nature, that which constitutes the basis of religion.

[1] This argument is more fully developed *infra*, chap. viii.

## CHAPTER V.

### THE PROOFS OF THE EXISTENCE OF GOD.

THE view which I have now attempted to express may be further developed and explained by a brief examination of the so-called proofs of the existence of God. For these proofs, in so far as they possess any real significance, are simply expressions of that impossibility of resting in the finite and of that implicit reference to an Infinite and Absolute Mind, which we have seen to be involved in our nature as rational and spiritual beings. Considered as proofs in the ordinary sense of the word, they are open to the objections which have been frequently urged against them; but viewed as an analysis of the unconscious or implicit logic of religion, as tracing the steps of the process by which the human spirit rises to the knowledge of God, and finds therein the fulfilment of its own highest nature, these proofs possess great value. This, by a brief review of them, I shall now attempt to show.[1]

[1] See on this subject Professor Edward Caird's *Critical Account of the Philosophy of Kant*, chap. xviii.

Taken in their natural order, the proofs of the being of God are the three following: (1) The Cosmological, (2) The Teleological, (3) The Ontological; and when we examine them we shall see that, stated in this order, they unfold the successive steps in the process which I have called the implicit or unconscious logic of religion.

1. The first, or *Cosmological* argument, is the argument *from the contingency of the world.* Reduced to its briefest expression, it is simply this:—The contingent world exists, or, the world of our immediate experience is contingent, therefore an absolutely necessary Being exists. It starts from the thought that the world as presented to our immediate experience has in it no substantiality or independence. Its existence cannot be explained from itself; and the mind in trying to account for it is forced to fall back on something outside of it, and finds rest only in the idea of a Being who is necessary, self-dependent, substantial. The movement of thought which this argument involves may be stated in various forms or under different categories. It may be put as an argument from the world viewed as phenomenal, to an absolute substance out of which all phenomena spring; or from the world viewed as an effect to a First Cause; or more generally from the world viewed as finite and relative to an infinite and absolute Being on whom it rests. But in all these and other forms, the gist of the argument is the

same. If we take it, for example, in the form in which it turns on the idea of causality, it is the argument, that whatever does not exist necessarily exists only through another being as its cause, and that again, if itself not necessary, through another: and as an infinite regress of finite or contingent beings related as causes and effects is unthinkable, the mind is compelled to stop short and place at the head of the series a First Cause, a Being which is its own cause, or which exists unconditionally and necessarily.

Translated out of this abstract form, this argument is simply the expression of the fact that the first dawn of religious feeling may be traced to the impression which our experience of life forces upon us of the transitory, unsubstantial, evanescent character of the world on which we look and of which we form a part. "The world passeth away and the lust thereof": "The things that are seen are temporal": "Our life is but a vapour that appeareth for a little and then vanisheth away":—such words as these express a feeling old as the history of man, which the fleeting, shifting character of the scene on which we look, the transiency of life, the inadequacy of its satisfactions, the insecurity of its possessions, the lack of any fixed stay, of anything enduring and real on which our thoughts and desires can rest—which, in briefer terms, the contingency and unsubstantiality of the world and the things of the world inevitably awaken in the mind, and which impels us to seek after a reality beyond the world of shadows, an enduring and eternal rock on which, amidst the stream that bears us away, we may plant our feet.

Now in this very feeling of the instability and illusoriness of the world, there is something which betrays the presence in the mind of what may be called the germ of the idea of God. The very consciousness of our finitude, as we have seen, indicates that we have already transcended it. If we were wholly finite we should never be conscious of our finitude. We could have no sense of imperfection but for the presence in us of a standard of perfection. The discernment of vanity and illusion is already the implicit recognition of a truth and reality by which we measure the world of appearances. That we regard the world only as the domain of "the things seen and temporal," implies at least a latent reference to the idea of an invisible and eternal life, an existence in which is no variableness or shadow of turning.

But when we attempt to translate this experience into the language of formal reasoning, and to give it, as above, the form of a syllogistic proof of the existence of God, we altogether misinterpret its meaning, and our argument becomes open to the objections which have been urged against it.

The most important of these objections is, that

the result which, in strict logic, it gives is purely negative, and that the positive result which it pretends to give is not legitimately reached. You cannot in a syllogistic demonstration put more into the conclusion than the premises contain. Beginning with an infinite or absolute cause, you might conclude to finite effects, but you cannot reverse the process. All that from a finite or contingent effect you can infer is a finite or contingent cause, or at most, an endless series of such causes. But if, because the mind cannot rest in this false infinity, you try to stop the indefinite regress and assert at any point of it a cause which is not an effect, which is its own cause, or which is unconditioned and infinite, the conclusion in this case is purely arbitrary. True, indeed, it is through the negation of the finite or contingent that thought rises to a higher conception—to the idea of that Being who is really a *causa sui*, in whom cause and effect are united. But in a process of deduction such a transition—such a leap from a lower to another and higher idea or principle—is of course inadmissible. To drag in, because of a mental incapacity to go on thinking that false infinity which is merely an infinite series of finites, a name that seems to indicate a true infinity, is simply to conceal under a phrase the break down of the argument.

Another way of stating the objection is to point out that, from the nature of deduction, the infinite or necessary Being of this argument is not really infinite or necessary. He is not infinite: for the world from which we conclude to him, inasmuch as its existence remains as a positive existence outside of the supposed infinite, constitutes a limit to it or reduces it to something finite. He is not necessary: for he is related to the world as a cause to its effect; but in the relation of cause and effect, the cause is as much conditioned by the effect as the effect by the cause. Even if this argument proved necessity, it would not be a necessity of existence but merely a necessity of causation. You may form a conception of two beings of which, if they existed, one would be the necessary cause of the other; but this does not prove that the former, though it has a necessity relatively to the latter, possesses any absolute necessity of existence.

Though, however, the argument fails as a logical demonstration, it has, in another point of view, a real and deeper value. It is, as I have said, a step in the process by which the mind is led to the realisation of that Infinite Being, of whom, in its very perception of the world's evanescence and finitude, it shows itself implicitly conscious. We deny the finite because, as spiritual beings, we secretly know the Infinite and are under an irresistible inward impulse to seek after Him. The conception which in this first movement of thought we reach is not so much false as inadequate. The idea of an infinite which negates or annuls the finite, however insufficient, is true and necessary as a stepping-stone towards a higher idea. And when we have taken this first step, the same necessity forces us on to a second, the hidden logic of which is that which is represented to us in the second of the arguments above enumerated, viz., the *Teleological*, or, as it is commonly called, the *Argument from Design.*

2. Considered as a logical proof we have seen that the Cosmological argument fails, but that its truth and significance consist in this, that it is the first step of the movement by which, according to the secret logic of religion, thought advances to a higher and richer idea. That advance may be represented by saying that the Infinite we reach by the denial of the finite is not the true Infinite, for the true Infinite must embrace or explain the finite, instead of annulling it. At first, indeed, the mind, in the search for an absolute reality, seeks it in the mere negation of the unreal and transient. When we cannot find the real or substantial in the world of immediate experience, we naturally look for it in that which is the opposite or contradictory of that world. But an Infinite which is merely the negation of the finite, a necessary Being who is merely the negation of the contingent, is not truly infinite or absolute. The idea thus

attained contains in it nothing positive; it is derived from and determined by that to which it is opposed. If we cannot think the contingent save in relation to the necessary, neither can we think the necessary save in relation to the contingent. The latter depends as much on the former as the former on the latter. And, on the other hand, though we have reduced the world of experience to a mere appearance or accident, yet, *as* appearance or accident, it has an existence which still needs to be accounted for. Say that it is but a vain show, a vapour that appeareth for a little and vanisheth away; yet, the question still arises, Whence came it? Why is it? What is the reason of its existence? If we are such stuff as dreams are made of, yet our very dreams have a relation to a real and waking life, and even the vagaries of slumber, in their extravagance and fleetingness, point to a something more substantial of which they are the reflection. The world of experience may be insubstantial and phenomenal, still, in the reality which we seek beyond that world there must be something that accounts for it, and does not merely annul it; and that is *more* infinite, if we may use such an expression, which contains and explains the finite, than that which denies or ignores it. That necessity is higher which contains in it the reason, both of itself and the contingent, than that necessity which is merely the contradiction of the contingent.

By its own necessary movement, therefore, thought goes in quest of such an idea—the idea of an Infinite whose existence explains both itself and the existence of the finite world.

Now, in the attempt to reach such an idea, the first solution is that which is represented by the argument which conceives of the relation of God to the finite world as that of Creator and Contriver. The transition to this idea is explained by the need which the mind feels to get beyond the alternatives of Contingent and Necessary, and the first effort to satisfy that need is expressed by the notion of a necessity which is not conditioned by the contingent, which is complete in itself and self-determined. In the idea of an all-wise Creator or Designer we have the conception of a cause which is not merely the correlate of an effect outside of itself, but which is self-conscious and self-determined before it determines anything else. God is thus thought of as a Being, self-conscious and self-contained, who freely, or of His own will and pleasure, creates and works out certain purposes or ends in the world; and as these ends indicate skill, contrivance, ingenious adaptation of means to the accomplishment of a foreseen plan, we infer in Him not only infinite power but also infinite wisdom or forethought.

Now, it is to be noticed that that which gives to this argument its plausibility and attractiveness to the popular mind is just that which greatly impairs its force for the scientific mind. To the former, the most striking manifestations of spiritual power are those in which it brings about arbitrarily, by the mere exercise of will, results which the materials employed have no natural tendency to produce. The ingenuity and deftness of a human artist are shown in moulding into accordance with a preconceived plan rude material elements which could never by any possibility, from their own nature, have so shaped themselves. If stone and wood and mortar had any natural tendency to grow into houses; or iron, brass, zinc, and other metals, into watches, steam engines, electric machines, the mechanist would lose his credit for contrivance and dexterity, or would be entitled to only the inferior honour of the gardener, who takes advantage of the natural capacities of seeds and plants to produce fruits and flowers, or of the teacher who successfully educates a mind rich in natural gifts. In the former case, it is because, as it is said, the mere pieces of dead matter could not shape themselves into correlations of means with useful or beautiful ends, that the skill of the external designer is rendered so striking. In like manner, when we see the rough materials of the world, which have no inherent tendency to frame themselves into such results, wrought up into planetary systems, vital organisms—into innumerable and diversified structures, each often in itself, in form and function, a marvel of exquisite combination and contrivance, and finding itself also in wondrous correspondence with the other existences around it––this view of a world in which things having no natural connection are adjusted, in a marvellous way, to each other for a definite purpose, at once suggests to us the presence of an External Designer of infinite power and wisdom, by whose agency alone such results can be conceived possible.

But though there is much in this view which, taken as a pictorial or popular representation, may furnish materials for pious feeling, yet, regarded as a logical argument, it is by no means unexceptionable. For the relation of God to the world on which it turns is a relation which, in the first place, is a merely external, and, in the second place, a purely arbitrary one.

(1.) The notion of an external designer is something far short of perfect or absolute wisdom and power. It is beset by limitations which pertain to its very essence, and render it incapable of application to a Being, by supposition, infinite. A human contriver works on materials prepared to his hand; the thought or idea which he works out is something that is in him and not in them. In dealing with these materials he is limited by their inherent nature, and his ingenuity is displayed either in overcoming their intractableness, or in taking dexterous advantage of their natural qualities, so as to impose upon them an ideal form foreign to their original nature. When, again, the human designer has completed his machine, his thought and power do not continue any longer with it; he commits it to the custody of 'laws of nature,' of natural forces and energies which are altogether foreign to the thought and power that were at work in its construction. It cannot be said that these are limitations which apply only to a human or finite designer and which vanish when the designer is to be conceived of as himself both creator and sustainer of the materials with which he works. On the contrary, they are limitations which cling to the very conception of an external designer, and which do not admit of correction by the rude device of supplementing the notion of design by the additional notions of creation and providence. Our admiration of the power and skill of a human designer is, as above said, enhanced by the supposed intractableness of the materials with which he works; but when the divine designer is conceived of as himself the creator of these materials, he must, according to this anthropomorphic notion, be himself responsible for that original intractableness which he is supposed afterwards to manifest his skill in overcoming. Where difficulties are of one's own creating, no credit for wisdom can be due to the act which evades or vanquishes them.

Even when the designer is conceived of, not as overcoming the resistance of matter, but as taking advantage of natural tendencies and laws, the thought which he brings to bear upon them has still the character of an *after*thought. There is nothing in these supposed original tendencies—nothing in matter as matter—which makes it necessary that it should develope into the organised structures and systems of nature; if there were any such necessity, the whole force of the argument would be gone. The form of thought, therefore, under which we are forced to conceive of this designer is, at best, that of an agent who comes in with a second idea, or a subsequently struck-out device, not present to him in his original or creative thought; of one who improves upon or corrects his first conception. Finally, though by the supplementary notion of Providence, we get rid of the limitation above referred to in the case of human contrivers, viz., that their thought and power cease to be in or with their work as soon as they have finished its construction and surrendered it to the keeping of the ordinary laws of nature, yet this device does not wholly purge the primary idea of its finitude. The Providence that comes in to sustain the mechanism which the Divine Contriver has completed is something outside of that mechanism itself, and therefore limited by it. The work has a definite nature of its own, apart from the power that merely props it up or keeps it going. As we cannot think of the Divine Contriver as going on perpetually re-creating the same work, but must think of the completed work as having a particular character and form of its own which He has merely to sustain, it is obvious that there must be something in the work which lies outside of or apart from Him.

There is, indeed, another kind of teleology—what may be designated as inner or essential teleology—to which the foregoing objections are not applicable, and of which, as I formerly said, we have an example in the animal organism. The thought or design which is at work in the growth and development of organised structures is not a mere mechanical power or cunning acting from without—shaping, adjusting, putting together materials prepared to its hand, constructing them according to an ingenious plan, after the manner of a maker of machines. Here, on the contrary, the idea or formative power goes with the matter, and constitutes the very indwelling essence of the thing. Instead of coming in as an afterthought, to give to existing materials a new use and purpose not included or presupposed in their own original nature, the idea or design is present from the very beginning, inspiring the first minute atom or cell with the power of the perfect whole that is to be. Nor, for the building up and completing of the structure, is there any call for the interposition of external agency. From first to last it is self-formative, self-developing; the life within resists all merely outward interference, and subordinates all outward conditions to its own development. In this case, therefore, we do not need to go beyond or outside of the thing itself in seeking for the explanation of it. The thought or reason that explains it is within itself, nay, *is* its very self; so that to perceive or know the thing at all, is to perceive or know the reason and ground of its existence. Nor, lastly, can we here separate the notions of existence and preservation —the nature of the thing, and the providence that keeps it up—so as to make the one a limit to the other. The idea, or active formative thought, in which an organism lives, needs no second or foreign idea to preserve or sustain it. It is, in a certain sense, its own providence. The continuous existence of the organism lies in the perpetual activity of the vital principle, which is, so to speak, ever re-creating it, ever engaged in that process of continuous self-differentiation and integration, the cessation of which would be the extinction of its very existence.

Now, if it were possible to extend this teleological idea to the whole finite world, we should be able to see in the world the manifestation of a kind of design to which the objections urged against the ordinary design argument would no longer be applicable; for what we should then have before us would be one vast, self-consistent system, one organic whole, one self-evolving, self-realising idea, infusing the lucidity of reason into all things, potentially present in the lowest order of existences, slowly advancing itself, without cleft or arbitrary leap, from lower to higher; so that the lower, though not the cause, would be the presupposition and the unconscious prophecy of the higher, the higher the explanation of the lower, and the highest of all that in which the meaning, end, or aim of the whole would be clearly seen. Such a teleological view of the world would not involve a representation of Divine Intelligence as an arbitrary agency brought in from without to fill up gaps or improve on its original products, nor as a power acting in different isolated capacities—now as creator, now as contriver, now as sustainer—but as the inward life and reason of all things anticipating and foreshadowing the end from the beginning, and moving onwards in its own continuous, self-conditioned process to an end which itself determines. But whilst it may not be impossible for us to rise to such a conception of the world and its relation to God, yet it is obvious that this is not an idea which can be reached empirically or by any such method of proof as that on which the design argument proceeds. We cannot conclude to the final cause of the world from any special adaptations or ingenious correspondencies which its particular phenomena exhibit; for the very notion of a final cause implies that, short of itself, no such perfect adaptations exist, that all lower ends are incomplete and imperfect viewed in themselves, and that, so far from furnishing independent proofs of the final order or Divine thought, they are themselves only intelligible by means of it. It is only in the light of the Divine idea that for the first time we see the design or end of nature and man; how then can we build our belief in God on any prior perception of design or end in them? The God we could logically infer from any or all of them would only be an imperfect God, inasmuch as it is their very nature, viewed as individuals, to be incomplete, and to find their complements, each in the other parts of the system to which it belongs, and all alike in its perfect realisation. Even if the argument were otherwise unexceptionable by which we infer a design in each of the innumerable instances of adaptation with which the world abounds, yet a thousand finite designers would never make up the idea of that Being, of whom and through whom and to whom are all things.

2. A second defect of the Design argument is, as I have said, that according to the view it gives, the relation of God to the world is a purely arbitrary one. To see in the world a manifestation of infinite wisdom, both the existence of the world

and all that is in it must be traceable to something in the *nature* of God, and not to mere arbitrary will and power. If we knew beforehand the nature of God we might conclude, even where we could not trace the connection between that nature and His works, that everything in them is consistent with perfect wisdom; but we cannot reverse the process. We cannot conclude, apart from any discernment of the reason and meaning of the thing, that the inexplicable or anomalous must be grounded in infinite wisdom and goodness. Unsolved enigmas and contradictions are inadmissible in an empirical induction. Knowing you to be good and wise, I may believe that conduct of which I cannot understand the reason, or which, at first blush, seems to be unwise and perverse, must yet be somehow in perfect consistence with goodness and wisdom; but if I know nothing of you save through your actions, if I am to divine your character only from these, unmeaning or ambiguous actions either tell me nothing about it, or tell me that it is so far imperfect. At best, amidst conflicting or inexplicable manifestations of character, I can only suspend my judgment. And this difficulty has still greater force when, as in the case before us, we have not to determine from his actions the character of a Being we know, but to discover whether the Being we call God actually exists. Now, it is obvious that from a merely arbitrary product—from works or actions that are, by supposition, the result simply of will or power—we can infer nothing as to the essential nature of their author. A result which is not necessarily involved in the nature of its cause, but which we try to connect with it by the notion of mere creative will, proves nothing as to that cause, not even so much as its existence. Having convinced ourselves from independent reasons of the existence of an Infinite Intelligence, we may be content to ascribe the existence of the world to such a Being, though its creation be to us a notion altogether incomprehensible. But when we attempt to demonstrate the existence of Infinite Intelligence from the existence of the world and its contents, a final appeal to an inexplicable creative will and power vitiates the argument. It will not suffice to say, 'Matter, or a material world, could not make itself, therefore it must have an all-wise Creator;' for this is not to find the proof of Infinite Mind in the world, but merely, when the traces of mind fail us—when we cease to see reason in things finite—to substitute assertion for reason, or to call in, to aid our otherwise incomplete proof, a *deus ex machina* of arbitrary power.

The imperfection of this idea of the relation of Infinite Mind to the world may be seen by comparing it with that which is involved in the Christian doctrine of the Logos. For, according to the latter,

God is not a mere abstract Infinite shut up in barren self-sufficiency, but an Infinite which, by its very nature, must reveal itself in, and communicate itself to, a world of finite existences. From such a point of view, the creation of the world becomes not a mere arbitrary inexplicable act, but a thing grounded in the nature of God, having its reason in the very nature of Infinite Reason; and a proof of Infinite Mind from the existence of the world is impossible, unless we can thus perceive that Infinite Mind would not be what it is without it. This, however, is a point of view beyond that to which the Design argument can bring us. For not only is it impossible to trace everywhere the marks of design amidst the seeming imperfections and terrible anomalies of the present system of things; but, as we have seen, all the adaptations and contrivances of which the argument speaks presuppose the existence of matter or material forces, of which it can give no other account than to ascribe them simply to creative will or power. But though the result we reach is thus, in one point of view, a failure, yet, as in the case of the Cosmological argument, it is a failure which leads us to something better, or which constitutes a necessary step in the mind's progress to a higher and truer idea. The first argument, the argument *a contingentia mundi*—in which the mind rises from the perception of the transitory, contingent, finite character of the world to the notion of an absolutely necessary or Infinite Being—is, we have seen, inadequate, because the Infinite or necessary Being to which it points is simply the negation or contradiction of the finite; and the perception of this inadequacy impels us to seek after a higher notion of the Infinite, as that which embraces or explains, instead of denying or annulling, the finite. In like manner, the logical flaws which vitiate the Teleological argument—in which we rise from the world as a manifestation of design to an all-wise Designer—become, in their turn the impelling motive towards another and higher solution of the problem. That solution we seek therefore, finally, in the last of the above-enumerated arguments, the so-called Ontological argument, the form and significance of which we shall now briefly consider.

3. *The Ontological Argument*, as commonly stated, finds in the very idea of God the proof of His existence. The thought of God in the mind demonstrates His Being. This conclusion from Thought to Being constitutes the gist of the argument, though it is presented in different forms by different writers. Sometimes, as we find the argument stated by Anselm and others, the idea of an "absolutely perfect" Being or "most real" Being, which, it is said, we have in our minds, is held to prove His existence, on the curious and, at first sight, not very conclusive ground, that if such a

Being did not actually exist, we could conceive of another who does exist, and who would therefore be more perfect. Or again, with a slight variation of form, it is maintained that, Existence being one of the attributes which must be ascribed to an absolutely perfect or infinite Being, the Being of whom we think as absolutely perfect, if He did not actually exist, would lack one of His essential attributes. Once more, the argument, as in the representation given of it by Descartes, takes the form of an argument from effect to cause; and the idea of infinite perfection, inasmuch as nothing in the finite world could originate it, is held to imply the existence of an infinitely perfect Being as its author or inspirer.

At first sight, this mode of reasoning involves the most glaring of paralogisms, and scarcely admits of serious criticism. To argue that, because a notion in my mind includes existence as one of its elements, therefore a Being corresponding to it must actually exist, seems to be only a foolish play upon words. If the mere fact of my thinking anything does not prove its actual being, the proof does not become any better when the thing I think of is what I call 'existence.' A notion or conception of existence is not a proof of actual or objective existence, any more than a notion of food or clothing can conjure a banquet on to an empty table or persuade us that a naked body is warmly clad; or—as it is put in Kant's well known illustration—any more than the notion of three hundred dollars in my mind proves that I have them in my purse. If existence is an element of perfection, no doubt the idea of a Perfect Being must include the *idea* of His existence; but the presence in my mind of the idea of existence or of anything else, says nothing as to its objective reality.

It is difficult, however, to conceive that an argument of which the refutation seems so easy and obvious, could have imposed itself on thinkers such as those above-named: and on closer examination we shall find that, imperfect as may be the form in which it has often been presented, the principle of this argument is that on which our whole religious consciousness may be said to rest.

It is quite true that there are many things of which, from the mere idea or conception of them in our minds, we cannot infer the objective existence. If existence means, as in the case of Kant's dollars, the accidental existence of particular objects for sensuous perception, such an existence we cannot infer from thought. It is, indeed, of the very nature of such things that, regarded simply in themselves, they either may or may not be; and to infer their necessary existence from the idea of them would be in direct contradiction with that idea. But there are other ideas with respect to which this does not hold good; and there is especially one idea, which, whether we are explicitly or only implicitly conscious of it, so proves its reality from thought that thought itself becomes impossible without it. Its absolute objective reality is so fundamental to thought, that to doubt it implies the subversion of all thought and all existence alike. In a former chapter I attempted to point out the self-contradiction ultimately involved in materialistic theories of mind, viz., that in making thought a function of matter, they virtually made thought a function of itself. In other words, they make *that* the product of matter which is involved in the very existence of matter, or which is the *prius* of matter and of all other existences. Neither organisation nor anything else can be conceived to have any existence which does not pre-suppose thought. To constitute the existence of the outward world, or of the lowest term of reality we ascribe to it,—say in 'atoms,' or 'molecules,' or 'centres of force'—you must think them, or conceive them as existing for thought; you must needs pre-suppose a consciousness for which and in which all objective existence is. To go beyond, or attempt to conceive of an existence which is prior to and outside of thought, 'a thing in itself,' of which thought is only the mirror, is self-contradictory, inasmuch as that very thing in itself is only conceivable by, exists only for, thought. We must think it before we can ascribe to it even an existence outside of thought.

But whilst it is true that the priority of thought, or the ultimate unity of thought and being, is a principle to doubt which is impossible, seeing that, in doubting it, we are tacitly asserting the thing we doubt; yet it must be considered, further, that the unity thus asserted, when we examine what it means, is not the dependence of objective reality on my thoughts or yours, or on the thought of any individual mind. The individual mind which thinks the necessary priority of thought can also think the non-necessity of *its own* thought. There was a time when we were not; and the world and all that is therein we can conceive to be as real though we, and myriads such as we, no longer existed to perceive and know it. All that I think, all objective existence, is relative to thought in this sense that no object can be conceived as existing except in relation to a thinking subject. But it is not *my* thought in which I am shut up, or which makes or unmakes the world for me; for in thought I have the power of transcending my own individuality and the world of objects opposed to it, and of entering into an idea which unites or embraces both. Nay, the unity of subject and object, of self and the world which is opposed to it, is implied in every act of thought; and though I can distinguish the two, I can no more divide them or conceive of their separate and independent existence, than I can think a centre existing without or independently of a circumference. In thinking myself, my own individual consciousness and an outward world of objects, I at the same time tacitly think or pre-suppose a higher, wider, more comprehensive thought or consciousness which embraces and is the unity of both. The real pre-supposition of all knowledge, or the thought which is the *prius* of all things, is not the individual's consciousness of himself as individual, but a thought or self-consciousness which is beyond all individual selves, which is the unity of all individual selves and their objects, of all thinkers and all objects of thought. Or, to put it differently, when we are compelled to think of all existences as relative to thought, and of thought as prior to all, amongst the existences to which it is prior is our own individual self. We can make our individual self, just as much as other things, the object of thought. We can not only think, but we can think the individual thinker. We might even say that, strictly speaking, it is not we that think, but the universal reason that thinks in us. In other words, in thinking, we rise to a universal point of view, from which our individuality is of no more account than the individuality of any other object. Hence, as thinking beings we dwell already in a region in which our individual feelings and opinions, as such, have no absolute worth, but that which alone has absolute worth is a thought which does not pertain to us individually, but is the universal life of all intelligences, or the life of universal, Absolute Intelligence.

What, then, we have thus reached as the true meaning of the Ontological proof is this, that as spiritual beings our whole conscious life is based on a universal self-consciousness, an Absolute Spiritual Life, which is not a mere subjective notion or conception, but which carries with it the proof of its necessary existence or reality.

And now, finally, if we consider what is involved in the idea of God and of His relation to the world which we have reached as the true meaning of the Ontological argument, we shall find that we have here the deepest basis of religion and that in which lies its necessity for man as a spiritual self-conscious being. If we think of God merely as an Infinite which is the negation of the finite, or which is related to a finite world only by the bond of arbitrary will, there is no room under such a conception for any religion which is spiritual or which involves a conscious relation of the human spirit to the Divine. But if we conceive of God as Infinite Mind, or as that universal infinite Self-consciousness on which the conscious life of all finite minds is based, and whose very nature it is to reveal Himself in and to them ; then we have before us a conception of the nature of God and of the nature of man which makes religion necessary by making it, in one sense, the highest realisation of both.

## CHAPTER VI.

### THE RELIGIOUS CONSCIOUSNESS.

IN the foregoing Chapter we have found that the basis of religion lies in the very essence of man's nature as a thinking, self-conscious being. We are rational or spiritual beings only in virtue of our power to transcend our individuality, to rise above the region of feeling and sensation, and to enter into communion with that which is universal and objective. The conscious self is that which remains constant in its pure universality through all particular, changeful experiences, and, in its relation to outward objects, it is not only conscious of itself and of a world of objects opposed to it, but it has in it the capacity to transcend that opposition and to think a higher unity which comprehends both these elements. As a thinking being I can make my individual self as well as the world which is external to it, the object of thought. In thought, in other words, the hard opposition between self and not-self is broken down, we rise above our petty individuality—above the narrow limits in which the mere creature of passing impressions and impulses is confined—and we enter into a region which is universal and infinite. We *feel* as individuals, but we *think* only as sharing in the universal life of reason. It is thought, as the activity of the universal, which gives to man the capacity of that self-abnegation and self-surrender to an infinite object in which religion may be said to consist.

But whilst it is true that the basis of religion lies in man's rational or intelligent nature, or that it is thought or intelligence which makes him capable of religion, this is not equivalent to the assertion that religion is a purely intellectual thing. To say that man is religious because he is rational, is not the same thing as to say that religion has its seat in the intellectual part of man's nature, as distinguished from the emotional or the active. In truth, the question about which so much has been made, as to what special faculty or division of human consciousness it is to which religion distinctively belongs,—whether, in other words, religion is characteristically a thing of knowledge, or of feeling, or of volition and action,—is one which rests on a false or defective psychology. The spiritual life and consciousness of man cannot be broken up, as this inquiry implies, into independent divisions or departments existing side by side, or into separate powers and faculties having a common substratum in something which is called 'the mind'; nor is it possible to assert with respect to any of the concrete manifestations of man's spiritual nature, that it is confined to any one form of activity to the exclusion of other and cognate forms. There is no feeling or volition which does not contain in it implicitly an element of knowledge, nor any kind of knowledge which does not presuppose feeling, or in which the mind is in an attitude simply passive and receptive, without any element of activity. A spiritual unity cannot be conceived of as a repository, like a case of instruments or a box of tools, in which so many things are placed side by side, but rather as a unity of which the various elements necessarily involve each other or are the correlative expressions of a common principle. And if we ask what is that central principle which is present in all the many-sided aspects of our spiritual life—in our sensations, feelings, desires, imaginations, conceptions, notions, &c.—and of which these are but the various or successive specifications, more or less concrete, the answer can only be, that that principle is *Thought*. Thought, intelligence, self-consciousness, is not one among many co-ordinate faculties, having its own peculiar functions, its own particular times and ways of action, but it is that which runs through, characterises, gives organic relation to, all our spiritual activities. That which makes the simplest essentially one with the most complex of these activities, that which gives a distinctive character to the rudest impressions and impulses of a human being and makes them different from the impressions and impulses of an animal, is that they are referable to a conscious self, or contain in them, at least implicitly, an element of thought. I feel, I desire, I imagine, I reflect; but through all these changing experiences the unchanging element is the "I," the conscious, thinking self, to which they are all alike related. It is as a thinking being, and not as an animal, that I feel, or desire, or will, or act. And in an especial manner must this hold good when the object with which any human experience is concerned is itself universal,—when, as in religion, we have to do, not with that which is particular, accidental, finite, but with a Being who transcends all that is finite and phenomenal. A universal object appeals to and can be apprehended only by an organ which is itself universal. God and divine things may touch our feelings, kindle our emotions, awaken in us desires and impulses, dominate our practical activities: but underneath and throughout all these there must be present the activity of that organ which alone can raise us above ourselves, which alone can bring us into relation to the things unseen and eternal, and that organ is thought.

But admitting that it is thought, or the intelligent, rational nature of man, which makes religion possible for him, the question may still be asked what is the special form of thought to which religion belongs? In religion, as in all the experiences of a rational, self-conscious being, an element of thought must be present, but its presence does not necessarily take the form of pure thought—of ideas or doctrines scientifically apprehended, and developed into a reasoned system. As it is possible to reason correctly without being able to trace and logically defend the intellectual process by which our conclusions are reached; as the idea of beauty or of goodness may manifest its power over many a mind which has never translated its experience, or is incapable of translating it, into an explicit theory of morals or æsthetics; so it is conceivable that religious ideas may implicitly dominate the heart and life, even when the subject of them has not grasped, and cannot grasp them in the form of objective thought. And it is a question by no means unimportant, whether and to what extent this is actually true,—whether, in other words, the ideal element of religion may be wholly implicit or unconscious; or, if not, to what extent religious ideas must be consciously and definitely apprehended by the mind that is swayed by them. May religion manifest its reality and power simply in the form of *Feeling*—of sensibilities that are touched and affections that are moved, blindly and all but instinctively, without any intelligent recognition of the nature of their objects, or rational proof and determination of the ideas which underlie them? Or, on the other hand, is *Knowledge* of the essence of religion? Can there be no reality in religion without the presence of definite and accurate notions concerning God and divine things? Does ignorance or intellectual error vitiate religion, or, if not, to what extent may they intrude without affecting that which constitutes its real essence? It will enable us to answer these questions if we examine briefly the nature of the religious consciousness—the various ways, that is, in which religious objects or ideas can be present to our consciousness—and some of the theories which have been held as to that which constitutes the peculiar province of religion.

I. In the first place, it has often been maintained that religion is exclusively a matter of *Feeling*. Its seat is not in the understanding—in that form of consciousness which deals with terms, propositions, arguments, with logically defined notions or systematically arranged doctrines; nor again, though religion leads to practical activity and indeed constitutes the leading principle and motive of human conduct, does it primarily lie in the will or in the province of practical life; but its distinctive essence is in a condition of the heart or the emotional nature. We are religious, not in virtue of thinking accurately or willing rightly, but simply and essentially in virtue of a certain state of our feelings and affections towards God.

The grounds on which this view is based have been partially discussed above in our examination of the theory of immediate or intuitive knowledge, and need here only be briefly referred to. That the essence of religion lies in Feeling is held to be proved, either (1) simply by an appeal to ordinary popular convictions, or (2) by certain considerations of a more scientific character.

(1.) We need not go beyond the ordinary consciousness of men to be convinced, it is said, that neither knowledge nor outward practical activity constitutes the measure of piety. The logical or scientific faculty, we instinctively feel, is not the organ of communion with God, nor, by its greater or less acuteness and activity, can a man's spiritual state be tested. It is possible to possess ratiocinative powers of the highest order—keen and penetrative intelligence, capacities of observation, comparison, reflection, the cultured intelligence which renders a man a competent literary and historic critic, a subtile apologist, a deft framer of theological dogmas and systems of divinity; and yet with all this intellectual equipment, to lack that element of 'living faith,' that state of the heart and affections, which constitutes the essence of true piety. On the other hand, we are constrained to recognise the presence of that element in minds at a very low point of intellectual development—in natures which may be profoundly sensitive to spiritual objects, without the capacity to verify their own convictions, to analyse the process by which they have reached these convictions, or to define, in intelligible form, a single doctrine of the faith in which they believe. Indeed, if religion is a thing possible for all, if it is a relation of the soul to God not conditioned by any special gifts or arbitrary acquirements, its essence must obviously be altogether independent of that intellectual ability and culture which are far from universal. It must come to the human spirit in a way possible for the simplest and rudest alike with the most acute and cultured intelligence. Religion thus cannot be identified with knowledge or regarded as having its seat in the intellect. But as little, it will be said, can its essence be found in action or in the sphere of practical activity. For not only is outward activity dependent on the accidental conditions and opportunities of life, but it obviously takes its complexion from the inward principles and motives of which it is the expression. And if, as already shown, the inward principle of religion is not an intellectual one, where can it lie but in the region of feeling or emotion? The principle of human activity is not in the will itself, but in the affections, desires, sentiments, which lie behind it and impel it. It is the fire of genius, the susceptibility or sentiment of the beautiful, which constitutes the true artist, not the scientific knowledge of the principles of art, or practical skill and deftness of hand in dealing with the outward materials of art. And so, the ultimate source and secret of the religious nature is to be found neither in the philosophic intelligence nor in the sphere of external achievement, but in the feelings of self-abnegation, of conscious dependence, of awe, reverence, aspiration—in that disposition or attitude of the heart towards God, call it what you will, which often gives moral elevation to the humblest intelligence, and sheds spiritual grandeur around the homeliest and obscurest life.

(2.) But, setting aside these and similar considerations, which lend popular attractiveness to the view that identifies religion with feeling, the same thesis may be defended on more scientific grounds.

Religion is defined as the elevation of the human spirit into union with the Divine. But this, it may be maintained, necessarily implies that the principle of religion lies in feeling. For it is here, and here only, that the deepest union between different natures can be achieved. It is only in feeling that any object ceases to be merely external, and becomes implicated with the very nature and consciousness of the subject itself. So long as a thing is merely known, it is still something outward and foreign to my consciousness. Knowledge implies the distinction of subject and object. In knowing I put myself in opposition to the object—I coolly contemplate and examine it. But in feeling, this opposition vanishes, the determination of the object becomes one with the determination of my own inmost nature, so that, in a sense, they are no longer two, but one. When a being or object reveals itself to feeling, it, so to speak, loses any vestige of foreignness or estrangement, and becomes blended with the consciousness to which it is revealed. The nature of the object is not argued about or inferred, but is reflected in the inward movement of the spirit, the joy or satisfaction, the awe or aspiration or ecstatic elevation, of which it is immediately conscious. In other words, knowledge, strictly so called, can never be immediate, but is attainable only by the mediation of grounds or reasons or steps of proof. But when an object is given in feeling, its existence is no longer a thing reached only by intermediate steps, as the conclusion of an argument or the result of a process of thought. Above all is this true of the highest object, God. It is not when He is set before us as an object to be thought of or reasoned about that we have the deepest consciousness of union with Him. It is when His presence penetrates the soul with love, joy, admiration, when boundless exultation or ecstasy suffuse the spirit, that all division and intermediation are at an end. For then we are through and through determined by the object, it takes possession of us, the assurance of its existence becomes identified with the certainty of our own, it becomes, in a sense, spiritually one with us.

Now there is much in the foregoing arguments which we are not concerned to dispute. It may be admitted that knowledge without feeling is not religion, nor the measure or criterion of religion; and again that, inasmuch as religion is for all, and cannot be conditioned by any special gifts or attainments, whatever element of knowledge enters essentially into the nature of religion, must be a kind of knowledge possible for all men alike. What we dispute is, that these and similar arguments afford any ground for restricting the essence of religion to the sphere of feeling, to the exclusion of intelligence and will; in other words, for leaving out of religion, as such, the elements of knowledge and of practical activity. That we have valid reasons for denying any such limitation the following considerations may serve to show.

(1.) To place the essence of religion in feeling is self-contradictory, for a religion of mere feeling would not even know itself to *be* religion. Without a distinct conception of, or reference to, a known object, religious feeling is incapable of discriminating itself from any other kind of feeling, of ascribing to itself any special character, or justifying its own existence. What, within the sphere of feeling, I am conscious of is simply the fact that I have such and such emotions of pleasure or pain, joy or grief, elevation or dependence, etc. What the objects of these feelings are, or whether, indeed, there be any objects to which they are referable, or whether these objects are good or bad, worthy or ignoble, real or imaginary—as to all this the feelings themselves give me no information. The objects which call forth feeling may be of the most different kinds, but unless I have had some intelligent insight into the nature of these objects, and on rational grounds have qualified and distinguished them, the mere feelings they excite give me no right to characterise them, or to say anything about them, save, at the most, that they are the unknown counterpart of certain subjective emotions. I cannot say of any one class of feelings that they are moral or religious, in distinction from another class which are purely sensuous; for, apart from a conscious reference to and definition of their objects, the utmost that I know of the feelings is that one feeling is more or less vivid, more or less pleasurable or painful than another. Within the sphere of feeling, the rapture of the sensualist and the devout elevation of the saint are precisely on a level; the one has as much justification as the other. If there be no common criterion, outside of feeling, to which we can appeal, any one man has as much right to his own religion as any other.

It may be said that, without going beyond the sphere of feeling, the varying intensity of our feelings does supply us with a measure of the nature and worth of the objects which excite them. But the answer is, that—even if distinctions of feeling were possible without an appeal to some higher standard—when we attempt to graduate feelings simply by their greater or less intensity, it might with some show of reason be maintained that the keenest and most vivid feelings are those which are most closely connected with our sensuous nature, that the more intellectual or rational the source of feeling, the more subdued and passionless does it become, and that thus the real elevation of the object is by no means to be measured by the vivacity of the feeling it creates. Besides this, it is to be considered that the intensity of feeling is determined as much by individual character and temperament as by the nature of the object. The same object calls forth feelings of different degrees of liveliness in different minds and in the same mind at different times. What gives keen pleasure to some, is indifferent and offensive to others. Natures of a soft, pliant, susceptible texture are ready to respond to every breath that sweeps the chords of feeling; they are elated or depressed, attracted or repelled, roused into superficial rapture or plunged into despondency and despair, on occasions when colder or deeper natures remain unmoved. And in religion as little as elsewhere can we extract from a thing so variable and capricious as feeling a criterion of objective worth. If intensity of emotion proves reality, or if religions are to be graduated according to the liveliness of the feelings excited in the breast of the worshipper, the purest Christian faith will have no advantage, not only over the more corrupt forms of the same religion, but over any other religion down to the grossest nature-worship or fetishism. 'My religion must be true, for I feel it to be true': 'Of this or that doctrine I am convinced, because it touches and thrills my heart': 'The irrefragable reality of my idea of God is certified to me by this, that it penetrates with strange emotion the inmost depths of my being, fills my spirit with unspeakable wonder and joy, or rapture and elation':—this is a kind of argument which the adherents of all religions alike can employ, and the more sensuous and materialistic religions with even greater force than the more rational and spiritual. In short, feeling in religion merely shows the religion is *mine*, that it is part of my experience. But the value of this experience, as an evidence for any religion, depends on the stage of moral and spiritual culture I have attained. That

*I* feel anything, supplies no objective criterion till you first determine who or what the 'I' is. There is indeed some element of truth in all religious feeling, not because it pertains to a being who feels, but because the feeling is that of a spiritual or self-conscious being: for religious feeling, as such, is beyond the range of the merely sensitive or feeling subject.

(2.) As a further consideration fatal to this theory it might be shown that if religion be a relation between the human spirit and the Divine, and if, therefore, we are in search of that on the human or subjective side which most fully corresponds to the infinite object, then least of all can we find that which meets this requirement in mere feeling. For that side of my nature, the characteristic of which is to be individual, variable, accidental, cannot be that which corresponds to, or is capable of entering into relation with, an object the very idea of which is to be universal, immutable, necessary. On this ground also, it is impossible to claim for feeling the character of the exclusively or distinctively religious faculty.

II. The foregoing considerations lead obviously to the conclusion that in its essence religion must contain in it an element of *knowledge*, or that religous feeling must be based on objective truth. Religion must, indeed, be a thing of the heart; but in order to elevate it from the region of subjective caprice and waywardness, and to distinguish between that which is true and false in religion, between the lowest and most corrupt and the highest and purest forms of religion, we must appeal to an objective standard. That which enters the heart, must first be discerned by the intelligence to be true. It must be seen as having in its own nature a right to dominate feeling, and as constituting the principle by which feeling must be judged and regulated.

But if this be so, the question immediately arises, What is that form of knowledge which is of the essence of religion? Is it that to which alone, in the highest sense, the word can properly be applied —scientific or speculative knowledge, truth grasped in its absolute necessity and coherence as an organic system or process; or again, is it that form of knowledge which we commonly understand by the words 'dogma,' 'dogmatic theology'—that in which the logical understanding educes from given materials precisely defined notions as to the nature of God and His relations to the world, carefully determines the point where in each case dogmatic accuracy is to be discriminated from heretical error, and sets forth the whole content of faith either as a series of independent propositions or articles of belief, or woven together into a connected system or body of divinity? Or, if we are constrained to admit that the religious is something essentially different from the philosophical or the logical attitude of mind, is there, it must be further asked, any lower or less elaborate form of knowledge which is possible for all men, and in which spiritual truth may be conceived to become the possession of every pious mind?

Now there are various ways in which a mind, by supposition incapable of grasping spiritual truth in a scientific form, may yet attain to a knowledge of it which is substantially true, and which may suffice for moral and religious ends—nay, may for these ends be more potent and inspiring than scientific or purely speculative knowledge. To a spiritual, self-conscious being, to whom by the very idea of his nature truth is already, from the beginning, an implicit or virtual possession, it may be apprehended in a *representative* form—in the form of fact or figure—long before it is seen, or, failing the capacity to see it, in a purely scientific form. Many things of an outward, finite character may become the vehicles of truth, may have power to touch the springs of thought and to awaken in us conceptions far transcending their own immediate content and significance. Material objects, things in space, actions and events in time, may become to us the images or symbols through which we contemplate things infinite and eternal. They may, in a certain figurative, pictorial, suggestive manner, embody and enable us to rise to the apprehension of spiritual realities.

In so far, for instance, as the earlier nature-religions contained any element of truth in them, it was truth which reached the human spirit through what may be called the suggestive power of outward and sensuous things. Even the stock or stone, the rudest fetish before which the savage bows, is at least, to him something more than a stock or stone; and the feeling of fear or awe, or abject dependence with which he regards it is the reflex of a dim, confused conception of an invisible and spiritual power of which the material object has become representative. In the more advanced nature-worship of the early Indian religions, again, the grander forms, objects, and aspects of nature were fraught with a spiritual significance, became in a subtile, unconscious way, the suggestive symbols of divine realities to the gradually developing religious consciousness. It was not that by any process of proof, by any syllogistic demonstration after the manner of the modern Natural Theology argument, men inferred the existence of an anthropomorphic creator and designer adequate to the production of observed results; but simply that nature, natural objects and appearances—the bright and cloudless firmament, the starry heavens, the dawn, the rushing wind, the teeming earth, the shimmering sea—had for the awakening spiritual consciousness a representative significance immeasurably transcending anything that could be educed from them by formal proof.

It was not the notion that the heavens and earth needed an omnipotent architect to construct them that awoke the religious susceptibilities of the Indian worshipper hymning the praises of Dyaus and Prithivi, of Mitra and Indra and Varuna ; but then as now, men, impressed with the sense of human weakness and dependence, and groping about unconsciously for something permanent, unchangeable, universal, amidst the finitude and fleetingness of earthly things, found in Nature that which, in an undefined yet wonderful way, was the symbol of what they sought after — found in the overarching sky and the ever-expanding horizon and the inexhaustible earth, images of invisible and eternal realities. And at all stages of spiritual culture, in modern alike with primitive times, Nature and natural objects are, in this indeterminate way, the symbols of spiritual ideas and the vehicles of religious thought.

But again, spiritual truth may be represented, spiritual ideas called up in the mind, not merely by material objects in space, but by events in time. The actions and events of the individual life, the facts of history, may become to us the embodiment of ideas of a richer and more complex character than those which are conveyed to us by the objects and appearances of Nature. The moral significance which the ordinary consciousness discerns in the actions of individual men, and in a vague and indeterminate way, in the events of history, though it is not apprehended by any process of philosophical reflection, constitutes a kind of knowledge far transcending anything which, viewed in themselves, these facts and events contain. Literally construed, one series of facts is of no higher or more spiritual significance than another. Every such series is merely a certain succession of phenomena occurring in time. But however we explain the process, the ordinary consciousness can and does read into such outward phenomena of human history conceptions, notions, ideas, which possess something of that universality and self-consistency, that absoluteness and necessity, which are the characteristics of truth. When, for instance, from the outward incidents of an individual life we rise to an idea of *character*—of purity, integrity, heroism, self-devotion—these incidents become to us representative of spiritual realities far beyond their literal compass. We are weaving them into a unity, supplying to merely isolated things the hidden link of spiritual continuity and coherence, penetrating beneath the outward husk of facts to a something deeper, richer, more permanent, which underlies them. It may be possible for philosophy to justify in a speculative way the ideas we have thus reached and to give them the higher form of necessary truth, but the knowledge we have gained is not less entitled to be characterised as knowledge, though it is not in the form of speculative truth. Thus, the events of the life of Christ are for the Christian consciousness the outward representation of a spiritual content. Considered as mere facts, they are of no more value and significance than any other series of events in the individual lives of his own or other times. But what a new impulse have they given to the moral and spiritual consciousness of mankind, to what a world of new spiritual ideas have they given birth in the common thought of the world! What the meaning of that life is for ethical science, in what respect the Christian ideal contains moral elements in advance of the ideas of pre-Christian times—these and similar questions it may be the function of philosophy to investigate. But to the thousands of minds for which such investigations have neither meaning nor interest, the life of Christ has been the symbol and suggestion of the richest treasure of moral ideas. It has supplied to them, not abstract principles of morality, but an ideal of moral beauty which not only captivates their affections, but, passing into the spiritual intelligence, constitutes for them the absolute standard of perfection. It is true indeed that for the religious mind at the stage at which we are at present contemplating it, there is no formal distinction of the fact or symbol from the idea which it represents. The universal principle or idea is not in any conscious deliberate way separated from the material object, the historical event, the individual personality, which is the immediate object of thought. But though the universal and particular are thus blended or confused together, yet, in a certain unconscious way, through the particular the universal is really present to the mind, and its attitude is no longer that of subjective feeling, but of knowledge.

There is yet another way in which it may be shown that the ordinary consciousness is capable of an apprehension of spiritual realities, which, though it falls short of science or speculation, is yet entitled to the designation of Knowledge. The popular as distinguished from the scientific or speculative consciousness dwells, as we have seen, in the region of images, symbols, figurate or pictorial representations of ideas under a sensuous form. But even popular thought is capable in one way of rising above the mere figurative or metaphorical reference of the signs it uses, of emancipating itself from what is sensuous, empirical and accidental in its own representations, and so, of elevating them into a nearer approach to the universality of scientific thought. Language even in its ordinary and unscientific use, may become an organ of thought which deals with ideas, no longer through the medium of material images, but in their own pure and ideal form. When in the language of common life we speak of things spiritual and supersensuous, we use expressions derived from the world of sense, based on material types and analogies. But though the instrument of thought is pictorial or metaphorical, we need not, in employing it, *think* metaphorically. From much of common speech the material or pictorial basis has died away; its terms have ceased to be metaphorical; the mind in using them is no longer conscious of their sensuous reference, but has elevated them into the immediate exponents of spiritual or supersensuous things. The very words, for instance, by which in various languages thought represents to itself that which is its own principle or essence, *spirit*, ψύχη. πνεῦμα, *animus*, *Geist*, etc., though originally expressing the effort to depict that which is above sense by the aid of that which in the world of sense is most impalpable and etherial, have lost, even for popular thought, almost every reference to their material origin, and have become endowed with a certain ideal significance. So again, when we use as the signs of mental and spiritual acts and processes, such words as *attention*, *reflection*, *consideration*, *aspiration*, or, in the province of religion, such words as *repentance*, *conversion*, *regeneration*, *sanctification*, etc., or when we speak of things or ideas as 'producing an impression on our minds,' or 'softening or hardening our hearts,' of the 'enlightening, subduing, transforming, influence of divine truth,' of 'turning from sin to righteousness,' of 'beholding the face and the glory of God,' it is obvious that such forms of speech have disengaged themselves, in a great measure, from the pictorial or figurative element that lurks in them; they have become clothed from the inner resources of thought with a real though supersensuous significance which renders them fit expressions of things transcending the outward and the sensuous.

Again, it is obvious that very much of what is anthropomorphic in the form of our religious ideas, receives a silent corrective from the advancing religious consciousness, till finally no suggestion of anthropomorphism remains attached to the language in which such ideas are expressed save what pertains to the truth itself. Language which, literally construed, would ascribe to the Divine nature the conditions of space and time, the physical and mental limitations, the ignorance and changefulness, even the desires and passions of our finite sensuous nature, is tacitly stripped of its primary and grosser import, and transformed into the expression of purely spiritual ideas. Even in earlier times, when mythological personifications were not impossible objects of belief, the conception was ever something more elevated than the coarsely humanised form in which it was expressed; and as the religious education of the world advances, it becomes impossible to attach any literal meaning to those representations of God and of His relations to mankind which ascribe to Him human senses, appetites, passions, and the actions and experiences proper to man's lower and finite nature. When we read of a Divine Being who has eyes to behold the righteous, ears to listen to their prayer, to whom the smell of incense or the savour of sacrifice is sweet; when He is represented as seated on a throne, according a place of honour at His right hand, having a local dwelling called heaven, coming down or despatching emissaries from heaven to earth; as working, being fatigued and taking rest; or again, when we are told of His wrath as being roused or abated, of His avenging personal insults and offences, of His repenting of former acts or intentions, of His being induced by persuasion, intreaty, or interposition, to give up His former purposes, of His making and revising schemes, contracts, covenants, with mutual stipulations and penalties for breach of bargain;—in all these cases, even in its most immature stage of spiritual culture, the religious mind passes beyond the anthropomorphic figures to seize, in an indefinite but not unreal way, the hidden spiritual meaning. The representation conveys a general impression which is of the nature of knowledge, though, literally construed, it expresses what is untrue. Finally, when we use as expressive of the essential nature of the Godhead such terms as *Father, Son, First-born, Only-begotten;* when we speak of God as 'the Father of spirits,' and of all men as 'His offspring'; when He is represented as forming the body of man 'out of dust,' and as communicating life by the act of 'breathing into his nostrils'; when we conceive of Him as a Legislator or Governor who forms a code of laws, gives them due publicity, keeps a record of criminal offences and affixes to them appropriate penalties, and who finally summons all mankind to a solemn function of justice, opens books, examines witnesses, and passes sentences of acquittal or condemnation—there is in all this much which, even when religious feeling is absorbing the latent nourishment contained in it, is perceived to belong to the domain of materialised and figurate conception. The paternal and filial relation cannot be literally predicable of the divine nature or of divine 'Persons'; God is not and cannot be maker or father, or ruler, or judge, in the sense in which human beings fulfil these functions; nor does the religious mind, in dwelling on such representations, accept them as exact equivalents for spiritual realities. What it does is simply to let them suggest, or in the way of imaginative indication, awaken in us conceptions of spiritual things. The knowledge thus obtained, though, considered simply as knowledge, it is limited and defective, is yet adequate to the wants of the religious nature. It rescues religion from the purely subjective and accidental character which would pertain to it were its essence placed merely in feeling, and it gives us an objective standard to which feeling must conform, and by which it can be measured. In estimating the religious character of individuals, or the point of progress which at any time has been attained by nations or races in the religious history of the world, the fundamental inquiry is, therefore, as to the objective character of their religious ideas and beliefs. The first question is, not how they feel, but what they think and believe—not whether their religion is one which manifests itself in emotions, more or less vehement and enthusiastic, but what are the conceptions of God and divine things by which these emotions are called forth. Feeling is necessary in religion, but it is by the content or intelligent basis of a religion, and not by intensity of feeling that its character and worth are to be determined. In other words, in considering what is the nature of the religious consciousness, we must regard as of primary importance, not the element of feeling, but the objective character of that about which we feel; we must look beyond feeling to that intellectual activity by which feelings are determined.

# CHAPTER VII.

## INADEQUACY OF RELIGIOUS KNOWLEDGE IN THE ORDINARY OR UNSCIENTIFIC FORM.

THERE is, we have seen, a mode of apprehending spiritual things, to which, though it differs from philosophical or speculative thought, the term 'knowledge' may be applied. We have seen, further, that this kind of knowledge—the knowledge of which ordinary thinking, embodied in the language of common life, in a great measure consists—may and does enter as an essential element into the idea of Religion. But ordinary thinking consists, for the most part, of generalised images, of conceptions derived from the outward and phenomenal world, and charged more or less with the inherent characteristics of their sensuous origin. Now, though the spiritual mind rises in a certain instinctive and unconscious way above the poverty of the medium it employs, yet that medium, considered in itself, falls far short of that which is required in the instrument of scientific thought.

It may suffice for practical piety, but it is insufficient for the purposes of philosophy. If it is possible to advance from faith to science, in other words, to attain, in the sphere of religion, to knowledge in the philosophic sense of the word, there must be an organon of thought by means of which we can perceive and correct the inadequacy of ordinary thinking, and apprehend spiritual realities in their purely ideal form. Before, however, we attempt to show that there is such an organon, and in order to prepare us for understanding more clearly the function it has to fulfil, it is necessary to consider a little more closely wherein the inadequacy of ordinary or unscientific thought consists.

The relation between popular and scientific thought in religion—between those conceptions of spiritual things which are accessible to the ordinary consciousness and those which are possible only to speculative or scientific insight—may be said to be this, that they agree in substance or content, but differ in form. It is the same distinction which we have before our minds when we speak of the difference between illustration and argument, between description and definition, between the picture of a thing addressed to the eye or reproduced in the imagination and the idea of it grasped by the mind. In both cases thought is present, but in the former it is apprehended through a medium that is outward or foreign to itself; only in the latter is it apprehended *as* thought. The transition from the one to the other may be imperfectly exemplified by that which our view of an object undergoes when instead of merely understanding the description of it, we come to apprehend the law or principle of its being; when, *e.g.*, instead of merely looking at the sections of a material cone or the diagrams which represent them, we come to know in each case the equation of the curve—to grasp, so to speak, its genetic idea, and to produce or re-create it for ourselves.

To understand this distinction more clearly—to see, in other words, wherein that representative knowledge which suffices for ordinary thought differs from that higher knowledge which it is the aim of philosophy to reach—it is necessary, in the first place, to consider in what respects the former is an imperfect or inadequate form of knowledge; and then, secondly, to trace the steps of the process by which this inadequacy is corrected, and thought, emancipated from every foreign element, attains to the purity and freedom of scientific knowledge.

The defects of that representative form of knowledge which is, as we have seen, the highest to which ordinary thought can attain, may be said to be chiefly these three :—

1. Its material or sensuous origin still clings to it, and tends to betray the mind into illusion and error;

2. It fails to give real or organic connection and unity to the objects with which it deals;

3. It is incapable of solving the contradictions—of reconciling the seemingly antagonistic elements—which, closely viewed, all thought contains. To state these defects more briefly, ordinary thinking is, or tends to be, (1) Metaphorical, (2) Abstract, (3) Self-contradictory.

1. It is the characteristic of that knowledge which is the highest attainable by ordinary thought, that it is got through the medium of images or illustrations. We see, for instance, in the example above given, that thought, at this stage, has not grasped the genetic law of the curve, but that whatever knowledge it has of the circle, ellipse, parabola, etc., is derived from, and dependent more or less on, the perception of diagrams or figures in space. And although, as above shown, what thought here discerns is ever something more and deeper than the mere sensuous sign—though outward facts and events, regarded in their bare externality, are but the suggestive materials on which the imaginative and generalising intelligence builds its conceptions—yet thought, whilst it thus rises above what is merely outward and sensuous, is seldom wholly emancipated from the limiting and illusory influence of the means with which it works. What it gives us is a spiritual content under a sensuous form; but it is ever in danger of carrying the con-

ditions of the form into its apprehension of the content, of ascribing to spiritual objects the limitations that belong only to the world of sense and sight. That by means of which thought rises above sense is itself a thing of sense; the wings by which it seeks to soar above matter are themselves material, and they tend to become a burden and to drag it back into the world to which they belong. Thought, indeed, at this stage, is unconsciously trying to work itself clear of the sense-image, to drop from its content that which is not universal; but its effort is never wholly successful. The idea is beginning to subordinate to itself the material form, but it never completely subdues it, and we are still apt to be led into error by unconsciously introducing into our conceptions of things spiritual, conditions which apply only to the things of space and time.

Of this tendency to substitute metaphors for thoughts, and of the erroneous results to which it leads, the history of philosophy and of theology supplies many illustrations. Thus, in the inquiry concerning the origin and nature of human knowledge, many of the errors and misconceptions into which sensationalist theorists have been betrayed, are traceable to the latent influence of the metaphor or materialised conception which lurks under the term 'impressions,' employed as an explanation of the relation of outward objects to the mind or thinking subject. Under this figure, mind and its object are conceived of as related to each other in the same external and spatial manner as, *e.g.*, the wax to the seal, or the paper on which letters and words are 'impressed' to the printer's types. But, obviously, in whatever way the origin of ideas, or our knowledge of an external world is to be explained (and with that question we are not here concerned), no real explanation of a mental or spiritual process can be got from a theory which treats the subject 'mind' as capable of being acted on by physical impact, or of receiving dints, marks, spatial deepenings and elevations, in the manner of a softened or prepared material substance. When we speak of 'the deep impression made on us' by an external scene or event, or of a past impression as being 'indelibly imprinted on our memories,' or as 'becoming fainter and fainter,' etc., such expressions may serve well enough, in a figurative, analogical way, to embody a knowledge which suffices for practical purposes; but when regarded as exact accounts of a psychological process, they are either attempts to explain a relation of two things essentially different, in terms only of one of them, or they presuppose and insinuate a materialistic theory of the nature of mind. Thus the philosophic systems above referred to, while seeming elaborately to demonstrate a particular theory or doctrine, are in reality only bringing out in abstract terms, and with an air of demonstration, the theory which was assumed at the outset in a metaphor. The same tendency to carry metaphors, or materialised conceptions, into the domain of ideas, and so to apply the laws and conditions of matter to spiritual things, shows itself in the controversy as to the freedom of the will. The human will is subject to conditions in common with the falling stone, or the ball which moves when another impinges on it. But when you say that force is the cause of motion, and that education is the cause of temperance, avarice the cause of theft, revenge the cause of murder, or in general, that certain 'motives'—appetites, desires, passions—are the causes of human volitions and actions, it is only to the ear that there is any similarity between the two kinds of relations, and only by an unconscious confusion of what is physical with what is spiritual, that we can argue as if relations so different could be embraced under a common formula. By a false analysis of the supposed phenomena of the will into motives and volition we are led to represent the former as something spatially external to and acting on the other—motives as pushing, impelling, restraining the so-called faculty of will in the same fashion in which one physical agent acts on another. But, in all this, we are really imposing on ourselves by a fiction of externality and necessity; and the results which we reach by such a method are not true of things spiritual, but only of things spiritual dressed up to our minds in the semi-pictorial forms of things physical.

The same unconscious fallacy, to give one other example, besets many of our theological controversies as to the nature of what is called 'grace' —whether, *e.g.*, it is to be conceived of as ordinary or extraordinary, supernatural and sovereign, or natural and common, prevenient or co-operative, etc.—and in general the theological treatment of the relation between divine and human agency in the spiritual history of man. Arguments on such questions gain often a superficial clearness and conclusiveness from no other cause than the material and mechanical significance with which the language of the controversialist is charged. One mind or one spiritual being is conceived of as related to another under conditions which are only applicable to inorganic matter. Thus it is supposed to lend elevation and grandeur to our idea of God, to conceive of Him as dwelling in some supernal, celestial space, from which He acts on and sways finite intelligences, which are conceived of as occupying terrestrial space; it is regarded as more manifestly a divine operation or agency, or as indicating a more special interposition of God, if He thus acts from above, and in some immediate way moves and sways the human spirit, than if He were present merely in the normal processes of thought, in the 'natural' influence of truth over the mind and heart. Now, in the case of an intelligent agent, it is obvious that that influence which is conceived of simply as inexplicable, supernatural force, is really lower and less divine, because more material and mechanical, than the ordinary and intelligible suasive power of moral and religious ideas. It would, indeed, be impossible to think otherwise were it not that, insensibly, we carry into our theological reasonings a criterion or measure of power which is really derived from the materialistic metaphors under which our spiritual conceptions are couched. A force that controls other forces is physically greater than these, but a force that controlled minds and overruled moral and spiritual motives, would be not greater, but lower and meaner than they; and its successful interposition would imply, not the exaltation, but the degradation both of the agent who exerted it and of the nature on which he operated.

2. Ordinary representative thought has this further defect that, from the necessary conditions under which it acts, it is incapable of apprehending *that kind of unity* which belongs to spiritual things. If there is a kind of unity which is that not of things existing in juxtaposition or in succession to each other, but of elements which internally involve or contain each other, so that no one element can be known truly in abstraction or isolation from the rest, then that is a unity which, from its very nature,

ordinary or figurative thought has no means of apprehending, and which needs for its apprehension the deeper insight of speculation or philosophy.

The materials of ordinary thought are, as we have seen, generalised images derived from the external world. Its whole repertory consists of materialised conceptions got from the sphere of the senses, and they are to the last subject to the conditions of sensuous intuition, to that reciprocal exclusion which pertains to objects in space and events in time. "To the last," I have said; for even though at this stage the aid of logic—of the abstracting, generalising, classifying powers of the logical understanding—may be called in to give a kind of external order and unity to our popular conceptions, yet the inherent inadequacy of representative knowledge, its incapacity to grasp and exhibit the real internal unity of spiritual things, is not to be overcome by any such aid. Instead of solving the differences and oppositions of the spiritual world, logical analysis only brings them into harsher prominence. This ineradicable inadequacy of representative thought will be better understood if we consider for a moment whether and how far it is possible by means of sensuous images to represent to ourselves the complexity of mental or spiritual objects. It is possible, as we have seen, for truth to clothe itself in a sensuous form, but by the very fact that it does so, it must submit to the limiting conditions of sense; and the question recurs, Is there a point beyond which the forms of sense cannot go, a range of ideas which they are inadequate to express? Can we find in the realm of nature images, forms, figures, which will adequately represent things spiritual and supersensuous — the objects, relations, ideas, which belong to the realm of spirit? Now the forms of sensuous intuition, and of the imagination which deals with the materials supplied by it, are *space* and *time*. But under these forms the only way in which we can think of objects and events is as existing outside of each other, and taking place after each other. In other words, the general characteristic of sensuous or imaginative intuitions is that they are absolutely isolated or self-exclusive. They constitute a vast multiplicity of individual terms or units, each having an existence distinct and separate from the rest, and incapable of any other unity than the unity of the atom, or that which is produced by a merely external and artificial combination or aggregation of atoms.

But when we try by means of such materials to set forth or picture to ourselves spiritual objects, the poverty of the representative medium at once betrays itself. For, in mind or spirit, in the feelings, ideas, experiences of self-conscious beings, in their relations to each other and to the Infinite Mind, there emerges a new kind of unity—*a unity of differences*, in which all trace of that self-externality which pertains to nature and the world of sense has disappeared. In the realm of mind, in the spiritual life of conscious beings, there is infinite multiplicity and diversity; but it is a multiplicity or diversity which is no longer that of parts divided from each other, each of which exists and can be conceived of by itself in isolation or segregation from the rest, or in purely external relations to them. Here, on the contrary, the multiplicity and diversity is that of parts or elements, each of which exists *in and through* the rest, has its individual being and significance only in its vital organic relation to the rest, or each of which can be known only when it is seen, in a sense, to *be* the rest.[1] You cannot, for example, take the combination of two externally independent things in space and employ it as a representation of the relation of mind and its object, or of love and the being who is loved, or of the union of one soul with another, or of all finite spirits with God. For, though thought be distinguishable from its object, it is not divisible from it; the thinker and the object thought of are nothing apart from each other, they are twain yet one; the object is only object for the subject, the subject for the object; they have no meaning or existence taken individually, and in their union they are not two separate things stuck together, but two that have absolutely lost or dissolved

[1] This point is more fully treated *infra*, chap. viii.

their duality in a higher unity. The same thing is true of spiritual feeling and its object. You cannot represent or figure to yourself the union of souls by the combination of things that have an existence outside of each other; for a being into whose nature the element of love, sympathy, self-surrender, enters as an essential characteristic, is not intelligible as an isolated thing, or without taking into our notion of it the other beings to whom it is related. We do not get first the idea of man, and then add to it the further idea of society or the social union; for man is not man, the idea of human nature cannot be expressed apart from the social relation in which alone that nature is realised. The existence of a spirit in pure individuality apart from other spirits is not conceivable, for a spiritual being is one that finds itself only in what is other than itself; it must lose self, its isolated individuality, in order truly to find or be itself. And still more vain would be the attempt to find in images borrowed from external things an adequate representation of the relation of all finite souls to God. Religion is not the pantheistic identification of the finite spirit with the Infinite; on the contrary, it is in religion that the individuality of each human spirit reaches its intensest specification. But as no adequate conception of the individual human spirit can be formed apart from its relation to other finite spirits, so must any representation of the finite spirit be inadequate and incomplete apart from its relation to the Infinite. As rational, spiritual beings we have in us a nature which rests on the universal infinite reason—on a spiritual life which comprehends and transcends all individual lives, and apart from their relation to which they are themselves unintelligible. You cannot represent the finite spirit or its religious experience in terms of the finite, for in the very act of thinking that which is deepest and most real in the finite, you must think at the same time of the Infinite. You cannot, by any combination of things which are purely individual, adequately set forth a relation which is at once the most intense assertion of individuality and its absolute surrender and sacrifice. The religious relation is not conceivable as that of two terms limiting each other, for the very idea of each of the terms, in this case, is that which implies the other, and their true relation is that in which the limit is removed.

It is true, indeed, that even in the region of things finite and sensuous there are to be found shadows and reflexions of that deeper unity which belongs to the spiritual world—attempts, so to speak, of nature to break away from that reciprocal exclusiveness or externality which is the law of things natural, approximations to that self-transcendence which is the essential characteristic of the spiritual life. In chemical affinity, and still more in organisation and animal life, as we formerly saw, nature begins to overcome that spatial outwardness which is the condition of inorganic matter, and to become prophetic of a life which lies beyond it. In the animal we have not a unity which is a mere mechanical aggregate, for along with that spatial outwardness which still pertains to the matter of the organism and which matter, as such, can never wholly transcend, we find in the animal a unity in which each part or member is bereft of all individual or isolated existence, and has its meaning and life only in its active relation to the other members and to the whole. Accordingly, when religious thought endeavours to find an image to express spiritual ideas and relations, it is here, in this highest reach of the realm of nature, where it borders on the realm of spirit, that the least inadequate representations may be found. Spiritual relations are less imperfectly represented by expressions which turn on the conception of life and of corporate or organic unity than by those which are based only on the conceptions of outward contiguity, of mechanical construction and combination. When we speak of our relations to God in terms expressive of spatial distance or nearness, of subjection or resistance to external force, of physical transformation and transmutation; when we conceive of spiritual beings as related to each other as the stones of a building or as a building to its inhabitants,—in all such cases the form of our conceptions is derived from an order of things foreign to the content, and the representation is necessarily poor and inadequate. Spatial measures are not applicable to moral and spiritual relations: distance or nearness has no more to do with the relations of two spiritual beings than with the relations of two irreconcilable or congruous ideas. And when we attempt to express relations so heterogeneous in terms of each other, the representation necessarily falls far short of, or only vaguely and dimly adumbrates, the thing represented. But when spiritual ideas are expressed in forms derived from the phenomena of life—when, for example, the relation of the undeveloped to the developed, or of the finite to the Infinite spirit, is pictured in terms of the relation of the seed or germ to the plant, of the vine to the branches, of the vital principle to the members of the body; or when the origin of religion in the soul is represented as the infusion of a divine regenerative principle, and its progress as the growth or development in us of a divine or eternal life; when the action of new spiritual ideas is conveyed in terms expressive of the assimilation of food, and even a divine agent is conceived of as operating not as an external mechanical power or force, but as the 'bread of life,' 'the living water' which becomes inwardly incorporated with the very nature and being of the recipient,—in these and similar cases spiritual ideas are still expressed under sensuous forms, but these forms are derived from a region where sense is already transformed into something half-spiritual, and its forms are instinct with the life of that world whose hidden things they symbolise. They are not indeed one with it, they have not become altogether freed from the alloy of sensuous outwardness; for even in the organism there is that which is not taken up and dissolved into the self-inclusive unity of organic life. But in employing this medium of expression, we are at least approximating towards that higher mode of apprehension in which thought becomes its own organ, abides with itself, and in all its activity moves in the region of ideal purity and freedom.

3. Closely connected with that defect which we have just noticed as necessarily clinging to thought which is yet at this semi-pictorial stage, is this further inadequacy, that it is incapable of solving the contradictions or reconciling the seemingly contradictory elements of the spiritual world. If it is incapable of giving unity to the differences of thought, still more obviously incapable is it of apprehending in their unity its oppositions and contradictions. From the conditions under which the ordinary consciousness acts, the antagonistic tendencies which are the very life of the spiritual world can only be represented by it as irreconcilable opposites; and whilst simple feeling may be unconscious of their inconsistency, when reflexion has once been awakened to

the presence of such contradictions, the resource to which it usually betakes itself is either, with a narrow rationalism, to reject one of the contradictory aspects of thought, or to give up the problem as insoluble.

The spiritual world, we have seen, differs from the outward and natural world in this respect, that it cannot be conceived of as made up of individual things independently existing and only externally related to each other. Its lowest terms are not absolute, self-identical units, but unities which are the integration of diverse elements. It is only a further development of the same idea to say, that the lowest terms or unities of the spiritual world are unities which embrace and are the solution of opposite and apparently contradictory elements—complex unities the factors of which can be grasped, not in separate or successive affirmations, but each only by means of that which is its own negation. It is a world the harmony, the very existence of which, can be understood only as the perpetual play and reconciliation of antagonisms, as the harmony of discords. For when we examine the process of thought by which any true idea is reached, we find that it includes a negative as well as a positive movement, and that a spiritual truth cannot be grasped as a bare affirmation, but only as that which holds in it both negation and affirmation.

This is true, for instance, of the very notion of mind or intelligence itself. The idea of self is only possible as the counterpart of that which seems to contradict it, the idea of not-self. Mind or spirit can be known only in opposition to that which is given as non-spiritual. A mind without a world of external objects, an external world without a mind to think it, are equally incogitable. Materialism and a superficial idealism or spiritualism are only vain attempts to evade the solution, by denying one side of the contradiction; a true idealism is that which recognises both the contradictory elements, yet rises above them to lay hold of a higher principle in view of which the contradiction vanishes. It is but a foolish travesty of idealism to represent it as the doctrine that there is no such thing as an external world, and that the external world and all that looks so real in it is merely a phantasm or illusory creation of the mind. What, for any sober thinker, idealism does mean is, that both mind and matter, self and not-self, intelligence and its objects are, taken in isolation, nothing more than abstractions, that they have no conceivable existence save in opposition and therefore in relation to each other, and that a self which does not refer itself to that which is not-self, a not-self which is not for a self, is as much an impossible notion as an inside without an outside, an upper without an under, a positive without a negative. Thought or self-consciousness is that which at once posits and in its own higher unity solves the contradiction.

Take again an idea of a different kind—that of moral and spiritual freedom—and in this case too we shall find that the truth is one which involves or is reached only by the correlation of seeming contradictories. If we attempt to conceive of absolute freedom, a freedom which has no conditions or limits, which is not in any way determined either from without or by the nature to which it pertains, we are in search of a chimæra. Such a conception of freedom runs away into vacuity and non-entity. The thought of the purely indeterminate is the thought of nothing. When we think of freedom we must think it as the freedom of something or somebody, of that which has a nature of its own, of which freedom is predicated; and that nature, at least, is a limit to mere abstract, unconditioned freedom. In general, the notion of freedom, in order to be grasped at all, must call up that of limit, of conditions, of non-freedom; and the true idea, when it is reached—whether it be that of self-determination or self-activity, or liberty according to law, or conscious realisation of the law or idea of one's being—must be one which contains or subsumes under it its own opposite, the idea of necessity.

In like manner the words Finite and Infinite are only correlative terms, each of which carries with it a reference to the other; and the idea expressed by each is intelligible only when apprehended in the light of that which apparently denies it. As we have already seen, the consciousness of our finitude implies that we have virtually transcended that finitude. All religion starts from a sense of the insufficiency, vanity, unreality of the finite; and this would be an impossible experience, if in the very feeling of our finitude there were not contained a latent consciousness of that which denies and contradicts it. And when religion has reached its highest and purest form, that of the conscious self-surrender of the human spirit to the Divine, its deepest explanation is to be found only in the combined affirmation and denial by the finite of its own finitude, in the consciousness of a nature which finds itself only in losing itself, and which can express its experience only in such language as this, 'I live, yet not I, but God liveth in me.' On the other hand, equally impossible is the notion of a bare self-identical Infinite, of an Infinite which does not embrace in it that which seems to contradict it. A spiritual infinitude which merely fills, or spreads itself out, so to speak, through the universe, to the exclusion of all other being but its own, would not be truly infinite; for it would be an Infinite incapable of that which is the highest attribute of spirit—incapable of sympathy, of love, of self-revelation, of a life in the being and life of others. An Infinite, in other words, which is limited only by that which makes love possible, is, so to speak, higher, *more* infinite, than an Infinite, which is nothing but the boundlessness or absence of all limits. Nor, again, can we reach the true idea of the Infinite by merely exalting it immeasurably above the finite world, by conceiving each of the two in hard unmediated opposition to the other. For the very existence of an external finite destroys by limiting the notion of infinitude. The true Infinite is that which implies, or in the very idea of its nature contains or embraces the existence of the finite.

Now it is this characteristic of the things of spirit (viz., that they are only to be grasped in a thought which embraces and solves contradictory elements) which renders impossible any other than a merely analogical or pictorial representation of them to the ordinary consciousness. The language of the ordinary consciousness, as we have seen, is competent to express the nature of those things which are subject to the conditions of time and space. It lends itself naturally to that mode of thought in which the world is regarded as made up of individual existences, each of which has a nature of its own, self-identical, self-complete. But when we rise to a spiritual view of things, when it becomes necessary to apprehend objects which are no longer self-identical units, but each of which is, so to speak, at once itself and other than itself, when you cannot affirm without at the same time denying or deny without affirming, when seeming contradictions interpenetrate and give reality and life to each other—here obviously the resources of ordinary thought break down. Pious feeling may indeed rise, in an instinctive way, to this exalted region and furnish a practical solution of its contradictions. And so long as we remain in the sphere of feeling, or are content with that form of knowledge to which the ordinary consciousness can attain, contradictory elements may be accepted without any sense of their contradiction. At most they will betray their presence only by that paradoxical and mystical form of expression in which religious experience spontaneously clothes itself. "He that loseth his life shall find it"; "When I am weak then am I strong"; "We know God, or rather are known of God"; "I live, yet not I, but Christ liveth in me"; "I in them, and thou in me, that they may be made perfect in one"; "We which live are alway delivered unto death, that the life of Jesus might be made manifest in us"; "As deceivers and yet true, as unknown and yet well known, as dying and behold we live, as sorrowful and yet always rejoicing";—he who so speaks is one who has in his own experience realised the intense and incessant play of conflicting tendencies by which the spiritual life maintains itself, and who, at the same time, has found in the unity and permanence of that life their practical reconciliation.

But when reflection is awakened, and reason begins to seek its own satisfaction, that satisfaction is one which neither pious feeling nor the representations of the ordinary and unscientific consciousness can supply. In the endeavour to give inner connection and unity to the manifold and seemingly conflicting contents of religious belief, the first step we naturally take is to call in the aid of the logical, systematising faculty, we try to meet the craving for intellectual satisfaction by constructing theological definitions and dogmas, and weaving them into systems freed from anything that wars with logical self-consistency. But we speedily find that the unity of the spiritual world is a thing which lies beyond the scope of formal logic, and that instead of reconciling, our rationalising efforts only bring into harsher opposition and discordancy, the differences we seek to solve. Nor, from the nature of the thing, can it be otherwise. If the sphere of spiritual reality be that in which nothing exists as a self-identical entity, how is it possible that formal logic, whose fundamental principle is the law of identity, should be other than baffled in the endeavour to grasp them? Or how can an organ of thought which tests all things by the so-called law of contradiction, compass, or in the attempt to compass, do anything else than misrepresent, the realities of a world where analysis is ever revealing oppositions which, taken abstractly, *are* contradictions, and whose absolute opposition can only vanish in the light of a higher synthesis? The only resource of the rationalising intellect, in order to attain self-consistency, is to explain away or sacrifice one side or aspect of truth to another with which it seems to conflict, or to select some supposed fundamental principle or dogma as its starting point, and force everything else in the many-sided world of thought into external coherence with it. The only method, in other words, which logical ratiocination has for attaining unity is that of abstraction and generalisation — that which proceeds by the elimination or excision, rather than by the harmonising, of differences. In Philosophy, for instance, it seizes hold of one of the indivisible elements in the duality of consciousness, and rejects the other equally necessary element. It tries to evolve all things out of the objective element, and so produces a system of sensationalism or materialism; or insisting, with equal one-sidedness, on the subjective element, it is led into a spurious kind of idealism. In ethical controversies, it poises against each other the alternative notions of freedom and necessity, rejects everything that seems to conflict with a liberty of indetermination which is nothing more than an abstraction; or, becoming aware of the difficulty or rather impossibility of such a notion, it falls over into a mechanical necessity which is either equally incogitable or reduces mind to the level of matter. In the province of Religion and Theology the same tendency to pass all things in heaven and earth through the sieve of a narrow rationalising logic, leads to analogous results. The only Infinity of which it can conceive is that which is the negation of the finite, and therefore the only theory of the universe possible to it is either a Pantheism which reduces the world and man to an illusion, or a Materialism or Individualism which leaves no place for God. A free finite intelligence and will conditioned by an infinite or absolute thought and will is a contradictory notion, and accordingly, we have either a theology which, starting from the idea of divine sovereignty and foreknowledge, denies to man any real spiritual life; or, on the other hand, a theology which, in order to protect human responsibility, virtually limits and lowers the idea of God. The conceptions of the Divine and the Human are reciprocally exclusive or contradictory, and if we try to get rid of the contradiction, it is possible, according to this method, only by marring and undeifying the Divine, or by virtually annulling the Human. Hence we have, on the one hand, a shallow Deism clinging to the notion of a God who is but an abstract numerical unit; and on the other hand we have, through the long lapse of ages, controversialists spending the resources of a subtle logic in attempts to modify or refine away to a mere docetic phantom the human side of Christ's person so as to make it capable of union with the Divine. Lastly, to name no other example, the same attempt to apply to spiritual realities a method inadequate to their subtlety and depth is exemplified in those theological devices or 'schemes' by which different attributes of the Divine nature are supposed to be harmonised. Certain qualities or attributes, such as Righteousness and Mercy, are treated as independent entities, each having a fixed and definite existence and meaning of its own; and as, when taken thus abstractly, they seem to involve conflicting results—Righteousness being a principle which demands the infliction of deserved penalties, Mercy a principle which seeks their remission—a crude attempt is made to solve the contradiction by hypostatising both attributes, and inducing the one personified quality to accept fictitious concessions or compensations in order that the other may have its way. Obviously however, here as elsewhere, the unity which is attained is got not by any real conciliation of differences, but by explaining away one side or aspect of a complex truth, in order to hold by another with which it seems to come into collision.

In general, the conclusion we reach is that instead of giving any real unity to the differences of the spiritual world, logical ratiocination only serves to exaggerate them. It may dissect and exhibit in isolated detail the various members of the organic whole of truth, but it can no more reproduce the living unity than the anatomist can re-unite in harmonious vital action and reaction the *disjecta membra* of the organism he has dissected.

Is there any higher method of reconciliation? Has thought any organ by which it can not only reveal the differences and contradictions of the spiritual world, but cause them to vanish in a richer and deeper unity? Can we attain to a point of view from which every spiritual idea can be seen to be, from its very nature, a unity of differences—an ideality out of which, by an inherent necessity, diversities and contradictions evolve themselves, only by another equally necessary step to be reintegrated in the identity of another and higher idea? In short, is thought capable of grasping divine truth in such wise that all its constituent elements shall be seen, not as isolated notions, but as correlated members of an organic whole; in such wise that no element shall be conceived to have any independence or opposition to other elements of the whole, save an independence which is only a step in the process by which all independence vanishes, an opposition which is but a seeming discord in the universal harmony? That such a view is possible, it shall now be our endeavour to show.

# CHAPTER VIII.

## TRANSITION TO THE SPECULATIVE IDEA OF RELIGION.

THE inadequacy of ordinary thought has been shown to consist chiefly in this, that it does not rise above those external and accidental relations which belong to the sphere of the finite. Hence when it calls in to its aid the categories and methods of the logical understanding, the only result is to bring to light and give definite expression to the contradictions that lurk in our popular conceptions and beliefs, without furnishing any true reconciliation of them. Now, the definite notions of the understanding, if they may be said, in one point of view, to mark an advance upon the simple unreasoned conceptions of our first religious consciousness, yet in another seem to involve a retrogression in the spiritual life. They carry us a step onward in the necessary movement of thought, but if that movement were arrested at this point, it would only have deprived us of the satisfaction of uncritical and unquestioning faith without enabling us to reach that deeper satisfaction after which reason aspires. The highest ideal of knowledge, the only knowledge in which thought can rest as the realisation of its own demands, is a knowledge from which these defects have vanished,—in which the form is no longer foreign, but adequate to the content, and the ideal element is grasped in its purity, and in its internal coherence and harmony. It is only another way of stating the same thing to say that the highest and only adequate form of knowledge is that which has the characteristic of necessity. For necessary truth is that from which every external or given element has vanished, in which we not merely see that things are, but discern that they *must be;* and further, in which the constituent elements of knowledge are apprehended, not as isolated and independent terms or notions, accepted each on its own evidence, but as related to or flowing out of each other, so that, one being given, the others follow, and the whole body of knowledge constitutes one organic system.

In the last chapter we have indicated in a general way the incompetency of the ordinary logic as an organon of knowledge. Spiritual realities, it has been shown, are related to each other in subtler ways than its forms and methods can grasp, and the ultimate problem of thought is one which lies beyond its scope. We shall now proceed to consider a little more closely the reason of this incompetency, and to inquire whether, by any more adequate method, it is possible to reach that higher and only perfect form of knowledge which the logical understanding fails to attain.

The failure of the understanding as a final organon of knowledge may be said to be due to this, that it starts from presuppositions which make the unity of knowledge an impossible problem. It begins by so disintegrating the universe that it can never restore its scattered elements to unity. It postulates for all things and beings a self-identity, a reciprocal exclusiveness, which by no ingenious machinery of external relations it can ever overcome so as to bring them together again in one rational system or whole. In this view the reality of each thing or being consists in this, that it is, and ever remains, one with itself, that it has a sameness or self-identity which lies beyond and excludes from itself all difference, so that, when we think of it, we must think of it by itself, as itself, and no other than itself. Thus Nature, Man, God ; Matter and Mind ; the world of finite beings, and the Infinite or Absolute Being, have each an independent identity, a separate, self-contained reality, and whatever relations we may go on to predicate of any one of them towards the rest, we must, in the first place, think of it as what it is in itself, and altogether independently of these relations. But there is unity in the world as well as diversity ; individual things and beings through all their varieties of form and function are continually betraying relations to each other and to the whole which embarrass or baffle the attempt to think them as self-identical units. Hence, in the contemplation of the multiplicity of finite objects, even the ordinary consciousness refuses to be content with taking up each by itself in succession, passing on from one to another in interminable series ; and the difficulty becomes greater the more the reflective intelligence is awakened. The understanding is therefore driven to search for expedients by which it may reconcile unity with difference—may apprehend each individual existence as one, despite of its incessant phenomenal changes—may show how the unity of God is consistent with the boundless variety of determinations, which we must ascribe to the Divine nature—may be able to ascribe to each finite spirit a being of its own, without at the same time tampering with the idea of the infinitude of God. Let us examine for a moment some of these expedients by which, consistently with its fundamental canon of identity, the understanding attempts to give unity and self-consistency to its knowledge of individual objects and of the universe as a whole.

1. The slightest reflection makes us aware that many of the things and beings which present themselves to the unreflecting observer as separate individual unities are really not simple, but complex.

They are made up of parts which lie outside of each other in space; they do not remain absolutely the same through successive moments of time; they are continually betraying new phenomenal aspects when brought into new relations with the other existences around them. Even the lowest existences of the inorganic world, and *a fortiori* those possessed of life and intelligence, are not absolutely self-identical units, but existences which contain in them an element of complexity or difference. How then can we continue to think of them as individual things, how can we prevent our knowledge, either of particular objects or of the world as a whole, from falling asunder into a chaos of isolated points?

The answer often given is that we can combine diversity with unity in our conceptions of things by thinking them as individual existences each endowed with manifold qualities. They are substances which possess various properties—extension, solidity, weight, colour, mechanical attraction and repulsion, chemical affinity, etc. Or they are subjects to whom belong capacities of sensation, feeling, perception, memory, imagination, etc., or who are endowed with attributes of power, wisdom, goodness, etc. However numerous therefore the differences which we must connect in our thought of such individual existences, we can thus conceive of each of them as being a unity of which a variety of determinations may be predicated, but which, through all that variety, remains one and the same.

But, apart from other considerations for which this is not the place, this device obviously fails to give us any real apprehension, even of the simplest individual existence, and is found to be utterly inadequate when applied to the realities of the spiritual world. In trying to give unity to a number of unconnected determinations by ascribing them to a common substance, what we really do is only to add to these determinations one more determination equally isolated or unconnected with the rest. When we ask what is the connection between the different properties of a material object, or how extension, impenetrability, weight, colour, etc., unite to make up one thing,—to answer that they cohere in one substance is not to explain or give a rational idea of their unity, but merely to reassert that they are one. It is impossible to explain the known by the unknown: but whilst we know, or suppose we know, the different qualities, of the substance which, we say, unites them, we know and can say absolutely nothing beyond pronouncing the word substance, and repeating the assertion that it is that which makes them one. To apprehend the unity of different qualities, to think them as one, what the mind demands is that we should think or have a rational notion of the relation of each to each, that we should discern how the existence of any one involves and is involved in the existence of the rest and how all are so connected that this particular quality would not exist, except in and through the whole to which it belongs. If we are to have an idea of the thing which is more than a mere enumeration of its parts or properties, we must discern the principle from which this manifoldness of parts and properties necessarily arises, which has its very existence or being in them, and which thus links together in thought the differences that spring out of it. But to say that there is a common substance in which they cohere or of which they can be predicated, instead of making them one for thought, is only to tie them together with a string, and that too, a fictitious string. If in this case substance be for us any more than a blank term round which we string the various predicates, it is only a name for the bare abstraction of being or existence. And whilst it is, no doubt, true that when we abstract from any concrete object all its several qualities or determinations, there is still left, as the ultimate logical abstraction, the element of being or existence which is common to them all; yet in this abstraction we have nothing that could give to a particular object the unity which thought seeks; for the form or category of Being is common to all concrete objects alike, and cannot therefore be the notion which explains the unity of any *particular* object or combination of qualities. In short, instead of enabling us to think a given object as a unity of differences, to say that they are the differences of one substance is merely to say that the differences exist, or have existence in common.

It is, however, when we rise to the consideration of spiritual realities that the inadequacy of this method of thought becomes most palpable. It does not in any measure enable us to apprehend the spiritual unity of man's nature, still less does it give unity to our conceptions of the Divine nature, to think of mind or spirit as a substance with various capacities or attributes. For, in the first place, here as in other cases, the several qualities or attributes are left in mere outward contiguity and are only accidentally and arbitrarily connected with each other and with the unknown substance to which they are attached. Feeling, memory, imagination, reason, etc., or power, wisdom, righteousness and other predicates, remain, so far as thought is concerned, as unconnected as the separate stones in a heap, and the order in which they come, the fact that it is this precise number of items, neither more nor less, which come together to constitute the totality, is as much a matter of accident in the one case as in the other. Why the so-called powers or attributes differ from each other and yet are united together, is left as unexplained, as much a mere result of external and fortuitous conditions, as the coagulation of a certain number of bits of quartz and other pebbles in a mass of conglomerate. But further, in the case of rational and spiritual beings, there is this special reason for the failure of the notion of substance to give unity to the differences of things, viz., that *an element of difference enters into the very idea*, or if we may so speak, *into the very substance itself of mind.* You cannot think of mind as one single substance beneath all diversities of powers and attributes; for when you chase this very substance back to its furthest retreat, you find it to be *not one*, not a bare unit, but a complex unity which is the combination or inter-action of elements distinct yet indivisible. We are debarred from thinking of a spiritual nature as a substance behind all diversities, a unity which is and remains simple and unchangeable amidst all changes and differences; for spirit cannot be conceived save as containing in it an element of diversity, and the only unity we can ascribe to it is, not a unity *beyond* differences, but a unity which manifests itself *in* them. When we try to form a notion of mind or spirit as distinct from other existences, the most abstract, the least complex identity we can ascribe to it is that not of bare being, but of intelligent or self-conscious being. But self-consciousness is not a simple notion or one which can be thought of as excluding from itself all difference.

It includes in it of necessity two elements, a self which is conscious and a self which is the object of consciousness, a self which thinks and a self which is thought of; and these two not added to each other or in external contiguity, but in inseparable correlation. You cannot get farther in your elimination of difference, you cannot abstract either of these ultimate factors and think it by itself as the substance of mind, or get beneath them both and think of a substance or self of which they are only the properties. If you try to do so, if you say, *e.g.*, I can conceive of myself as a spiritual substance or self prior to any mental act by which I make myself or anything else an object of thought, I can conceive of the substance of my nature in its original and untroubled simplicity or unity; the answer is, *either* that what you are really thinking of here is not mind or spirit, but the mere blank potentiality of mind which slumbers in the unconsciousness of the embryo, which is not the self that continues and lives through your life as a rational and spiritual being, but that from which you must *emerge* in order to be spirit, and which, if it continued, would not be the self of an intelligent being, but of an animal or an idiot; *or*, if this is *not* what you are thinking of, then in the very act of conceiving or picturing to yourself this supposed simple, abstract substance or self prior to all consciousness, you yourself are reclaiming it from its abstractness, tacitly endowing it with your own subjectivity, and by making it an object of thought, contributing to it that other factor which is necessary to its existence *as* mind or self-consciousness. Lastly, and as a further development of the same thought, the impossibility of conceiving of a spiritual being as a self-identical substance distinct from all other substances, a unity apart from all differences, will be seen by considering that it is of the very essence of mind or spirit to contain within itself relation to other beings, and especially to other spiritual beings. Self-consciousness implies not only, if we may so speak, an *internal* dualism or difference, a self which is opposed to or object to itself, and so, distinguished from itself, but also an *external* difference, a self which knows or realises itself only through its consciousness of that which is not self. You cannot define mind or spirit as a substance which exists by itself, prior to or apart from its relations to other substances, for its very nature and essence is to exist in and through its relations to other substances. They are a part of its being. It discovers or realises its own nature only through natures that are foreign to or outside of itself. Its whole life *as* spirit consists in taking into itself that outward world which it at first opposes to itself. The very beginning, the earliest dawn of that life, is the awakening of the consciousness in one and the same indivisible act, of a self and a not-self, of a world without as opposed to a world within: and the whole subsequent development of that life consists only in the reclaiming or gathering back into the inner self of the rich content of that world which it first posits as foreign or external to itself, or, what is the same thing from the opposite side, in the unfolding or evolution of the consciousness of self, through the mediation of nature and other spiritual beings. Mind or spirit cannot be thought of as a substance distinct from all other substances, for it has no reality apart from them; or as an identity prior to all differences, for its very life and being is *in* differences. It is not a unity behind differences, but it is a unity *in* differences, and of differences. On this point, as we shall immediately recur to it, it is unnecessary at present to insist further.

2. We have seen then that the logical understanding fails as an organ of knowledge in this respect, that it cannot apprehend in their unity the differences which present themselves in individual things and beings. But its inadequacy becomes still more apparent when we pass from the differences which even individual existences contain to the deeper problem which is involved in the relations of these individualities to each other and to the whole. Rational knowledge cannot be a

knowledge merely of an unconnected succession of isolated objects, or of discordant, or even arbitrarily related elements of thought. To be rational, our knowledge must be coherent and systematic; our ideas, *e.g.*, of matter and mind, of things natural and things spiritual, of the world without and the world within, our ideas of Nature and Man and God, of the Finite and Infinite, must, in order to be held together in thought, be, not merely not discordant and contradictory, but so related to each other by necessary links of thought as to constitute one self-consistent body or system of truth.

Now so long as we look at things from the point of view of the logical understanding and under those laws of Identity and Contradiction which it adopts as its fundamental principles, it is impossible to attain to any such coherence and unity in our apprehension of the various objects of knowledge. All real knowledge is systematic knowledge, but the abstract logical method makes system impossible. Matter and mind, Nature and Man and God are thus isolated from each other, each in its own hard self-identical individuality, and must be regarded as independent entities existing side by side, or only outwardly and mechanically related to each other; and their co-existence in one universe, though it may be held as a fact, is not a co-existence for thought. The understanding, indeed, attempts to pass beyond individual existences and to give unity to its apprehension of the different objects of knowledge; but, as it cannot break through the hard self-inclusion in which at the outset it has shut up each individual object, the only expedient to which it can have recourse is that of abstraction and generalisation. Observing certain aspects or qualities in which individual things or beings resemble each other, it neglects or leaves out of view the points in which they differ and invents general names for those which they have in common. Thus it gives a kind of unity to its ideas of red, green, violet, etc., by the general term or abstract conception of colour, it unites the various individuals of the vegetable world by the conception of plant, those of another class by that of animal, those of a third by that of mind or spirit, etc. But very little reflection is needed to see that this expedient fails to attain the end at which it aims. The particular things or beings embraced under a general conception are not really, but only formally united. In themselves they remain different as they were, what unites them is only something in us. Their difference, their isolated particular existence, is the reality, and that which gives them unity is only a fiction of the observer's mind. There is no such thing in reality as an animal which is no particular animal, a plant which is no particular plant, a man or humanity which is no individual man. If plants, animals, men, are united by the general notion it is only in the arbitrary world of logical abstractions; in their own real existence they are still left, for aught that the understanding can discover, in their hard, self-included, reciprocally-repellent individuality. Generalisation, so far from apprehending reality, is a process which takes us away from it, and the further it advances, the more abstract our thought becomes, the further do we recede from the real, objective truth of things.

But thought is capable of another and deeper movement. It can rise to a universality which is not foreign to, but the very inward nature of things in themselves, not the universal of an abstraction from the particular and different, but the unity which is immanent in them and finds in them its own necessary expression; not an arbitrary invention of the observing and classifying mind unifying in its own imagination things which are yet essentially different, but an idea which expresses the inner dialectic, the movement or process towards unity, which exists in and constitutes the being of the objects themselves. This deeper and truer universality is that which may be designated *ideal or organic universality.* The idea of a living organism, as we formerly saw, is not a common element which can be got at by abstraction and generalisation—by taking the various parts and members, stripping away their differences, and forming a notion of that which they have in common. That in which they differ is rather just that out of which their unity arises and in which is the very life and being of the organism; that which they have in common they have, not as members of a living organism, but as dead matter, and what you have to abstract in order to get it, is the very life itself. Moreover the universal, in this case, is not last but first. We do not reach it by first thinking the particulars, but conversely, we get at the true notion of the particulars only through the universal. What the parts or members of an organism are—their form, place, structure, proportion, functions, relations, their whole nature and being—is determined by the idea of the organism which they are to compose. It is it which produces them, not they it. In it lies their reason and ground. They are its manifestations or specifications. It realises itself in them, fulfils itself in their diversity and harmony. Nor, again, can you reach this unity merely by predication or affirmation, by asserting, that is, of each part or member that it is, and what it is. On the contrary in order to apprehend it, with your thought of what it is you must inseparably connect that also of what it *is not*. You cannot determine the particular member or organ save by reference to that which is its limit or negation. It does not exist in and by itself, but in and through what is other than itself—through the other members and organs which are at once outside of and within it, beyond it and yet part and portion of its being. It can exist only as it denies or gives up any separate self-identical being and life—only as it finds its life in the larger life and being of the whole. You cannot apprehend its true nature under the category of 'Being' alone, for at every moment of its existence it at once is and is not; it is in giving up or losing itself; its true being is in ceasing to be. Its notion includes negation as well as affirmation. Lastly, in a still deeper way does negation or a negative movement of thought enter into the idea of an organic whole. Its ideal nature is not immediate, but is reached by a process of growth or development. But the notion of development is one which cannot be apprehended merely by affirmation or by a series of affirmations, but only by a process which includes affirmation and negation, or more precisely, perpetual affirmation, perpetual negation, solved in re-affirmation. At no moment of its progressive existence is it possible to determine a living organism merely as that which is, or to compass the idea of it by any number of positive predicates. A succession of affirmative predicates can no more give us the unbroken continuity of life, than a series of separate points the idea of a straight line, or a series of infinitely minute straight lines the idea of a curve, or than the successive positions of a body at infinitely minute intervals of time can give us what is equivalent to the idea of the motion of a projectile. At every stage of its growth, and at every minutest portion of that stage, the organism not only is, but is passing away from, that which it is. And when you have reached the perfect idea—the idea of the completely developed or perfect organism —it is found to be, not the sum or collection or affirmative generalisation of all its successive states, but the result of a process of perpetual affirmation and negation, which, whilst it has annulled all the prior stages of its history, at the same time has absorbed and re-affirmed each and all of them in its own perfect unity. Here then we have a kind of universality which is altogether different from the barren and formal universality of generalisation, and the indication of a movement of thought corresponding to an inner relation of things which the abstracting, generalising understanding is altogether inadequate to grasp.

Now, it is by the application of this principle to religion and religious ideas that we are enabled to apprehend these ideas in their essential nature, their reciprocal relations, and their harmony and unity as a whole. The attraction of Pantheism and of pantheistic systems of philosophy lies in this, that they meet the craving of the religious mind for absolute union with God and of the speculative mind for intellectual unity. But what Pantheism gains by the sacrifice of individuality and responsibility in man, by depriving the finite world of reality and reducing Nature, Man and God, to a blank, colourless identity, a true philosophy attains in another and deeper way. It gives us a principle in the light of which we can see that God is all in all, without denying reality to the finite world and to every individual human spirit, or without denying it except in so far as it involves a life apart from God —a spurious independence which is not the protection but the destruction of all spiritual life. Let us briefly endeavour to show how it may attain this result.

Nature, the finite Mind, and God or the infinite Mind, are not discordant or irreconcilable ideas, but ideas which belong to one organic whole or system of knowledge. It is with the last two that a philosophy of religion is specially concerned; for religion is that practical solution of the difference between God and man, between the Infinite Spirit and the finite, which it is the problem of that philosophy to explain. But the principle which solves the difference between the finite mind and Nature is the same which finds its higher application in the solution of the difference between the finite mind and God: or rather the movement of thought by which Nature relates itself to finite intelligence is only a lower stage or exemplification of that by which finite intelligence rises into union with the Infinite Mind. A brief consideration, therefore, of the relation of Nature to Finite Mind will prepare us for the analogous but higher problem of the relation of the Finite Mind to God.

(*a*) To the ordinary consciousness there is difference but no disharmony between the various elements of its knowledge, for they are all embraced in the uncritical and undoubting unity of immediate belief. The differences of things as they present themselves to outward observation, are instinctively recognised and their harmony or unity is tacitly accepted as a matter of fact. The ordinary consciousness does not inquire what these differences really are, nor how they can be solved, not merely empirically, but for thought. Nor does it ask, again, how nature and man, things and thought, the world without and the world within, are related to each other, what is the distinction between them, and how that distinction is overcome. Things are before us—matter and material objects existing apart in themselves just as I perceive them—a world of realities independent of any mind to know them: and on the other hand, I who perceive that world am here in my own equally complete and independent existence. Matter is matter, and mind is mind; and there is no thought of inquiring what each really is, or how consistently with their essential difference and independent reality, knowledge, and that communion which knowledge implies, are possible.

It is the province of philosophy to solve this

problem; but very often philosophic writers have been satisfied with formulating the uncritical assumptions of the ordinary consciousness, and restating in formal language as an ultimate belief the hard opposition of mind and matter, thought and things, in which common sense instinctively rests; or, if they have gone further, they have evaded the difficulty by explaining away one or other of the opposed terms, and thus have fallen into Materialism or into a merely subjective Idealism. Aware, for instance, that much of that which the ordinary consciousness ascribes to Nature is really contributed by the observer's own mind, such writers set themselves to analyse our knowledge of Nature in order to discover how much that contribution includes. The 'secondary qualities' of matter they give up as purely relative, the creation of our own sensuous organism; but they still assert that extension and solidity are actually and objectively in Nature just as we perceive them. Or again, finding this position untenable, and constrained to concede that what the mind is conscious of is simply its own sensations, they enlarge the subjective contribution to knowledge and reduce to its minimum that independent reality beyond thought which they still ascribe to Nature. Of that vast complex of realities which to the ordinary consciousness appear to exist in Nature just as we perceive them, it is now conceded that much the larger part is due to mind. What is given from without is only the raw material which sensation supplies; and the rest—the whole fabric of our seeming objective knowledge—is reared up out of sensation, either, according to one school, by certain mental laws of association, or according to another, by the activity of the understanding, guided by its own forms and categories. But all this wonderful system, whatever its value, is composed, not of realities but only of ideas about them. Behind and beyond our ideas lie the things in themselves, the unknown cause or source of sensuous impressions, the hidden reality of Nature, the world as it is in itself, independent of thought, irrespective of any mind to know it.

But even this last residuum of a world foreign to and independent of mind, it is, as we formerly saw, impossible to retain. For, whatever it is, it cannot even be imagined save by giving it relation to thought. The existence we try to ascribe to it beyond thought is itself a thought. Being or existence has no meaning save as being or existence conceived or thought about. To say that thought itself can think an existence behind thought, or which has no relation to thought, is a contradiction in terms. Even if there were such a thing as a world beyond thought, we, at least, could never know anything about it, even the bare fact of its existence; for that would be equivalent to knowing what we do not know, to knowing and not knowing in one and the same mental act. Starting, therefore, with the presupposition of the independent existence, both of the world without and of the world within, and inquiring what contribution mind gives to our knowledge of the former, we find mind successively claiming for itself one element after another of that knowledge, until at length the whole has been brought within its own province, and the last unresolved fraction, the ultimate residuum of a reality beyond thought, has disappeared.

Are we then driven to the conclusion that the external world is but a phantasm, the illusory assumption of common thought, which philosophy shows to be nothing more than the creation of the individual mind, coming into existence and vanishing with the thought of the mind that thinks it? As materialism tries to evolve all things, mind included, out of matter or material force, does idealism succeed in showing, on the contrary, that the whole objective world is but the phantasmal creation of mind? And if not, if we refuse to be argued out of our conviction that there is a real world which our thought neither makes nor unmakes, and which would exist without our existing to think it—if this be so, where lies the fallacy of the idealist's argument?

The answer is that it lies in the false presupposition with which he started, the presumption, namely, that Nature and Mind, the world without and the world within, constitute two fixed independent realities, each by itself, complete in its own self-included being. And the true solution of the problem lies in the surrender of this false Identity for that principle of Organic Unity which we have above attempted to explain. Beginning with two isolated existences separated by the impassable gulf of a rigid self-identity, no theory can ever force them into rational union or coherence. The only logical conclusion to which, from such premises, we can come is, either that there is no external world, or if there is, that we can never know even the fact of its existence. But when we cease thus arbitrarily to bar any solution by giving impossible conditions to the problem; when we begin to see in Nature and Mind not two independent things, but two members of one organic whole, having, indeed, each a being of its own, but a being which implies, and finds itself in living relation to, the other—then and then only can we bring the two factors or members into that union which any real knowledge of Nature implies. Nature in its very essence is related to Mind, Mind to Nature; therein lies the possibility of their coherence in one system. If Nature were a mere chaos, without law or order or intelligible constitution, knowledge would be impossible, thought could find in the outward world nothing to grasp. But it is because law, rational order and sequence, in one word, because reason exists in Nature, that

Nature yields itself up to thought or intelligence. On the other hand, Mind or intelligence is no mere abstract entity, self-contained, having its whole reality in its own self-included being; and a consciousness that is conscious of nothing—a thinking subject to which no object of thought is ever present, would be a mere blank—not mind, but only the unrealised possibility of mind. On the contrary, as Nature is realised Mind, so Mind finds itself in Nature, and in converse with Nature has awakened in it the consciousness of its own manifold content. The speculative solution of the problem which the opposition of Nature and finite Mind presents is, therefore, that Nature is not the hard antithesis, but the reflexion of Mind, and that Mind discovers itself in Nature *tanquam in speculo.* Further, it is only by self-negation or self-renunciation that the Mind enters into that relation to Nature which constitutes true knowledge. For it is but a spurious idealism which makes the world without only the illusory creation of the individual mind. Rather the truth is that the individual mind must renounce its own isolated independence, must cease to assert itself, must lose itself in the object before it can attain to any true knowledge of Nature. Scientific knowledge is the revelation of a world of objective realities which only he who abnegates his own individual fancies and opinions before the absolute authority of truth can apprehend. In order, therefore, to attain to the universal life of reason that is in the world, it is an indispensable condition that I renounce my own individuality, my particular thought and opinion, and find the true realisation of my own reason in that absolute reason or truth which Nature manifests. On the other hand if we naturally begin by opposing the outward world to ourselves, if, in other words, the first step which the finite mind takes is to affirm the independent objective existence of Nature in opposition to itself, the last is to deny that independence, to bring back Nature to unity with thought, to discover that Nature is essentially rational or that throughout the whole realm of Nature there is nothing irrational or unintelligible, nothing which thought may not claim as akin to itself. The principle, in fine, that solves the difference between Nature and Finite Mind is, that their isolated reality and exclusiveness is a figment, and that the organic life of reason is the truth or reality of both.

(*b*) The principle which, as we have thus seen, enables us to apprehend Nature and the Finite Mind, at once in their difference and their unity, we may now apply to the solution of the higher problem of Religion, or of the relation of the Finite Mind to God. Here, too, it will be seen that the understanding, which clings to the hard independent identity of either side, inasmuch as it starts from essentially dualistic conditions, renders any true solution impossible. If the law of non-contradiction is carried to its logical results, the only alternatives in which the mind can rest are, either Pantheism, which denies spiritual reality and life to man, or Anthropomorphism, which makes religion a mere subjective fiction and God the self-imposed illusion of the worshipper's own mind. A true solution can be reached only by apprehending the Divine and the Human, the Infinite and the Finite, as the moments or members of an organic whole, in which both exist, at once in their distinction and their unity.

To see this, let it be considered, in the first place, that even in the case of our social relations—of the relations of the individual to other individuals, we find it impossible to hold fast by that notion of individual identity with which popular thought contents itself. Just as the hard and fast distinction between matter and mind which is the unquestioned presumption of ordinary thought creates an impassable gulf between us and the outward world; so the ordinary conception of self-identity isolates the individual from his fellow-men. But as in the one case, so in the other, the attempt to follow out the conception to its logical consequences speedily discloses its insufficiency. The abstract individual is not truly man, but only a fragment of humanity, a being as devoid of the moral and spiritual elements which are of the essence of man's life, as the amputated limb of participation in the vital existence of the organism. The social relations are a necessary part of the being of the individual. He cannot realise himself within himself, but only in and through those who are other than himself; and it is only by the negation or surrender of his individual self, of his own isolated being and life, to a larger or universal self, that he comes to realise the true meaning of his nature as a spiritual being. It is not by supposing in the first place a number of individual human beings, each complete in himself, and then combining these individuals, that we reach the idea of the Family: rather must we first think the Family in order to know the individuals. The abstract individual, isolated from all other human spirits, would lack elements which enter essentially into the idea of humanity, would be nothing more than the undeveloped germ of human nature, the possibility of a spirit that has never become actual. Here, as elsewhere, the universal is the *prius* of the particular. Yet the universal must not be conceived as having any reality apart from the particulars, any more than the body apart from its members. The true idea is reached only by holding both together in that higher unity which at once comprehends and transcends them, that organic unity, whether of the Family or the State, which is the living integration of the individual members which compose it.

But man has relations not only to other finite

beings, but also to that which transcends the finite. If in order to understand aright the nature of the individual, we must take into account other finite beings and his relations to them, still more necessary is it, in order to know the meaning of his nature, that we take into account that Infinite and Absolute Being which is at once the presupposition and the end of all finite thought and life. And here again when we examine the relation, we shall find that it is intelligible only as one of organic unity, that the terms held apart are only abstractions, and that they find their truth in that higher idea which at once denies and includes them. The true Infinite is not the mere negation of the Finite, but that which is the organic unity of the Infinite and Finite. What therefore we are now required to show is (1) that Finite Spirit presupposes or is intelligible only in the light of the idea of Infinite Spirit, and (2) that Infinite Spirit contains, in the very idea of its nature, organic relation to the Finite.

(1.) The religious impulse, the aspiration after God and after union with Him as the soul's true life, is grounded in the very nature of man as a rational and spiritual being. Something more than the mediation of Nature and of other finite minds is needed in order to the unfolding of the latent content of my spiritual nature. My life as a rational and spiritual being would be impossible and my relations to nature and society would be baseless save on the presupposition of an Infinite and Absolute Intelligence on which all finite thought and being rest.

At first sight, indeed, when we consider merely the logical opposition expressed by the terms Infinite and Finite, it would seem that so far from the latter implying the former, it must be simply suppressed or annulled by it. If God be the absolutely unlimited Being, if there be no existence that is independent of Him, if all reality is comprehended in Him, where is there room for any such existence that is not a mere shadow and semblance? The contradiction may be softened and a place apparently found for the Finite, by representing God, not simply as Infinite, but under such notions as 'First Cause' or 'Creator and Governor of the world;' but these expedients do not really suffice for the end in view. If for example we conceive Him as 'creating the world out of nothing,' we do not by this device escape the dilemma of a Finite which either limits or is suppressed by the Infinite. For by the act of creation *either* the Creator calls into existence something external to Himself, something absolutely new and which is, so to speak, an addition to His infinitude, and then, neither before nor after the creating act can He be called infinite; *or* the created world is not a new existence, an addition to the pre-existing sum of reality—not really an existence different from its source—and then it becomes incapable of any relation to God, seeing it is not distinguishable from Him.

But when we pass from this mere opposition of the terms Infinite and Finite to view the opposition as that of Infinite and Finite *Spirit*, the contradiction is no longer one in which each term is the negation of the other, but one in which each is necessary to, and realises itself in and through the other.

Finite Spirit or Mind, so far from being incompatible with Infinite Spirit or Mind, presupposes it, and can realise itself only through it. As all scientific investigation proceeds on the tacit presumption of the uniformity of Nature, and as it is only on this presumption that any knowledge of Nature becomes possible, so all finite thought rests on and becomes possible only through the tacit presumption of the existence of an Absolute and Infinite thought or mind; and, as the former belief constitutes not only the condition of all inquiry but the secret impulse to every endeavour after fuller knowledge of Nature, so the latter belief constitutes the perpetual spring and motive of all spiritual life. In all thought, even the most elementary, we presuppose an absolute criterion of thought, an ideal of knowledge, an objective truth or reality, to which our thought must conform itself, and without which thought itself would disappear in a mere chaos of sensations. Science is nothing else than the gradual realisation by us of a self-consistent whole of truth, the objective reality of which, from the outset, every investigator must presuppose. In the very beginning of knowledge the mind has implicitly grasped the goal or end of knowledge, and has tacitly asserted that it is infinite and absolute. It would, indeed, be absurd to say that every inquirer sets out with the conscious recognition of this idea, but the principle here maintained is that, unconscious or vaguely cognisant as the mind may be of the ultimate basis of its own activity, yet in all thinking, in all mental action, in all inquiry and reasoning, there is involved the assumption of the ultimate unity of being and thought, and that it is the end and aim of finite intelligence to realise it. How then are we to conceive of this ultimate basis of thought, this reality on which all intelligence rests? This fundamental question is a question which cannot be answered directly, seeing that all human knowledge, which is the gradual bringing of this reality to self-consciousness, may be said to be the never-exhausted answer to it. But even from the general point of view in which we here contemplate the subject, two things may without difficulty be proved, viz., that this ultimate reality is an Absolute Spirit whose existence is presupposed in all finite existence, whose thought is the one condition of all finite thoughts; and conversely, that it is only in communion with this Absolute Spirit or Intelligence that the finite spirit can realise itself. It is absolute; for the faintest movement of human intelligence would be arrested if it did not presuppose the absolute reality of intelligence, of thought itself. It is not the product of human thought, for no thought could ever begin to be, save on the assumption of it. Behind all finite thought lies a reality which is inaccessible to doubt or denial, seeing that doubt or denial themselves presuppose and indirectly affirm it. Even the wildest scepticism appeals to a criterion of certitude which its doubts, unless they annul themselves, can never touch. Thought of any kind, positive or negative, doubting or asserting postulates itself—postulates, that is, not the thought of the individual thinker, but a thought or self-consciousness that is prior to all individual thinking, and is the absolute element or atmosphere in which it lives and breathes. When I pronounce anything to be true, I pronounce it, indeed, to be relative to thought, for, as above said, that thought should think or conceive of a truth or reality that is beyond or outside of thought, is a contradiction in terms; but not to be relative to *my* thought or to the thought of any other individual mind. From the existence of all individual minds, as such, I can abstract, I can think them away. But that which I cannot think away, that to which every other thought is secondary, the pre-condition that makes possible any thought whatever, even the thought of the nothingness of finite thought is thought or self-consciousness itself, in its independence and absoluteness, or, in other words, an Absolute Thought or Self-consciousness. On the other hand, it is just in uniting ourselves with this Absolute Thought or Self-consciousness, and in so far as we do, that we realise ourselves as rational and spiritual beings. That which raises man above the animal, and provides for him an escape from the limits of his own individuality, is that he can, and even, in a sense, that he must, identify himself with a Consciousness that transcends all that is particular and relative. If he were only a creature of transient sensations and impulses, or if his consciousness were, so to speak, the theatre of an ever coming and going succession of intuitions, fancies, feelings, then there would be in his nature nothing to raise him above himself, nothing could ever have for him the character of objective truth or reality. Beyond the empirical fact that such modifications of his consciousness happen, he could not go. His spiritual life would be broken up into fragments, without continuity or coherence, and witnessing to nothing beyond themselves. Even if the opinions, tastes, feelings, fancies of a merely sensitive subject could testify to so much as the fact of their own existence; yet in the conflict of different individual opinions, there being no objective standard to appeal to, each would have the same right to his own as another. But it is the prerogative of man's spiritual nature that he can rise above himself as this particular being, that he can cease to think his own thoughts, or be swayed by his own impulses, and can yield himself up to a thought and will that are other and infinitely larger than his own. As a thinking self-conscious being, indeed, he may be said, by his very nature, to live in the atmosphere of the Universal Life. From the first dawn of consciousness in which sense is already for him transformed into thought, he has entered into this life; and all spiritual progress is to live more and more in the conscious realisation of it. As a thinking being, it is possible for me to suppress and quell in my consciousness every movement of self-assertion, every notion and opinion that is merely mine, every desire that belongs to me as this particular self, and to become the pure medium of a thought or intelligence that is universal —in one word, to live no more my own life, but let my consciousness become possessed and suffused by the Infinite and Eternal life of spirit. And yet it is just in this renunciation of self that I truly gain myself, or realise the highest possibilities of my nature. When in the language of religion we say, 'I live, yet not I but Christ liveth in me,' 'It is God that worketh in me to will and to do of His good pleasure,' pious feeling is only giving expression in its own way to that which philosophy shows to be in strictest accordance with the principle of man's spiritual nature. For whilst in one sense we give up self to live the universal and absolute life of reason, yet that to which we thus surrender ourselves is in reality our truer self. The life of absolute truth or reason is not a life that is foreign to us. If it is above us, it is also within us. In yielding to it we are not submitting to an outward and arbitrary law or to an external authority, but to a law that has become our own law, an authority which has become enthroned in the inmost essence of our being. It is the fulfilment and the freedom of every spiritual being to become the organ of Infinite and Absolute reason. When we attain the ideal perfection of our nature, the self that is foreign to it is foreign to us too, it has become lost and absorbed in that deeper, higher self with which our whole life and being is identified. It is our highest glory that every movement of our mind, every pulsation of our spiritual being, should be in harmony with it, and that apart from it we should have no life we can call our own.

(2.) We have now attempted to show that Finite Spirit or Mind, considered by itself and apart from Infinite Spirit or Mind, is a mere abstraction, that the former presupposes and is intelligible only in the light of the latter. But now turning to the other side of the opposition, we shall find that an abstract, self-referent Infinite must, equally with an abstract, self-referent Finite, yield to another and higher idea. The Infinite of religion cannot be a mere self-identical Being, but one which contains, in its very nature, organic relation to the Finite; or rather, it is that organic whole which is the unity of the Infinite and Finite. In other words, an Infinite which does not extinguish the Finite as its bare contradictory or negation, must *contain in itself* the determination of the Finite.

If religion means that only in union with God can my spiritual nature fulfil or realise itself, it follows that there must be something in the nature of God on which the religious relation is based. A necessary relation cannot be one in which there is necessity only on the one side and mere arbitrary will on the other. But this would be implied in conceiving of God as a mere abstract Omnipotence, and of the creation of the world as simply the act of His 'mere will and pleasure.' According to this conception, as there is no reason in God why finite spiritual beings should exist rather than not exist, there can be nothing in man which is unfulfilled and unsatisfied save in union with God. To be spiritually united to God, is to find in God the end and reason of my being; and to say this is equivalent to saying that the existence of a finite world or of finite spiritual beings cannot be ascribed to a mere arbitrary creative will, but springs out of something in the very nature of God; or that the idea of God contains in itself, as a necessary element of it, the existence of finite spirits.

Now, that the trúe idea of the Infinite does contain in it the idea of the Finite, or in less formal terms, that the nature of God would be imperfect if it did not contain in it relation to a finite world, may be shown in various ways. The simplest way in which we can make this thought clear to ourselves is by considering that, conceived as a mere abstract, self-identical Infinite, God would lack that which is one of the most essential elements of a spiritual nature—the element of love. Without life in the life of others, a spiritual being would not be truly spirit. To go forth out of self, to have all the hidden wealth of thought and feeling of which I am capable called forth in relations to other and kindred beings, and to receive back again that wealth redoubled in reciprocated knowledge and affection — this is to live a spiritual life; not to do this is to take from our lives all that makes them spiritual. But all this we leave out of our idea of God if we conceive of Him as a self-identical Infinite, complete and self-contained in His own being. Nor does it mend the matter to say that we can separate in thought the capacity of love from the actual manifestation of it, and that, as we can think of God as possessed of creative power anterior to the actual exercise of it, so we can still think of Him, anterior to the existence of any finite intelligence, as having in Himself boundless capacities of goodness and love and mercy —of all those elements of spiritual excellence which are only revealed, not created, by His relations to a finite world. For a latent capacity or possibility of spiritual perfection is to a perfection which has actually realised itself, as the undeveloped intelligence of a child is to the intelligence of a mature-minded man. All the future of the plant is, in a sense, present in the germ, all the rich content of the cultured, scientific intellect slumbers in the nature of the infant or the embryo; but the full-grown plant is something more and higher than the seed or germ, and the mind that has awakened to self-consciousness and self-command, and through the mediation of nature, of society, of the history and experience of the race, has entered, in some measure, into actual possession of its original birthright, is something more and higher than the same mind whilst it is as yet nothing more than the blank unconscious possibility of intelligence. Nay, we may go farther and say that, inasmuch as it is of the very essence of intelligence to be conscious of itself, inasmuch as to *know* oneself is truly to *be* oneself, and as that which has not yet entered into my thought is that which for me does not as yet really exist, so it is only that in my nature which has passed out of possibility into actual self-conscious thought, that can be said to be reclaimed from non-entity and to have become a spiritual reality. And this is a principle which is applicable, not merely to human intelligence but to all intelligence; it enters into the very idea of spirit as spirit, and therefore into our idea of the nature of God. If it were possible, by any rude application to the Divine nature of the conditions of time, to think of a time anterior to the creation of the world when as yet the treasures of wisdom and love and goodness of which that world is the revelation, lay hid in God as an unrealised and unrevealed capacity, then it would also be possible to say that there was a time when God was less than He is now, and that the God of creation, providence, and redemption, is greater than the solitary, self-sufficient God, the abstract Infinitude of the eternal past. But if we shrink from applying such coarse conceptions of growth or development to the nature of God, if we must think of the knowledge of God as eternally adequate to the being of God, if He for ever realises Himself in all the infinite riches of His nature, then in the very idea of God is included all that of which a world of finite intelligence is the manifestation; in other words, the true idea of the Infinite is that which contains in it organic relation to the Finite.

Now this idea of the Infinite, if we apprehend its true import, is simply the idea of God as Absolute Spirit. Under no other category than that of Thought or Self-conscious Mind can we conceive of

God as an Infinite who manifests Himself in the differences of the finite world, and in these differences returns upon or realises Himself. It is in Thought or self-consciousness alone that we have a subject which is limited by nothing outside of itself, for here the only limit is a determination that is capable of being wholly retracted into that which it limits or determines. It is only in the Absolute Thought or Self-consciousness that we reach a sphere where the object is one with the subject, where the knower is also the known. In finite thought the being of the object is still posited as something external to the subject, and the knowledge of the object is something distinct from its knowledge of itself. But infinite Thought or Self-consciousness rises finally above this separation; the last element of foreignness, of external limitation or finiteness vanishes; the object becomes a moment of its own being, the knowing, thinking spirit becomes object to itself. All other categories than that of Thought or Self-consciousness are still categories of the finite, and when we endeavour to apprehend God by means of them, we leave in our idea of Him a still unresolved element of finitude. If, for instance, we think of Him as the infinite Substance of all, we must either conceive of Him as that unknown and unknowable substratum which lies behind the finite world, a unity which underlies all differences, but to which these are something external, and thus the predicate of our definition is left in unsolved contradiction to the subject; or we must reduce the finite world—Nature and the human spirit—to the mere evanescent accidents of His being, shadows of that substance which is the only permanent reality. If, again, we think of God as the absolute Cause or Creator of the world, inasmuch as, under this category, either we must think of the cause as having a certain independence or indifference towards the effect, and so as something separate from it, or we must think of it (as in the scientific doctrine of the convertibility of force) as that which wholly passes into and loses itself in the effect; it follows that here again our idea of God is either vitiated by an unresolved element of finitude, or becomes pantheistic. It is only when we think of God as Absolute Spirit or Self-consciousness that we attain to an idea of His nature which, while it gives to the finite the reality of an object ever distinguishable from, never lost in the subject, yet refuses to it any independence or individuality which cannot be brought back to a higher unity. In the light of this idea we see that the world and man have a being and reality of their own, even that highest reality which consists in being that whereby God reveals or manifests Himself; but we see also that their being is no limit to God's infinitude, inasmuch as the highest realisation of that being is found in the absolute surrender of any independent life, in its perfect return to God and atonement with Him. There is no higher creation of God than a spirit that is made in His own image, and in that spirit there is nothing higher than the knowledge and love of God. But what, as we have already seen, the knowledge and love of God mean, is the giving up of all thoughts and feelings that belong to me as a mere individual self, and the identification of my thought and being with that which is above me, yet in me—the Universal or Absolute Self which is not mine or yours, but in which all intelligent beings alike find the realisation and the perfection of their nature. If therefore we think of God as the Creator of man, as calling into being finite spiritual natures distinct from Himself, we see also that it is the very principle and essence of such natures to renounce their finitude, to quell in themselves the self that divides them from God, and to return not into pantheistic absorption, but into living union with Him from whom they came. There is therefore a sense in which we can say that the world of finite intelligencies, though distinct from God, is still, in its ideal nature, one with Him. That which God creates and by which he reveals the hidden treasures of His wisdom and love, is still not foreign to His own infinite life, but one with it. In the knowledge of the minds that know Him, in the self-surrender of the hearts that love Him, it is no paradox to affirm that He knows and loves Himself. As He is the origin and inspiration of every true thought and pure affection, of every experience in which we forget and rise above ourselves, so is He also of all these the end. If in one point of view religion is the work of man, in another it is the work of God. Its true significance is not apprehended till we pass beyond its origin in time and in the experience of a finite spirit, to see in it the revelation of the mind of God Himself. In the language of Scripture—'It is God that worketh in us to will and to do of His good pleasure;' 'All things are of God, who hath reconciled us to Himself.' The history of the world is but the manifestation of 'the eternal purpose which He purposed in Himself,' the consummation to which it advances is that 'God may be all in all,' and the most exalted of religious natures finds its consolation in passing away from the contradictions of the finite, from the enigmas which human life and history present, and in rising to that loftier point of view where they vanish away in the thought of Him, 'of whom and through whom and to whom are all things; to whom be glory for ever.'

# CHAPTER IX.

## THE RELIGIOUS LIFE: RELATION OF MORALITY AND RELIGION.

IN the idea of a spiritual, as distinguished from a merely natural being, is involved the notion not only of self-consciousness but of self-determination. Not what I am or find myself to be by nature, nor what I am made to be by any foreign or external power, constitutes my spiritual life, but that which, by conscious activity and will, I make myself to be. This does not imply that a spiritual nature is one which is absolutely self-created, or that the spiritual life of the individual has no limits or conditions imposed upon it from without. But it does imply that, so long as there is anything within or without—any element of my inner life which is simply and immediately given, and not taken up, transformed, and, so to speak, re-created by the free self-assertion of the rational will, any outward conditions which constitute a limit to my nature, and which have not become the means of its self-development and self-realisation—so long and to that extent I have not attained to the true life of spirit. The life of Nature and of all things and beings that belong to the realm of Nature is a purely immediate or objective life; at best, it is a life which contains only faint foreshadowings of the self-activity that belongs to the realm of spirit. Nature and natural existences neither know themselves nor have any share in the production of their own being. Inorganic substances have an existence that is simply and absolutely given and determined from without. They do not exist for themselves. What they are they are made to be, and the changes they undergo are imposed upon them by external forces which they can neither resist nor modify. In living organisms we have indeed the beginnings of self-activity—of an existence, that is, which is not complete from the first, nor wholly imposed and determined from without. A plant is *causa sui* in a sense in which a stone is not. The germinal matter is not the unresisting slave of external forces. It has an inner law and life of its own, in virtue of which it is not the mere plaything of external conditions, but so relates itself to the world without as to subdue and transform what is external into the materials of its own self-development. Its future is, so to speak, of its own making; the ideal perfection of its nature is a potentiality which is hidden from the first within itself, and which it realises or makes actual by its own self-productive activity. But the self-activity of plant or animal is only, at best, a faint foreshadowing of that free self-development which is the prerogative of the spiritual life. Here, too, we have an existence, the basis and conditions of which are given from without; here, too, we have a life which exists at the first only implicitly or potentially, and the ideal perfection of which is reached only by passing through the stages of a progressive self-development. But, besides other points of difference to which we need not here advert, there is one essential distinction between the spiritual and all inferior kinds of life;—*their* triumph over Nature is itself only natural. The plant or animal maintains and developes itself by the subjugation of external conditions to the law of its being, but it neither knows nor wills its own conquest. Neither the idea of its own future, nor the *nisus* which at each successive stage it puts forth in order to reach that idea, is consciously present to it. Its struggle with Nature is, from this point of view, only the struggle of one blind natural force with other and weaker forces. It is, on the other hand, the essential characteristic of a spiritual self-conscious being that the opposition between itself and the world, and between its empirical and its ideal existence, is a *conscious* opposition, and that the conflict by which it developes itself is not the conflict of one blind force with other blind forces, but the deeper strife of impulse with reason, the inward war with self which is possible only for a nature allied on one side to that which is universal and infinite, on the other controlled by the brute forces of instinct and appetite. In all organic life, indeed, contradiction and conflict are involved. But in the animal organism the contradiction is a comparatively superficial one, and its solution is one which is accomplished tranquilly. The forces of external Nature are at war with and ever striving to break up that unity of differences which the animal nature is. But inasmuch as that unity does not exist for the animal itself, or only reveals itself in the feelings and sensations of the moment, it is, at most, simply in the feeling of physical pain or want that it is itself aware of the strife of which its being is the prize. In the animal organism there is, further, the contradiction which all development implies between the actual and the ideal, the phenomenal and the real; between that which is and that which is to be. But here again the contradiction is one which gives birth to no internal strife. The ideal perfection of the animal is not present to itself, it is an ideal which moulds and dominates its progressive existence in a purely unconscious way. Nature *in it*, as Aristotle says, wills an end of which it knows nothing. The animal feels no bondage in the chain that binds it to the immediate life of appetite and desire. Its whole existence is in each successive impression, each isolated sensation and feeling. It is wholly identical with its impulses, and absorbed in each transient, fragmentary experience. It is never conscious of a self that is more than these—of a higher nature, with claims and aspirations of its own. The animal nature is therefore not divided against itself; its development is not a victory won, inch by inch, by a nobler contending with a meaner self, but is rather an unconscious and unimpeded progress towards an unknown goal. In a spiritual being, on the other hand, the contradiction which development implies is a far deeper one, and no such easy solution of it is possible. It is of the very essence of a self-conscious nature to be divided against itself and to win its perfection, its ideal freedom and harmony, as the result of a fierce and protracted internal strife. The very dawn of self-consciousness is the awakening amidst the natural desires and impulses of a consciousness which is other and larger than these desires, which cannot fulfil itself in them, and which is capable of satisfaction only by breaking away from their bondage and becoming a law to itself. Yet these conflicting elements are both included within the circle of one and the same conscious being—enemies who cannot be at peace and yet can never part. The appetites and impulses of the animal are mine, part and parcel of my nature, elements of it which I can neither annihilate or abjure. And yet, no less mine, or rather *me*, my truer, deeper self, is that spiritual consciousness which is something more and wider, not only than all my sensuous desires and impulses, but than all the experiences of my phenomenal life, and which in the rudest and most undeveloped nature is the silent prophecy and foretaste of a spiritual perfection to which it is ever urged to aspire. Thus the conflict of nature and spirit, of impulse with reason, of the lower with the higher self, is one from which, for a rational, self-conscious being, there is no escape. But it is just through this conflict that its spiritual development is attained. Moral and spiritual perfection does not and cannot come to us by nature, but only as the result of struggle and self-conquest. 'That is not first which is spiritual, but that which is natural, and afterwards that which is spiritual.' It is in the reaction against nature that the higher life of morality and religion is developed. We shall endeavour briefly to trace the steps of the process by which this spiritual development takes place—by which, in other words, man rises out of the life of nature, first into the moral, and then into the religious life.

I. Let us look a little more closely into the nature of that division or discord in man's being, of which morality is the partial, religion the perfect solution. The possibility for man of a moral life lies, I have said, in the fact that there is in him a universal nature, a self which transcends all particular experiences. He can distinguish between himself and his particular feelings, he is conscious that he is more than his desires and passions, that there is in him that which underlies and remains beyond all isolated gratifications of appetite and sense, and which these do not exhaust or fulfil. The merely animal nature has in it no such universal element. Its life is identical with and lost in the successive and isolated experiences of appetite and sense. There is no spiritual link which, for it, binds them together, no self-consciousness that interpenetrates and survives them and can think itself apart from them. The animal passes from one impression or impulse, from one immediate gratification to another, without comparing or comprehending them or bringing them together in any continuous, conscious history. It is without any past whose experiences are treasured up in the present and remain to determine the future. And though you, the observer, can think of its life as a unity, it is a unity of which itself is all unconscious.

If in man there were nothing more than this, he, too, would be capable, in the gratification of his natural tendencies, of a life of happiness undisturbed or disturbed only by outward causes. Or if the rational element in him were only one other natural and spontaneous tendency added to the rest, the harmony of his nature would be still unbroken, he would be only a greater animal, an animal capable of a wider range of enjoyments than other animals. There would be no heterogeneous element to mar the unity and simplicity of his nature or to disturb its serenity and innocence. In point of fact, there is a period in the history both of the individual and of the race when the division between the spiritual and the natural life can scarcely be said to have emerged, when the immediate unity of the natural life is all but unbroken. Such a period we may picture as a time when spontaneous impulse was yet an all-sufficient guide: imagination may dwell fondly on the golden child-dream of a state of innocence yet undisturbed by the fatal boon of knowledge, of a life of unsought happiness in which man, because he was little more than the child of Nature, was in harmony at once with Nature and himself. But the new element of thought, reason, self-consciousness, has this as its distinctive characteristic, that it not only claims a satisfaction different from that of all the natural desires and impulses, but that from its very nature it sets itself in antagonism with them, and can never be at rest till it has subdued and transformed them. That this antagonism is an inevitable one, in other words, that reason is, by an inner necessity, at war with the appetites and desires of our lower nature, may be shown by a brief examination of these two sides or elements of man's nature.

In the first place, the objects of natural desires and impulses are particular and limited, while the end to which reason points is universal and boundless. The appetites and desires look not beyond themselves and their immediate satisfaction. Each particular desire claims to absorb me, looks neither before nor after, seeks to bind me down to the feeling of the moment. In each particular gratification appetite or desire finds its fulfilment; and though the craving of appetite revives again and again, it revives only as another isolated experience, to imprison the subject again in a similar self-included, self-complete satisfaction. On the other hand, whilst the natural tendencies are thus particular and limited, reason is essentially universal. Even in the least developed spiritual nature the consciousness of self, the capacity to say 'I,' 'Me,' 'Mine,' is a consciousness which lifts it above all particular experiences, all passing desires and satisfactions, a consciousness which at once comprehends and transcends them. However poor and imperfect a man's actual intellectual and spiritual attainments, thought or self-consciousness is in him a capacity which no conceivable multiplicity of particular experiences can exhaust, it is the form of an infinite content.

Moreover in this very fact that thought is the form of an infinite content is involved this further contrast with the tendencies of the lower nature, that whilst the latter are self-contained and self-sufficing, thought is the silent prophecy of an ideal which makes satisfaction with the present or the actual (or rather with the present or the actual into which no deeper signification has been infused) for ever impossible. Appetite and desire have no ideal. The cloyed appetite is for the moment perfectly content. Satisfaction is fully adequate to demand. If man's animal desires were the beginning and end of his nature, there would be in him no element of unrest; or at least, rest and peace, the rest of satisfied desire, the peace of browsing cattle, would be within easy reach. But that which makes man a spiritual being makes him also a restless being. Reason is the secret of a divine discontent. Amidst all actual attainments, it is the implicit revelation of a future to which they are immeasurably inadequate, the call to be adequate to an ideal which dwarfs every realised height of knowledge and goodness, and which is perpetually breaking the bonds that appetite and desire would bind around the spirit.

Lastly, to name no other point of contrast, the tendencies of the lower nature seek their ends blindly; reason *knows* its own end or is ever seeking to know it. Appetite and desire grope in the dark, and are content to grasp instinctively at their destined satisfaction. But it is of the very essence of self-consciousness that it comes to see and know the end to which it surrenders itself, to find itself in its objects, to apprehend that by which it is apprehended. Reason, indeed, alike with appetite and desire, has an end or object in union with which it fulfils itself. But the consummated union of appetite and desire with their objects is achieved by a merely outward and natural necessity. The union of reason or self-consciousness with its end is never consummated till it sees and wills itself therein—till the light of truth without flashes back in response to the light of thought within. The relation of spirit to its object is a necessary one, but the necessity in this case is identical with the highest freedom.

Here then we discern some, at least, of the grounds of that internal division or antagonism which marks man's nature as a being at once of sense and spirit, of natural impulse and rational self-consciousness. No man can serve two masters, even when the two are kindred and congenial. But here, bound up together within our very being are two which seem to be essentially antagonistic. A being governed at once by reason and passion would seem to be at one and the same time, blind and seeing, limited and unlimited, fettered and free. To serve both principles, I must be at once the unreflecting creature of each transient impulse and the sharer of a universal life, conscious of an infinite hunger and cloyed with every isolated, shallow satisfaction, living in the light and liberty of the spirit and shut up in the darkness and bondage of sense.

But the discord in man's nature is something more and deeper than this. We cannot represent it simply as the conflict between two independent principles—the universal principle of reason or self-consciousness and the particular tendencies of the lower or animal nature. For, the moment the higher principle of self-consciousness is awakened, the lower tendencies lose their simplicity and become capable of a new and intensified hostility to the higher. To *know* my impulses is to make them more than impulse. To become conscious of natural and spontaneous desires is to transform them into something deeper than desire. The spontaneous life dies the moment I begin to *think* it. Confronted with self-consciousness, the natural tendencies lose their simplicity and innocence. If they continue still to dominate my nature, they assume the new and more complex character of conscious self-indulgence. They draw down into them, so to speak, from the higher nature, a kind of illegitimate universality, and in the strife with reason become armed with a force stolen from the power with which they are at war. Considered in themselves, the appetites and impulses of nature, though they point to different ends from that highest good which, as spiritual beings, we must seek, are not directly hostile to it. In themselves they are devoid of any moral significance. They are no more anti-rational, no more immoral or irreligious, than the forces of Nature or the phenomena of vegetable and animal life. But in a self-conscious being these natural tendencies lose their moral neutrality. They are no longer merely natural tendencies seeking their own ends, but natural tendencies related to a permanent self, and so reduced into forms of its will, modes of its self-manifestation. The merely animal nature is incapable of sensuality or selfishness; for these vices imply a relation of particular desires to a permanent, conscious self. The satisfaction of animal appetite is limited to the moment, it penetrates no deeper than the sensuous nature, and passes away without leaving any reflex influence behind it. But in a self-conscious nature the satisfactions of appetite and desire cannot thus lightly come and go. The thinking self that runs through and gives unity to all man's empirical life, is present to them, knows itself in them, can recall and reflect on them, anticipate and plan for their repetition, and so clothe them with something of its own universal and ideal character. Though, therefore, in itself, sensuous pleasure is as transient a thing in man as in the mere creatures of appetite and sense, it is capable of receiving in his experience an illusory reality, a deceptive show of permanence, and therefore of becoming to reason the rival of its own higher ends. Sensuous pleasure, raised by reflection and imagination to a fictitious universality, is thus an end to the pursuit of which it is possible for a conscious nature to abandon itself. And, though man is infinitely more than any particular desire, though no repetition of sensuous gratifications can ever be commensurate with spiritual aspiration, and the keenest joys of appetite and sense leave the infinite void still unfilled, yet the illusion is one which ever-recurring failure does not serve to dissipate. It was not the mere momentary satisfaction —the thrill of the nerve, the titillation of the palate —which was the object of attraction, but that ideal capacity of delight with which imagination invested transitory objects; and therefore even when the shallow and transient character of these satisfactions has again and again discovered itself, the ideal capacity is attributed to new objects, and remains to fascinate the imagination of the sensualist and to stimulate his will to a renewal of the vain pursuit.

The same remarks apply to those desires and passions, such as avarice and ambition, which are less immediately connected with the sensuous nature. In these the self-conscious nature finds still more easily that fictitious perfection which tempts it to self-abandonment. Wealth, power, fame, as being objects more ideal, more commensurate apparently with man's universal nature, lend themselves more readily to the illusion which draws that nature away from its own ends. If we cannot really serve God and Mammon, yet Mammon, in its seeming permanence and absoluteness, its mastery over time and space, its capacity to represent an unlimited range of enjoyments and to spread itself over the whole compass of human life, is more like the God we seek than those lower objects of desire which perish in the using. And therefore it is possible for man to surrender himself to the passion for gain with an abandonment even more intense and lasting than the purely sensuous desires can ever call forth.

Yet it is obvious that this infusion of a universal meaning into the animal appetites and desires only serves to deepen the discord in man's nature. For what we have now to contemplate is not two elements, a higher and a lower, side by side with each other, but a higher confronted by a lower which usurps its own inalienable rights. Reason has no controversy with the merely animal tendencies as such, any more than with the forces of inorganic nature. But it *is* in conflict with these tendencies when they would absorb man's whole being, and demand that entire surrender of the infinite subjectivity, which is due only to the higher ends of reason itself. As a spiritual being man is conscious of an end which transcends all particular and finite satisfactions, of a life above and beyond them, of being his own end and law. But the secret power of sensuality and kindred vices lies in this, that by the false universality they give to their objects, they seek to possess themselves of man's whole being, to imprison it in the finite, to leave it no higher life beyond. Yet, as man, without ceasing to *be* man and sinking back into the life of the brute, cannot cease to be rational; as the conscious spiritual self, with its indestructible claims and possibilities, can never be extinguished within him, there arises in his nature the terrible discord, the strain and strife of two selves, the higher and truer self of reason and self-consciousness, and the lower self of appetite and passion. The conflict here is no longer the conflict simply of spirit with nature, but of spirit or reason with nature rationalised, with appetite and passion armed with a spurious force of reason. And what lends its special character to this conflict is that the combatants are not two, but one. They cannot fly apart. They are locked up in the same consciousness. The particular and the universal self are both mine. It is *I* who am the self that condemns sensuality and passion; and it is *I* who am, at the same time, the self that is condemned. It is I who abandon myself to the satisfactions of the animal; and it is I who, conscious of an infinite ideal, regard these satisfactions with shame and self-disgust. Nay, inasmuch as consciousness in its unity embraces all that passes within it, it may be said that I am at once the combatants and the conflict and the field that is torn with the strife—the serf who struggles to be free, the tyrant that enslaves him, and the scene of the internecine conflict between them.[1]

How then can this division in man's nature be healed? How can the contradiction between the lower and higher elements be solved? It is the answer to this question which furnishes the key to man's life as a moral and spiritual being. In other words, we have here, as we have already said, the great problem to which morality or the moral life furnishes a partial solution, but which only religion can finally and completely solve.

II. Morality or the moral life may be described as that solution of the contradiction between man's higher and lower nature which is accomplished by the transformation of the lower into the organ or expression of the higher.

Can reason be a law to itself, realise its own universality and freedom, and yet leave to the natural desires scope for their proper activity? Can we live a life which is at once universal and particular? The answer to this question lies in the principle, on the one hand, that the highest realisation of our individual nature with all its tendencies and desires, is to be attained not directly, by making itself its own end, but by absolute surrender to a higher or universal end; and, on the other hand, that

[1] Ich bin nicht Einer der im Kampf Begriffenen, sondern Ich bin beide Kämpfende und der Kampf selbst. Ich bin das Feuer und Wasser, die sich berühren, und die Berührung und Einheit dessen, was sich schlechtin flieht, *etc.*—Hegel, *Phil. der Rel.*, I. 64.

reason or the universal nature, though it is the form of an infinite content, cannot realise itself by abstract self-assertion, but only through the mediation of the particular desires and the acts into which they enter as motives. Now this can be shown to be not merely a fact of experience, but a principle grounded in the necessity of the case, as will be manifest if we consider what the higher or universal life of man is, or in what way it can be realised, and then how it reacts on the tendencies of his lower nature.

That I am capable of a universal life, a life transcending the limits of my own individuality, I learn practically in my relations to other human beings, when I find it possible so to identify myself with them as to make their life my own. The capacity of love and self-sacrifice is the capacity so to escape from the limits of the particular self that the happiness of others shall become my happiness. Morality, or the moral life may be described as the renunciation of the private or exclusive self and the identification of our life with an ever-widening sphere of spiritual life beyond us. That I am more than this self-contained individuality, capable of a larger and fuller life, I realise, in the first place, when my private, personal self expands into a self that is common to all the members of the corporate unity of the family. Here the latent capabilities of love and sympathy are liberated, and the pulse of my spiritual life begins to beat with the movements of an organic life into which many individual lives now enter. We speak of certain duties which the individual has to perform as parent, child, brother, sister; but these duties are based on the fact that it is in and through the relations so designated that the true nature of the individual expresses or realises itself. Then only do I truly perform my duties when they are no longer a law imposed on my will, but a law with which I feel and know myself to be identified. And the same thing is true of the more comprehensive social relations—the relations of the individual to the community, the state, the common brotherhood of humanity. In one sense the members of the social organism in which I live, the institutions, the civil and political organisation of the community to which I belong, are outside and independent of me, and there are certain duties and obligations which they authoritatively impose on me. They constitute a moral order, an external or objective morality, to which I must submit. But, in another sense, they are not foreign to me, they are more truly me than my private self. Apart from them I have no real self, or only the false self of a fragment taking itself for a whole. It is when the moral life of society flows into me that my nature reaches a fuller development; and then only are my social duties adequately fulfilled when they cease to have the aspect of an outward law and pass, in love and self-devotion, into the spontaneity of a second nature.

For one who felt thus, selfish indulgence at the expense of others would be a greater self-denial, a thing fraught with a keener pain than any private suffering; it would be an injury done to a dearer self for the sake of a self he has ceased to care for, nay, which in one sense has ceased to exist. For social morality reaches its ideal purity only then when the individual not merely loves others as himself, but can scarcely be said to have any other or exclusive self to love. Few indeed are they who have realised this absolute merging of the individual in the universal life, but for the nobler spirits who have nearly approximated to it, pain and pleasure are words which almost cease to have any private or personal significance. It is no longer any pleasure to do what they please, and pain and sacrifice have become touched with a new sense of sweetness. There have been times when, by such men, their country's humiliation and loss have been felt with a far keener pang than personal suffering, and for them the offering up of life itself has had a strange sweetness in it, if the sacrifice could avert or retrieve her ruin. Finally, the capacity of a universal life finds its highest realisation when the individual rises above even the organic life of the community or state, to identify himself with the moral life of the race. The higher and more developed the organism, so much the richer and fuller is the life which flows into each individual member of it. If there is an escape from selfish isolation when the individual identifies himself with the larger unity of the family, or again, if his spiritual life is still more expanded and enriched when his happiness is implicated with the welfare and progress of the wider organism of the state,—then most of all will the individual nature become enlarged when the love of kindred and of country expands into an affection yet more comprehensive,—the love of humanity, and the life and happiness of the individual becomes identified with the spiritual life and perfection of the race. It is true indeed that, with most men, moral sympathy loses in intensity what it gains in width, and that, in comparison with the filial, fraternal, and other domestic duties, the obligation of universal philanthropy is but feebly felt. To be personally interested in the moral progress of the race, or in the welfare of men and nations connected with us by no bond save the bond of common humanity would, to many men otherwise good and virtuous, seem but a fantastic cosmopolitanism, at best a humanitarian enthusiasm which only exceptional natures can be expected to feel. Nevertheless it is the indication of a true moral progress when nationality has ceased to be the limit of individual sympathy, when the oppression or degradation of nations however remote begins to appeal to us with a sense of personal injury; or when, as has sometimes happened in modern times, the story of a great act of cruelty or injustice done to a single human soul breaks down for the moment the barrier of national and individual exclusiveness, and evokes from all lands a cry as of pain and indignation for a universal wrong. In such incidents there is a witness to the capacity of a universal life which every human spirit contains, and to the slow advance of mankind towards that ideal of goodness which all Christians have recognised in One who loved all men with a love more intense than the love of kindred and country, and who offered up life itself a sacrifice for the redemption of the world from evil.

And now, having seen that in morality or the moral life there is a realisation of the ideal or universal side of man's nature, let us inquire whether this view throws any light on that contradiction or discord in man's nature of which we have affirmed that morality is at least the partial solution. When I begin to live not for self but for others, does impulse cease to be at war with reason? In rising above my private self into identification with the organic life of the world, or, in plainer terms, in self-devotion to the good of mankind, do I find that my nature is no longer at war with itself? Do I find that reason can be a law to itself, while yet the natural desires and impulses are neither in antagonism with it nor unnaturally suppressed? That we can answer this question in the affirmative—that the life of duty does, and must bring to us self-harmony—is what we must endeavour to show.

Now, in the first place, may it not be said that, here as elsewhere, in that which gives me the consciousness of contradiction or discord there is already contained a virtual solution of it? It is only in beginning to live the higher life that we become aware of the bondage which the lower imposes on us. The selfish instincts betray their existence only in hostility to the unselfish aspirations and affections that are awakening within us. If we were wholly natural—creatures of appetite and impulse, sunk in the bondage of natural necessity—we should never know it *as* a bondage. It is the awakening of the higher life, the dawning consciousness of its claims and possibilities that breaks up the superficial unity and simplicity of the spontaneous life, and creates division and conflict within us. But the very emergence of the contradiction in our consciousness is at the same time the silent prophecy of its solution: the annulling of the difference is involved in the very act which reveals it. For here, as in other cases, that which knows or feels division or discord must be a unity which transcends division or discord. It is only by the latent reference of the opposed elements to a whole which embraces them that we know or feel their opposition. The 'I' which is conscious at once of itself and of the impulses which limit and resist it must be an 'I' which is beyond their difference, a unity which comprehends and annuls it. It is to itself the tacit witness to a whole or harmony of man's nature, which is presupposed in the antagonism of desire and reason, and which is the prophecy of its final reconciliation. As, on the theoretic side of consciousness, the knowledge of an external world in distinction from ourselves, of a not-self in opposition to self, is only possible through a unity of self-consciousness which transcends the distinction; so, on the practical side, the consciousness on the one hand of that blind natural necessity which is the characteristic of our desires and impulses, and on the other hand of a spiritual life which they cramp and limit, is possible only through a self-determination in which necessity and freedom are embraced. In other words, the consciousness of contradiction in my nature is itself the proof of its potential unity. It rests on a deeper consciousness for which the contradiction no longer exists, and which contains the impulse and energy to work out its reconciliation.

But, in the second place, not merely does the moral consciousness, which brings to light the contradiction in man's nature, contain in it the virtual solution of that contradiction; but, further, we can see how, from its very nature, it is a consciousness in which the contradiction or discord vanishes. If morality were attainable only by the suppression or extirpation of one of the antagonistic elements, it would not be the solution but the evasion of the problem which man's nature presents. Now, in the moral life there is indeed an extinction or annulling of the individual, private self, with all its desires and impulses; but it is an extinction or annulling which takes place not by extirpating these desires, but by transmuting them. In the life of love we die to self, or, to express it otherwise, the self as a thing of particular, exclusive inclinations and interests, dies out; but the death is one not of annihilation, but, so to speak, of transmigration. The extinct tendencies are not killed out, but transfigured by the subduing, dominating power of a new and higher principle. If we consider for a moment what the development of a spiritual, self-conscious being means, we shall see that it is a development in which the lower natural tendencies have an indispensable part to play, and that, with all their apparent discordance with the ideal of man's nature, the realisation of that ideal would be impossible without them. The higher self presupposes and rises out of the lower or natural self. In many ways, as we have seen, they are in contradiction with each other; but it is only by the emergence of the contradiction and the annulling of it that the perfection of the higher self is attainable. And that perfection when it is reached, is not the impossible perfection of an abstract spirituality (which is as inconceivable as the notion of affirmation without negation, of a positive pole without a negative), but a perfection in which both elements are at once annulled and preserved—annulled in their isolation or abstraction, preserved in a higher and richer unity.

If we examine the moral and spiritual history of man, we shall find that the attempt has often been made to solve the problem which man's nature presents in a summary way, by ignoring or suppressing one of the seemingly contradictory terms. As a false or subjective idealism evades instead of solving the contradiction which knowledge seems to involve, so an ascetic morality is the endeavour to bring back unity to man's inner life, not by the solution of the antagonism, but by the suppression of one of the conflicting elements. And the mistake is by no means an unnatural one. The possibility of a moral life for man lies in the consciousness of a self that transcends his particular desires. But if we *know* this self by abstracting from our desires, why should not we *realise* it in the same way? If the spiritual self is essentially greater than these lower tendencies, why should it not assert itself independently of them? If it is desire and passion that drag me down from my ideal life, why should I not escape from their thraldom, and seek, apart from them, the realisation of the boundless possibilities which the ideal life contains? It is the conditions which my animal nature imposes on it that thwart and enslave my higher nature; let me fly from these conditions, and shall I not at once be free? Snap the ties that bind me to the satisfactions of the moment, that absorb me in the transient and perishable, and shall not the universal nature gain at a bound its own proper sphere? So thinking, the ascetic, weary with the conflict of the flesh with the spirit, the law in the members with the law in the mind, begins the impossible effort after an abstract spirituality by the suppression of natural desires; so thinking, the mystic dreams, by the silencing of all that binds thought and feeling to the world of sense and sight, to soar at once and immediately into communion with the Infinite.

But the attempt is and ever must be an abortive one, and the reasons of its failure are obvious. We cannot if we would, effect any such violent and forced self-diremption; and if we could, the result would be, not the fulfilment but the extinction of our moral life. To seek perfection in a life without desire and passion is to seek the *ideal* moral life by the destruction or elimination of that which makes *any* moral life possible. Morality is conditioned by the natural tendencies, first, because apart from these, it would not be a reality, but an abstraction; and in the second place, because it presupposes relations created by the natural desires, and of which they furnish the material basis. As to the former point, it is to be considered that to isolate the spiritual from the natural is to attempt to divide elements or factors which can only be ideally distinguished; it is to give independent reality to that which exists only as an element of a concrete whole. An ideal or universal nature, a moral will which has no relation to particular desires is but the blank form of moral life without any positive content or the possibility of acquiring it. Though reason is its own end and law, it is by particular acts that the blank form of rationality receives any actual content. Reason cannot realise itself merely by willing to be rational; it can only do so by willing particular acts that express or come under the form of rationality. But no particular act can be done merely from the general desire to be rational: along with or underlying that general principle, in every act we must seek some special end, be moved by some particular desire, without which the activity of reason would swim in the air. The lower nature is, it is true, the seeming opposite or contradictory of the higher, but it is that very opposition which constitutes it the means to the realisation of the higher. The one is particular, limited, blind; the other has in it the characteristics of universality, freedom, self-determination. But a universality which is simply universal and nothing more is an impossible notion. A real universal is reached only by the opposition of the particular and the negation of that opposition. The higher self, the moral nature, realises its own universality only by the opposition to it of a particular or private self, with its particular impulses and desires, and by the negation or absolute surrender of the latter to the former. So again, a freedom which is only freedom and nothing more, is as unreal and impossible as a lever without a fulcrum, a balance without a counterpoise. The higher self can only realise its moral freedom by the strain or opposition of tendencies which have the character of natural necessity, and by the annulling or absorption of that necessity. The moral will is a law to itself, but it cannot assert itself in and by itself. To know or realise its autonomy it must overcome and infuse its own inherent powers into the blindness and passivity of the natural desires.

In the second place, the moral life, though more and higher than the natural, presupposes relations created by the natural desires and rises out of them as its material basis. A living organism is more than inorganic matter, but the idea or principle of organisation presupposes inorganic matter with its mechanical and chemical conditions and laws, and would be nothing without them. But the matter of which the organism is composed, when taken up into its membered unity, no longer retains its original form, but becomes assimilated, transformed, suffused with the presence and power of a new and higher principle. In like manner, the moral life presupposes the natural life, and could not exist without it. To live a human life at all is to live a life of natural wants, of relations to nature and man, which call forth and are possible only through the mediation of natural appetites and desires. If morality be conceived of as the identification of the individual with the universal life, the surrender of the private to the social self, it implies the existence, as the raw material out of which it is to be wrought, of the individual self and of the various social relations, and therefore of all the natural tendencies out of which these relations rise. But here, too, the lower elements, when taken up into the higher organic unity, are not left as they were. The natural self does not continue to exist in all its original crudeness side by side with the spiritual, as if in separate compartments of a common nature. It still lives, with all its feelings, appetites, desires, passions, *in* the higher self,—not in outward or mechanical combination with it, but transformed into the organ of its spiritual life. The family union through which the individual first realises himself as capable of a life beyond himself, has its external basis in appetites that are common to man with the brute. But the new life which rises out of this union, and of which the merely animal nature is incapable, reacts on the crude material out of which it emerges. Love and self-surrender transfigure appetite into a spiritual affection, and purge it of its baseness. Appetite in a rational nature cannot remain what it was in a merely animal nature. The very capacity of a universal life changes its character. The rational being either sinks lower than the animal, because of the spurious universality which reason lends to nature, or rises infinitely above it by the elevation of the animal tendencies into essential unity with the universal aspirations and ends of reason. The spiritual nature is not mechanically severed from the carnal, any more than the plant from the common earth out of which it rises, but it transfigures the carnal into its own essence as truly as the life of the plant transmutes into fruit and flower the grossness and foulness of the soil from which it springs. And the same thing is true of all the natural desires and passions. The moral life is not a passionless life. Benevolence, patriotism, heroism, philanthropy, are not the unemotional pursuit of abstractions, virtues which live in a vacuum. The noblest moral natures, the men who live most and do most for mankind, are not strangers to feeling, untouched by the desires and passions that move the common heart. On the contrary, their very greatness is often due, in part at least, to the keenness and quickness of their susceptibilities, to the intensity of that original element of impulse and feeling which is the natural basis of their spiritual life. But though neither the sensuous appetites and impulses, nor the wider and more comprehensive desires, such as the love of wealth or honour or power, are extinct passions in the nature that is governed by moral principle —they have lost in it their original character. They are no longer impulses either blindly seeking their own ends or seeking no other or more general end than individual pleasure and satisfaction. The universal nature now seeks its own higher ends through them, and so rationalises and ennobles them. They lose their merely natural character as impulses by relation to the life of the individual viewed as a whole, still more by regarding that whole as an organic part of a wider whole. Wealth, honour, power, and the like objects lose their narrowness and sordidness when sought after only as resources for the advancement of that other and larger self in which our individual self is merged, when they are surrendered to that end or sacrificed for it. They may even be said to undergo a still more subtle transformation when the desires of these and kindred objects are felt only, so to speak, as reflected passions of the larger organic self; when, *e.g.*, the love of power or honour is transmuted into moral ambition for the greatness of country or nation, or better still, when the heart thrills only in response to the advancement, the welfare, the happiness of mankind.

III. In the moral life, then, we find the solution of the contradiction between the natural and spiritual, the actual and ideal, the individual and universal nature of man. But morality is, and from its nature, can be only the partial solution of that contradiction; and its partial or incomplete character may be said, in general, to arise from this, that whilst the end aimed at is the realisation of an infinite ideal, the highest result of morality is only a never-ending approximation to that ideal. It gives us, instead of the infinite, only the endless negation of the finite.

The spiritual life of man, we have said, rests on the fact that reason or self-consciousness is the form of an infinite content, and has in it the never-ceasing impulse to make the actual life adequate to its ideal form. In other words, the spiritual nature of man has in it a potential infinitude in this respect; not that there is nothing which limits it, but that nothing by which it is limited or determined is or can be foreign to itself, and that it is ever finding or realising itself in all things and beings that seem to limit it. As on the theoretical side, thought, whatever it thinks, can never go beyond itself, and ever as it advances in knowledge is only reclaiming the inheritance of which from the beginning it is virtually the heir: so, on the practical side, whatever I will and do for the good of others, I am still and ever willing and doing that which reveals and realises my own true nature. I am not one individual in a world of individuals, having a will of my own which is not theirs, as they have wills which are not mine, so that where my will ends their will begins; but on the contrary, it is in ceasing to have a will of my own—to will only what pertains to my own private, exclusive self, in entering into the life, identifying my will with the will and welfare of others, that I realise my own spiritual nature and become actually what, as possessed of a moral will, I am potentially. All truth is knowable as *my* knowledge, all good willable as *my* will; and in the impossibility of being determined by anything foreign to my own thought and will, of being negated by any thing or being in which I am not at the same time affirmed, lies the infinitude of man's spiritual nature.

But when this has been said, it is only a partial solution of the problem in question which we have gained. Social morality, even at the best; love and self-sacrifice, even if they reached the point of the absolute extinction of any private self-will, are the identification of our individuality, not with an infinite, but only with an indefinitely progressive life, not with the Infinite whole, but with a definite form of its objective realisation. Though the member of an organism may be unlimited in the sense that the other members which seem to limit it are really a part of itself, and that its own life is one with the life of the whole; yet if that whole, if the organism itself be limited, the unlimited or infinite life of the member is only a relative infinitude. The individual, at any period of human history, may identify himself by absolute self-devotion with the life of the family, the state, with the organic life of the world, but that life itself is ever far short of perfection. Beyond the corporate life of mankind there is a wider life of which all nature and history, all finite existences present and future, are the manifestations. Beyond the highest point to which the moral life of our age has attained there is ever a far-off goal which recedes as we advance. There is thus an infinite ideal which neither society, nor the individual who reflects its moral life, has attained—an ideal which it would seem to be man's everlasting destiny to pursue, and which therefore must remain for ever unrealised.

Is there, then, no solution of the contradiction between the ideal and the actual? Is there no way in which man's spiritual nature can become more than the blank form of an infinite content, or in which the impulse to make our life adequate to its ideal can ever be satisfied. We answer, There is such a solution, but in order to reach it we are carried beyond the sphere of morality into that of religion. It may be said to be the essential characteristic of religion as contrasted with morality, that it changes aspiration into fruition, anticipation into realisation; that instead of leaving man in the interminable pursuit of a vanishing ideal, it makes him the actual partaker of a divine or infinite life. Whether we view religion from the human side or the divine—as the surrender of the soul to God, or as the life of God in the soul; as the elevation of the finite to the infinite, or as the realisation of the infinite in the finite—in either aspect, it is of its very essence that the infinite has ceased to be merely a far-off vision of spiritual attainment, an ideal of indefinite future perfection, and has become a present reality. God does not hover before the religious mind as a transcendental object which it may conceive or contemplate, but which, wind itself ever so high, it must feel to be for ever inaccessible. The very first pulsation of the spiritual life, when we rightly apprehend its significance, is the indication that the division between the spirit and its object has vanished, that the ideal has become real, that the finite has reached its goal and become suffused with the presence and life of the Infinite.

But is not the religious life, alike with the moral, a progressive life? Do not imperfection and sin cling to the holiest of men; and even at its highest conceivable point of advancement, must not the finite spirit be still at an immeasurable distance from the Infinite? Is not the attitude of humility, reverence, aspiration, that which is and must be for ever proper to the most exalted finite spirit before God? Is not, therefore, endless approximation to God the only and the highest possible destiny for man?

To this we answer: the religious life is indeed a progressive one, but if we examine what is the nature of religious progress, we shall find that it is in no sense inconsistent with the assertion that religion is the sphere in which the contradiction between the ideal and the actual has vanished, in which the infinite ideal is no longer a for ever distant goal, but a realised end. If a finite nature could reach or realise its ideal only in the way of adding perpetually to the sum of its spiritual attainments, then, indeed, that ideal would be for ever unattainable. Continuous progression could no more bring us nearer to a quantitative infinite than continuous motion could bring us to the end of space, or endless additions of years and millenniums enable us to exhaust eternal duration. But to conceive thus of the religious life and its ideal is simply to substitute for God a metaphysical figment, and for spiritual perfection the solution of an arithmetical puzzle. That the finite can never attain to such an infinity is only to say that the finite can never attain to that which has no other meaning than the negation of the finite. A quantitative infinite, a perfection made up of endless additions of finite magnitude, is a contradiction in terms. There can be no such thing as endless or infinite quantity, for such a notion involves an absolute contradiction. Quantity is always that which is finite and bounded, always that which has an end. What is real in the notion of infinite quantity is only the finite; and the epithet we attach to it does not make it cease to be finite or ended, but only puts the end farther off. It is not the greatness of such an ideal which causes its unattainableness, but simply its incoherence or impossibility. On the other hand, as we have frequently seen, the true infinite, the only infinitude that can pertain to the sphere of spiritual existence, the infinitude of thought, of love, of goodness, is not that which has no element of finitude or determination in it, but that which is determined by nothing external or foreign to itself, that which in the object of thought or love only realises itself or the latent riches of its own being. Now, this is the ideal of religion,—not, therefore, an ideal which is for ever unattainable, because attainable only by interminable progression, but an ideal which, if we may so express it, is eternally realised, and *the attainment or realisation of which constitutes the very meaning and essence of religion.* For religion is the surrender of the finite will to the infinite, the abnegation of all desire, inclination, volition, that pertain to me as this private individual self, the giving up of every aim or activity that points only to my exclusive pleasure or interest, the absolute identification of my will with the will of God. Oneness of mind and will with the Divine mind and will is not the future hope and aim of religion, but its very beginning and birth in the soul. To enter on the religious life is to terminate the struggle between my false self and that higher self which is at once mine and infinitely more than mine, it is to realise the latter as that with which my whole spiritual being is identified, so that 'it is no longer I that live'—not any 'I' that I can claim as my own —'but God that liveth in me.' The ideal of religion, when we thus conceive of it, so far from being, like the false infinite, only the negation of the finite—so far, in other words, from implying the suppression of the finite in order to reach it--is an ideal in reaching and realising which, and only in doing so, does the finite spirit truly realise itself. As it is the very life of thought or intelligence to abandon all opinions and notions that pertain to it merely as the thought of this particular mind, and to let itself be dominated by the absolute thought or intelligence so as to have no other mind than that; so it is the glory and life of the finite will to abnegate all impulse, desire, volition, that is merely its own, and to become the transparent medium and organ of the infinite and absolute will, one with it, indivisible from it. Religion rises above morality in this, that whilst the ideal of morality is only progressively realised, the ideal of religion is realised here and now. In that act which constitutes the beginning of the religious life—call it faith, or trust, or self-surrender, or by whatever name you will—there is involved the identification of the finite with a life which is eternally realised. It is the elevation of the spirit into a region where hope passes into certitude, struggle into conquest, interminable effort and endeavour into peace and rest.

It is true, indeed, that the religious life is progressive: but, understood in the light of the foregoing idea, religious progress is not progress *towards*, but *within* the sphere of the infinite. It is not the vain attempt by endless finite additions or increments to become possessed of infinite wealth, but it is the endeavour, by the constant exercise of spiritual activity, to appropriate that infinite inheritance of which we are already in possession. The whole future of the religious life is given in its beginning, but it is given implicitly, as a principle which has yet to unfold its hidden riches and its all-subduing power. The position of the man who has entered on the religious life is that which pious thought expresses when it speaks of having put off the old man and put on the new, of being dead and having our life hid with Christ in God, of faith being counted for righteousness, of sin being no longer imputed to him who believes. The form of the old or finite life is still present to such an one, the raw material of natural desire and affection is far from being wholly wrought up by the transforming power of the divine principle that is now dominant within; but in so far as it remains unassimilated, it is present as a thing foreign, alien to the true self with which in the inmost spirit of his being he is identified. Evil, error, imperfection do not really belong to him: they are excrescences which have no organic relation to his true nature: they are already virtually, as they will be actually, suppressed and annulled, and in the very process of being annulled they become the means of spiritual progress. Though he is not exempt from temptation and conflict, though the shame and pain of temporary defeat may often mark the strife with evil, these belong but to the vanishing form of his outward and temporal life: in that inner sphere in which his true life lies, the struggle is over, the victory already achieved. Imperfection and finitude remain indeed, and must for ever remain, in this sense that the individual is not the whole, that the member is less than the perfect organism, that the life of God is greater than the life of man. But, in another sense, even that limitation has ceased to exist for him. As the life of the organism is one and indivisible, because the whole life, and not a part or portion of it merely, is present in every member, so it is not a finite but an infinite life which the spirit lives. It is a divine spirit which animates and inspires it. In all its activities it is a divine will that moves it. Every pulse-beat of its life is the expression and realisation of the life of God.

Is there any special form in which the religious life must express itself? Can it claim for itself any outward acts in which its essential character is distinctively embodied? We have seen that it is a life which is ideally or in principle complete from the beginning, and yet that in the outward, phenomenal life it can only express itself in the continuous, never-ending succession of acts of which that life consists. Is there, then, no outward form in which, as distinguished from the finitude and imperfection of our ordinary life, the infinite principle and essence of the religious life can manifest itself? The finite spirit, when it enters into the sphere of religion, has surrendered and annulled its finitude, and has no longer any life save that of absolute oneness with its divine ideal; yet on the other hand, as above said, not only is there in the individual life much which has not yet been subjected to the transforming power of the principle of religion, but that principle can never, under the conditions of the outward and temporal life, fully and adequately realise itself. The ideal unity in which the spirit lives is refracted in the brokenness and disharmony of our daily life, and there is no one act or moment of our ordinary experience in which we can realise and enjoy all that is involved in the consciousness of our oneness with God. The satisfaction and blessedness of the divine life is thus, so far as our common experience goes, ever only a goal to be reached, the result of a process ever renewed and never consummated.

Now it is here that we find the place and function of religious worship. Private devotion, common prayer, the offices, rites, symbolic acts of religious worship are expressions of the religious life in its principle and essence, as a thing realised and complete. In acts of devotion we give manifestation and embodiment to our inward elevation to that unity which lies beyond all differences; we gather up our fragmentary temporal life into its anticipated eternal harmony; we forecast and enjoy amidst the efforts and struggles of time, the sweetness and rest of the blessed life that is to be. It is possible, indeed, to carry the finitude and imperfection of our temporal life into the sphere of devotion, to make prayer only a reflection of our earthly anxieties and wants. But the peculiar significance of prayer lies in this, that therein we rise above ourselves: we leave behind the interests which belong to us as creatures of time; we enter into that sphere in which all the discords and evils of the time world are but deceptive appearances and illusions, or possess no more reality than the passing shadows of clouds that lie here beneath our feet. The world in which we outwardly live is only the unreal and the evanescent making believe to be real; the true, the real, the world of unchangeable and eternal reality, is that in which we pray.

Nay, in the sphere of devotion we may even leave behind the wants of the spiritual life—desires for the communication of spiritual good or the averting of spiritual evil. Prayer and acts of devotion may be, indeed, the vehicle of our immediate spiritual desires, of our penitence, our gratitude, our longings for spiritual strength and help, our aspiration after moral growth and improvement. But even when we pray that evils may cease, it is, if our prayer be the prayer of faith, because in spirit we realise that they have already ceased, because we are in a sphere in which we discern the nothingness of all that is not of God: even when we pray that new blessings may be communicated to us, it is because we realise that already all things are ours. Our prayer for spiritual improvement, for growth in faith, in purity, in knowledge, in love, is efficacious, just because of the deeper conviction on which it rests, and which constitutes the hidden reality of all devotional acts—the breath and life of that sphere into which prayer lifts us—the conviction that we are already perfect, even as our Father in heaven is perfect.

## CHAPTER X.

### RELATION OF THE PHILOSOPHY TO THE HISTORY OF RELIGION.

THE relation of the Philosophy of Religion to its History may be determined by the general consideration that all Philosophy is simply the intelligent study and apprehension of human experience. For this implies, on the one hand, that philosophy neither neglects experience, nor attempts by any *a priori* method to reach truth independently of experience; and on the other hand, that philosophy has a function of its own for which the observation and recording of empirical facts is only preparatory. In religion as elsewhere, philosophy is based on experience, but it is something more than a mere result of empirical induction. It enables us to put intelligent questions to experience, and it furnishes the principles by means of which these questions can be answered. The truth of this statement will be made obvious by looking at the subject from the opposite points of view, first, of experience, and secondly, of philosophy; in other words, by considering what elements are contributed (1) by history to philosophy, and (2) by philosophy to history, in the Philosophy of Religion.

I. There are certain branches of knowledge in the study of which we are independent of the history of the past, others into which a historical element necessarily enters. In some cases the laws which science unfolds are relations of phenomena which are immediately before us, the results which it reaches are generalisations from present observation and experience, and the means of verifying these results are ever ready to our hand. The Astronomical and Chemical student deals with objects the knowledge of which is independent, or all but independent, of the history of their genesis. The order of the material universe does not change, the general properties and relations of material substances remain the same from year to year and from age to age. The successions of phenomena which the physical sciences observe are ever repeating themselves, and there is no need, in order to understand the meaning of what is taking place before us, to go back to the past history of nature. Instead of recurring to the past to help us to interpret the present, in their case it is more true to say that it is our knowledge of the present which enables us to understand the meaning of the past.

It is the knowledge of the laws of nature to which modern science has attained that throws light on the imperfect observations and hypotheses of former times.

There are, however, other departments of knowledge into which, by their very nature, a historical element necessarily enters. Wherever science deals with phenomena which, instead of being constant or ever recurring, are the manifestations of a process of *development*, there it is impossible to understand the present without reference to the past. To attain adequate knowledge we must not merely observe the phenomena before our eyes; we must retrace the whole past history of the object, carefully follow it through all the progressive changes it has undergone, and see that which it is in the light of all that it has been. It is obvious that this is a point of view in which the Biological differ from the Physical and Chemical sciences. When we examine the nature even of an individual organism, a plant or animal, it is not enough to observe the phenomena it exhibits at any one stage of its existence—its form and structure, its various organs, their functions and modes of action, etc. For not only do the phenomena of its past history constitute part of the nature of the plant as well as those which are immediately present to the observer, but the latter cannot be truly observed and understood save in their relation to those prior facts and phenomena by which they are the rigorously conditioned, and it is only by recurring to these that we can detect the deepest fact of all relating to an organism—the law or principle of its development. Again, if we pass from individual organisms to the various species and orders of living beings of which the Biological sciences treat, it cannot be questioned that one of the most fruitful sources of knowledge has been the application to the history of species of the principle of development. Whatever view we may take of the form in which theories of development have been presented by particular writers, we must admit, what all competent naturalists seem to be agreed in asserting, that the doctrine of development has cast a flood of light on many phenomena in vegetable and animal life which formerly were unintelligible (such, *e.g.*, as the existence in almost all animal and vegetable bodies of what are called 'rudimentary organs,' —organs which have no present function and which seem adapted for special purposes which they never fulfil) that it has led scientific Biologists from the mere empiric study of organic forms to the investigation of the active causes of these forms and to the endeavour to trace them back to their origin; and that in many ways it has contributed to that remarkable advance which the natural sciences have in recent years attained.

It is however when we turn from nature to man,

and especially to man considered as a spiritual, self-conscious being, that the principle of development finds its most important application. Of man above all other beings it is true that to know what he is, we must know what he has been. Even as an individual it is impossible to understand his nature by looking at it simply as an object of immediate observation. A spiritual intelligence is not a thing which we can observe or analyse like a piece of metal or a chemical compound. Consciousness is not a mere collection or aggregate of 'faculties' existing side by side, each complete and self-contained, but a membered or organic whole every part of which exists only in and through its relation to the rest, a unity of differences which has developed itself by a necessary process and which has, in the actions and reactions of that process, its very life and being. To know even the individual mind, therefore, you must look not merely to what it is, but to what it has been. You must see how one stage of spiritual development or one form of consciousness rises necessarily out of another, you must retrace through all its course the genetic movement or process which has made the individual intelligence what it is.

But the individual is himself a part or member of a larger whole, and it is only by viewing him in relation to that whole—to the world in which he lives, the social environment which surrounds him, and the history of the race to which he belongs,—that we can ever really understand him. Man in the present is incomprehensible unless we know the process whereby his consciousness of himself and of the world has come to be what it is. The individual mind cannot be studied or understood as if it had grown up in a vacuum. Its consciousness is steeped in the thought and life of the age in which it lives. It is this which constitutes the atmosphere of its intellectual life, the formative principle by which its complexion and character are determined. Even the greatest and most original minds, though they may be the foremost exponents of the spirit of their time, can never isolate themselves from it or be understood independently of it. And that spirit again is no self-originated thing. It is the living result of all the stages through which the thought and culture of the world has passed to become what it is. Every step by which the consciousness of mankind has emerged from the life of nature and from the rudest primitive notions of itself and the world up to its present point of advancement, lives in the present consciousness of the race, transmuted but not annihilated. The form of time has dropped from those intellectual and moral struggles, those events and actions which through successive ages have distilled themselves into great movements of thought; but there is not one of them which, in its vital results, has not been absorbed into the progressive life of the world. In the case, therefore, of any one of those great branches of knowledge which deal, directly or indirectly, with the spiritual life of man —in the study of Language, of Art, of Politics, of Philosophy—it may be maintained that without widening the field of observation beyond the present, and embracing in it what men have been and thought and done in the past, our apprehension of the object of investigation will be superficial and inadequate. Is this true also of Religion?

Now, the question whether and how far the principle of organic development holds good in the province of religion, cannot be fully answered without a detailed inquiry into the history of the various positive religions, and such a task is beyond the limits of the present work. Meantime it may suffice to recur to the fact which has been pointed out in reviewing the proofs of the existence of God, viz., that these proofs are truly interpreted only when they are taken as representing the successive steps of that process in which the human spirit rises above the finite, and in which it is forced onward by the immanent logic of the religious life, from imperfect to gradually higher and more adequate conceptions of the object of religion. In other words, the highest proof of the reality of an idea is that in which reason grasps the inner, genetic nature of its object, enters into the very process of its formation, and so recreates it for thought. When we have thus proved a truth, not by the mediation of other and arbitrarily selected notions, but simply, so to speak, by looking on and following the path which thought takes in its own necessary movement, then the result we reach is grasped with a clearness and certitude which it is impossible to exceed; for this is a process in which the intelligence identifies itself, so to speak, with the very object to be known; or in which the process by which we reach the truth is, at the same time, the proof that it is the truth. Moreover — what we are here specially called to notice—the firmness with which we grasp the result is in proportion to the clearness with which we retrace its genesis, the stages or moments which it presupposes and without which it could not be what it is. Now we have attempted to show in general outline that it is by such a process that our idea of God has been reached, and this is a process in the study of which philosophy necessarily leans on history. The religious experience of the world is, in one point of view, the philosophy of religion ready-made. The speculative criticism of religion is the history of religion rightly understood. To follow intelligently the movement of human thought concerning God and divine things which the successive positive religions represent, is to find a philosophy of religion prepared to our hands. It is true indeed, as we shall immediately see, that history so contemplated contains an element which is more than the series of facts and events which constitutes its outward form. The ultimate origin of religion is not one to which tradition or historic research, however exact and recondite, can penetrate. The development of religion —the way in which the present ever rises out of the past—is a process which cannot be exhibited by a record, however comprehensive and accurate, of the successive phenomena which constitute the religious history of particular nations or races, or of the chronological order in which the various religions have succeeded each other in the general history of the world. But, whatever philosophy may contribute to the explanation of history, it is still on history it rests, its highest function is to follow history and to discern its real significance; and though it may finally translate an evolution in time into a process of thought which transcends time and of which the former is but the outward expression or symbol, it is only by beginning, not with any audacious attempt to spin a philosophy out of subjective thoughts and reasonings, but by an exhaustive study of the data of history, that a true philosophy of religion can be constructed.

It may be objected that, though the highest proof of any idea may be an account of the process by which it has been reached; yet to trace that process, to follow out in their organic connection the successive steps or moments which are latent in our present religious intelligence, does not necessarily imply any recurrence to outward history. We who have reached the present stage of religious thought have all the essential elements of the historic movement in our own consciousness. The microcosm of the individual mind reflects and reproduces in short-hand the whole of that process which has taken place on the grander scale of the world's spiritual history. But though this is true — though, in a sense, the dialectic of history reproduces itself in brief compass in the mind by which its results have been assimilated; yet, it serves to give us a new and wonderful appreciation of these results, when we look back and observe the long struggle, the slow and cyclical movements by which, step by step, they have been gained, and when we study the inner connection and filiation of ideas, not in our own minds merely, but as they are represented on the moving canvas of history. Nor is this all, for as we have seen, the historical method of study is fraught with important practical results. It is by recurring to the *sources* of our individual experience that we find the key to its significance and the corrective of its errors and vagaries. To know ourselves and the content of our spiritual life, we must needs go beyond ourselves. Instead of retiring into our own inner experience to find there the key to the moral and spiritual life of the world, it is nearer the truth to say that without knowing the life of the world we have no key to the meaning of our own. The consciousness of self and of all that self contains is not to be got by mere self-observation or introspection, it is rather the long and ever advancing result of our converse with the world without, and especially with that which is highest in it, the thoughts and actions of men, and the manifold, ever changing life of humanity. It is true that all the knowledge of the objective world which I thus gain is brought back into and becomes the content, of my individual experience. But that is simply because, as a spiritual being, I am more than individual, because the universal nature that is in me can break through the isolation of a merely individual existence, and go forth to find itself,—the objective reflex of its own being,—in that universal thought and reason which moves and lives in nature, in the infinitely diversified interests of human life, and in the progressive history of the race. We may add that the religious ideas which the individual mind works out in the laboratory of its own consciousness *need* the corrective of a wider and more general experience. The basis on which such ideas or convictions rest is not easily distinguishable from individual feeling, opinion, sentiment. They may be only the reflection of the intellectual fashion of a time—of the dominant but transient tone of thought of a particular age or society; and their apparent clearness and certitude may be only the factitious authority which social consent has lent to them. It is when we rise above ourselves and the intellectual or spiritual atmosphere in which we breathe, to live in the light of the universal mind, and to test the movement of our own thought by the surer and more unerring march of an intelligence in which individual aberrations are lost, that we find in the historic movement of thought its own criticism, in the process of reason its own verification.

II. We have seen then, that the history of religions or of the progressive religious experience of mankind constitutes a necessary element of the science of religion; that it is not religion only, but the history of religion which the philosophy of religion has to explain, and that, in one point of view, the history of religion might even be said to be itself the philosophy of religion. But if so much must be credited to experience, what function is left for philosophy? If the contribution of history to philosophy be what we have just represented it to be, what in its turn is the contribution which philosophy renders to history in a philosophy of religion?

It has been implied in what has been said that a true philosophy is not open to the reproach of disdaining experience—of attempting by any *a priori* method to construct a system of religious ideas,—or even of approaching experience with its own presuppositions and forcing the facts which it finds into a ready-made mould. Yet it is easy to exaggerate the place and value of experience; or rather, to put the matter more exactly, it is easy to misconceive what experience really is. To the uncritical mind there is great plausibility in the contrast sometimes drawn between the empirical and the speculative methods. 'Make your mind the mirror of experience, abjure all preconception, take the humble place of the minister and interpreter of nature, and let the facts speak for themselves:'—nothing surely can be more wholesome or unexceptionable than such counsels as these? Why should we attempt to excogitate from our minds a theory of the nature of religion, when we can go to the history of the world and see what religion actually has been? Metaphysical theories and systems are notoriously uncertain, but the solid results of modern research into the religious notions and practices of primitive races, the facts which have been elicited by the recovery and critical examination of the Vedas and other sacred books, by the deciphering of inscriptions and monuments, by the investigations of Comparative Philology, etc., as to the religious beliefs and rites of the ancient nations of the East, and the still more abundant resources accessible to the student of other religions—these fruits of modern inquiry have created a Science of Religions resting on the same sure basis with the other sciences of experience.

In this science there is no place for mere subjective theories and speculations. The humbler but safer function to which scientific investigators in this field have had to restrict themselves is the same as in the other inductive sciences. They have endeavoured to reduce the vast store of facts to some clearly defined groups and classes, and to elicit from a comparative study of the various religions of the world some general principles as to the nature of religious ideas and the conditions of their rise and development. In this way the subject of religion has been transferred from the domain of metaphysical or theological speculation to the sure ground of science.

Now, it is no doubt true that a science of religion must be based on experience, and that we can no more create such a science by *a priori* methods than we can create out of our own consciousness a science of Astronomy or Chemistry or Biology. Nevertheless, in this as in other cases, it is possible to make good the claim of philosophy to be something more than a reproduction of experience or a classification and generalisation of facts. Let us endeavour to see what that 'something more' is.

1. When we are told to 'observe facts,' to make our minds simply 'the mirror of experience,' we must, at least, know in a more or less definite way, what sort of facts we are in search of—what, amidst the manifold varieties of human experience, is *the*

*particular kind of experience* we are to observe. It is not any or every fact or class of facts that are relevant to this special inquiry, and we must start with, at least, so much preliminary knowledge of the object of investigation as will enable us to pronounce whether the facts which present themselves have or have not any bearing upon it. It is not Astronomy or Botany or Physiology — not the phenomena and laws of Nature, which we intend to study, neither is it Art or Politics, or Ethnology or Comparative Philology; it is that special department of human experience, those facts and phenomena of man's nature and life, which, as distinguished from all others, belong to the province of what we call 'Religion.' What then *is* Religion? What do we mean when we speak of a particular attitude of the human spirit and its outward manifestations and expressions as 'religious'? It is not the facts themselves or the history of them which can furnish the answer to these questions; for it is our presupposed knowledge of the answer that lends special interest to the facts. Facts pertaining to other provinces of experience may be in various ways related to this particular subject. The phenomena of Nature, the productions of Art, may have been either themselves the objects of religious worship or inseparably connected with these objects in the mind of the worshipper; the religious sentiment may have expressed itself through the medium of poetic fiction or of mythical personification; but it is not *as* natural phenomena or works of art, or mythological explanations of nature, that the science of religion has to do with them. In order to be contemplated in this special point of view, these and other objects of observation or products of human activity must become related to each other and to our minds as manifestations of that attitude or activity of the human spirit which we term 'Religion.' And to discover what that is, it is not to experience we can betake ourselves, for that which we are in quest of, though indivisible from positive experience, is presupposed in experience and logically prior to it.

It is true indeed, that when we ask what is the general idea or principle of religion, the answer must, in one sense, come from experience; for the general idea of religion is not a thing which has any existence or reality apart from experience. There is no such thing as religion in general apart from all particular or positive religions; it is only in and through particular or positive religious experience that we have come to know anything about religion. But neither, in like manner, is there any such thing as an abstract cause which is no particular cause or force, or an abstract principle of life which exists outside of all particular living beings, or an abstract beauty and morality separate from beautiful objects and from the actions of rational or moral agents. In all these cases the universal, the idea or principle, is not a thing in the air, a metaphysical entity, with an independent being of its own, but it is that which exists and is known in and through the particular or the multiplicity of particulars which express it. On the other hand, there is present in all particular experience an ideal or universal element which is not due to experience, inasmuch as no experience would be possible without it—an element, therefore, which experience itself cannot explain or interpret. It is, for instance, from observation and experiment that we learn what are the sequences and co-existences of phenomena in nature—what particular causes are connected with what particular effects. But the idea or category of causality itself is not given by experience, inasmuch as no science of nature would be possible save on the presupposition that the order of nature is constant, that its sequences are not arbitrary but invariable. When therefore we desire to know what is the nature and significance of that idea which every scientific observation or experiment presupposes—that hidden ideal element which constitutes the impulse to all scientific investigation, and gives to outward experience its reality and rationality—it is not to outward experience itself, nor even to the sciences which record and generalise experience, but to that which is the science of sciences, which deals with those principles of thought on which all science rests, in short, it is to philosophy, that we must have recourse.

In the same way, whilst religion has no existence as a mere abstract notion apart from the positive religions or the religious experience of the world, yet that experience would have no meaning or interest for us *as* religious, but for the fact that, consciously or unconsciously in all our observation of it, the idea of religion is presupposed. Here, as elsewhere, the universal or ideal element does not exist apart from, but realises and expresses itself in the particular. And here, as elsewhere, it is not experience or a so-called science of experience, but philosophy, which is the highest interpreter of experience, that must examine into the nature of that ideal element and determine its import. It is this function of philosophy which in the foregoing pages we have attempted to fulfil. There is involved, as we have seen, in man's spiritual nature a consciousness which goes beyond his consciousness of himself and of things without—an absolute self-consciousness which is the unity of all thought and being. It is of the very essence of man as a spiritual, self-conscious being to transcend the finite, to rise above the world of inner and outer experience, seeing that neither would have any meaning or reality if they did not rest on and imply a consciousness deeper than the consciousness of the individual self, deeper than the consciousness of Nature, a universal Mind or Intelligence which is the *prius* and the unity of both. It is this capacity of transcending the finite, this affinity to that which is universal and Infinite, which constitutes the latent grandeur of man's nature and has been the secret impulse to all that is great and noble in the individual life and in the history of the race. It is this relation to the Infinite which, above all, gives meaning to the outward history of religion. Man's spiritual nature is the form of an infinite content, and morality and religion are the practical, as philosophy is the speculative, effort to realise it. When we contemplate the religious experience of man as the endeavour to make himself one with that Infinite life which his spiritual nature presupposes, to renounce himself and all finite ends, and to become the organ of the Infinite Mind,—or, in briefer terms, when we conceive of religion as the self-surrender of the human spirit to the Divine,—we have the key to the religious experience of mankind. In this idea we find the answer to the question, why we isolate certain facts of human history as belonging to *religious* experience in distinction from all other experiences. It is in recognising them as the progressive manifestations of this idea, the attempts, more or less imperfect, to give expression and realisation to it, that we discern the true significance of the various positive religions as stages in the religious history of the world.

2. It is, then, one function of philosophy to

apprehend and define the fundamental idea of religion, that idea which determines what special phenomena of human experience are relevant to an inquiry into the history of religions. But the colligation of appropriate facts is something far short of a science or philosophy of religion. When that task has been accomplished we are as yet in possession only of the materials out of which such a science is to be constructed. It is the function of science not merely to observe and register facts, but to interpret them—to give them rational significance and systematic coherence and order. What we want to know is not merely the historical fact that the religious principle has at various times and amongst various nations and races manifested itself in certain rites, observances, notions, institutions,—at one time apparently running riot in a mere indiscriminating and arbitrary consecration of material objects; at another expressing itself in a more regulated nature-worship, by offerings, sacrifices, words and acts of adoration addressed to the sun, the moon, the bright heavens, the dawn, the winds and storms; at another, embodying its conception of the Divine, not in the powers of nature, but in a multiplicity of humanised divinities—individualities invested with human qualities and relations, and represented in the idealised forms of Art; or, once more, transcending all material and finite things and beings, and finding its object either in a mysterious essence which is the negation of the finite world, or in a living all-controlling power or personality to whose absolute will the whole finite world is subjected. What we are in search of is not simply these and other facts of man's religious history, but the clue to the spiritual meaning and relations of these facts—some principle by which we can discern why at one time and place religion took this form, at another that; what is the characteristic genius and spirit of each religion, and what is meant by its particular notions and observances. Finally, we ask of a science of religions that it shall enable us to estimate the measure of truth which the various positive religions contain, and to determine what is the place and value of each religion, and its relation to the other religions, not merely as respects the time of its appearance in history, but as respects its inner, ideal character. We ask that it shall tell us whether we are to regard the religious history of the world as a series of accidental phenomena, *i.e.*, of phenomena determined or modified only by external conditions, or whether we are to regard it as the organic evolution of one spiritual principle advancing through definite stages to a predetermined end and goal.

Now it is obvious that, if the 'science of religions' is to meet these demands, it can only be by viewing the materials which history supplies, that is, the facts of the religious experience of man, in the light of the fundamental idea of religion itself. It is this idea which furnishes the only adequate criterion of the value of each religion and the only adequate means of determining the relation of the various religions to each other. Even if the only function of science were the comparison and classification of facts, it would be impossible for it to fulfil this function without some *principle* of comparison and classification. But the only adequate principle is that which carries us beyond accidental resemblances and differences, and enables us to penetrate to the essential nature of the thing itself. Apart from such a principle, the mere outward form of fact may easily mislead us. Superficial resemblances may lead us to connect religions which are essentially different, apparent differences to dissociate those between which there is the closest affinity. A common but inadequate classification, for example, is that by which religions are divided into Monotheistic and Polytheistic. In this classification the various religions are arranged and graduated by the application of a mere numerical criterion to the object of worship. But, from a point of view so external and superficial, we can learn nothing as to the essential relations of religions to each other. It would not be difficult to show that all religions alike are, in one sense, monotheistic, in another, polytheistic—that they ascribe to the object of worship at once unity and plurality. The early religion of India, the religion of Greece, are polytheistic religions. But the most eminent English authority on the Science of Religions has shown that the Gods of the Vedic Pantheon lose, on close examination, their separate individuality, and that each for the time becomes to the mind of the worshipper the representative of all that is Divine. "Each God is felt at the time as supreme and absolute, in spite of the necessary limitation which, to our minds, a plurality of Gods must entail on every single God."[1] Greek polytheism, again, can be understood only by one who looks not merely to the many Gods—'the fair humanities of old religion,' with which the religion of Beauty filled the earth and the heavens—but also to the dark unity of Fate or Necessity hidden behind, yet enthroned above all, and in the presence of which the Gods of Olympus sink into finite and transitory forms. Nor is the mere numerical principle of distinction less fallacious when applied to those religions which are usually classed as monotheistic. The God of Christianity is not a numerical unit. In whatever way we conceive of the doctrine of the Trinity, it forces us to ascribe distinctions to the Divine nature, to include plurality as well as unity in our conception of the Godhead. And even in the abstract monotheism of the Jewish religion the idea of God is not a bare unit; for Jehovah is a Spiritual Being who manifests Himself in a diversity of attri-

[1] Prof. Max Müller's *Hibbert Lectures*, p. 285.

butes or names, and therefore His nature can only be apprehended as that which involves diversity as well as unity.

In contrast with this and other arbitrary and inadequate classifications, the true classification of religions must turn, not on accidental differences, but on those that have reference to the essential idea of religion itself, and to the measure in which that idea is expressed or realised in the various positive religions. In other words, it is the idea of religion which gives us the key to the significance of each of the particular religions and the principle which determines their relative place and worth. For all religions may be regarded as the unconscious effort of the human spirit in various forms to express that elevation above ourselves and the world, that aspiration after and rest in an infinite unity of thought and being, in which the essence of religion has been shown to lie. To distinguish therefore one religion from another, to apprehend their reciprocal relations, to pronounce what religions belong to the same group or class, and whether one religion or group of religions is higher or lower than another, is possible only when, passing by external and arbitrary resemblances and differences, we ask in what manner and to what extent each religion fulfils or realises the fundamental idea of all religion. Moreover it is in the light of this idea, if at all, that we shall be able to perceive whether the various religions of the world and the successive stages in the history of individual religions, rise out of each other, not arbitrarily or in obedience to merely external conditions, but by a natural transition, as the stages of one organic process. For whatever in the history of religion we may ascribe to accident and the force of circumstances, it is only when we approach the facts and phenomena of religion with a clear apprehension of the principle which underlies them that we can hope to discern in their apparently arbitrary succession the steps of a rational order, the inherent, all-dominating activity of an ideal and spiritual development.

III. The view we have now suggested of the relation of the philosophy of religion to its history could not be fully vindicated and elucidated without a detailed examination of the various positive religions. But in order to illustrate what is most important in it, it will be sufficient to take a single example from that silent movement of thought which the researches of modern writers enable us to trace in the successive phenomena of the early religions of India. The religious consciousness which is reflected in the sacred hymns of the Veda is, at first view, a polytheistic Nature-worship. But it is not merely that; for, in the first place, we do not find here, as in Fetishism, a mere arbitrary and indiscrimating ascription of mysterious powers to material objects—an expression of man's craving for spiritual help which is little better than the instinctive grasping of the drowning man at any stick or straw which in his vague terror he can lay hold of. "Fetishism," says Professor Max Müller, "is not a primary form of Religion."[1] The phenomena of

[1] *Hibbert Lectures*, p. 126. Prof. Max Müller controverts the once popular notion that all religion begins with Fetishism; and the above-quoted phrase, as he employs it, means that Fetishism as we find it among barbarous races, is not a low or primitive form of religion, but only the corruption of something higher and better. Barbarism, indeed, is not relapsed civilisation, nor the religion of savages the corruption of a primeval revelation common to all mankind. But Fetishism has in all cases 'its historical and psychological antecedents,' and it is only by the careful study of the latter that Fetishism can be understood. 'The first impulse to religion proceeded from an incipient perception of the infinite pressing upon us through the great phenomena of nature and not from sentiments of surprise or fear called forth by such finite things as shells or bones.' A Fetish can only be a sign or symbol of 'some power previously known, which power was originally distinct from the Fetish, was afterwards believed to reside in it, and in course of time came to be identified with it.' When the Fetish-worshipper calls a stone his God, the important thing is not the piece of matter but the predicate he attaches to it. The idea of God must be in his consciousness before he could call his Fetish divine.

Now, no doubt Fetishism may and does exist as the degenerate form of a purer faith, as the fossilised form of what was once instinct with spiritual life. If Fetish-worship means, as Prof. Max Müller describes it, 'a superstitious veneration for rubbish,' if Fetishes are material objects regarded as the means of procuring benefits or averting evils, irrespectively of any spiritual relation to these objects in the mind of the worshipper, then it must be admitted that there is scarcely any religion in which an element of Fetishism is not to be found. Not even the spiritual purity and elevation of the Christian faith has been able to protect it from the intrusion of this unwholesome taint. But though Fetishism is often the corruption of something better, and is a disease to which all religions are liable, I venture to think that it may exist, and that evidence is not wanting that it has existed, independently,—not indeed as the earliest form of religion, but as something lower than anything that can be called religion. It may be conceded that 'an incipient perception of the infinite' must, in one sense, precede

savage life are equally irrelevant to the religious and to the moral history of mankind. If morality takes its rise in the conflict between the ideal of duty and the life of animal instinct, then we can scarcely say that man, when he is still almost wholly imprisoned in the circle of natural wants and impulses, has yet entered on his career as a moral being. And for the same reason the Fetishist can scarcely be said to have entered into the sphere of religion. The savage has fears, wants, weaknesses, he is conscious of dangers which he cannot avoid, desires which he cannot gratify, a sense of dependence and incapacity, and a longing, blind and instinctive, for help amidst the ever-recurring exigencies of life. But he has not yet awakened to any consciousness of any other life than the life of impulse and desire, he has not risen to

even the savage's veneration for sticks and straws. But the Infinite is in the mind of the savage only in the sense in which all science and art are in the mind of the infant—not, that is, as an object of positive belief or of any attitude of mind that can be called religion, but simply as an undeveloped capacity or possibility. At best, the savage's worship of bones, sticks, straws, &c., implies a knowledge or 'perception of the infinite' in the same way and to the same extent as his attempting to count five on his fingers implies a knowledge of mathematical science, or as his tatooing his face or smearing his person with woad implies a knowledge of the Fine Arts. It is the measure in which this latent or implicit idea of the Infinite is *evolved* in any religion that constitutes its value as religion ; and whatever pure or true religious ideas may in some cases be found to accompany Fetishist observances, if we ask what religious value these observances taken by themselves possess, or what religious knowledge they indicate, the answer, it would seem, can only be that above indicated, viz., that they possess no religious value whatever.

any sense of the vanity and insufficiency of the things that are seen and temporal, and therefore to that need of an object of spiritual reverence, of an unchanging and abiding reality beyond the shows of time, in which religion has its birth. The fetish which he cherishes as the means of gratifying desires or averting dangers and calamities, and on which, when disappointed, he vents his irritation by blows and expressions of impotent anger, or by exchanging it for some other equally arbitrary object, is not, in any true sense of the word, an object of *religious* reverence. It is no medium of elevation above the finite and sensible world, it expresses nothing more than a vague groping after the supernatural, springing from weakness and fear. At best, it indicates only the transient, purposeless rise for one moment into the realm of the invisible, of a being who the next moment quits his hold of it, and sinks back into the world of sense. Wonder and fear may be emotions which precede religion as they precede scientific knowledge, but in themselves they are no nearer approximations to religion than they are to science.

It is an altogether different type of human experience which meets us when we turn to such religions as the early religion of India. If in it the objects on which the religious instinct fastens still belong to Nature, they have at least a special and distinctive character indicating a principle of selection and the rise of a new spiritual consciousness in the mind of the worshipper. It is not any or every object in Nature which the Indian worshipper finds capable of satisfying his spiritual aspirations; what he reverences or adores is something which can be fitly represented only by *some* material objects in preference to others—by the Sun, the Dawn, the daily and nightly Firmament, the fertile Earth, the Element of Fire, the Winds and Storms; above all, by that from which, as comparative philology has shown, all Aryan languages derive their name for the supreme divinity—the bright, all embracing Heavens. The effort to rise above the finite and variable—above human change, imperfection and frailty—the longing for some permanent stay amidst the flux, some boundless and inexhaustible object of trust amidst the narrowness and insufficiency of earthly things, expresses itself here in the worship of an object which has at least a relative permanence and boundlessness. For in the material Heavens we have a presence which, go where we may, is ever above and around us, expanding as we advance, impenetrable in its liquid depths, and amidst the instability and evanescence of human life, pouring down from age to age, with no sign of impoverishment or exhaustion, its wealth of bounty and blessing on the world.

But a polytheistic nature-worship—the worship, that is, of a number of distinct divinities identified with different natural objects, or even of any one of these selected for special reverence—can furnish at best only a very inadequate satisfaction for the religious consciousness. Nature as a whole, the visible universe in its unbroken completeness, may be to the religious aspirations the symbol of that infinite unity after which they are groping, but not that universe broken up into parts. Accordingly we find, especially towards the close of the religious epoch reflected in the Vedic hymns, an effort manifesting itself to correct this inadequacy by breaking down the limits which isolate each of the particular divinities from the rest, and by blending them in one fluent, indivisible whole, of which the particular divinity invoked at any one time is regarded as the type or representative. 'All the rest disappear for the moment from the vision of the poet, and he only who is to fulfil his desires stands in full light before the eyes of the worshipper.' Nay 'the consciousness that all the deities are but different names of one and the same Godhead' is sometimes enunciated in express terms in the Veda. "One poet, for instance, says, 'They call him Indra, Mitra, Varuna, Agni; that which is and is one the wise name in diverse manners.'"[1] The multiform character of the objects of worship thus becomes evanescent, or there is a latent recognition of a unity beneath the multiplicity, of an invisible real-

[1] *Hibbert Lectures*, p. 311.

ity which is neither the Heavens nor the Earth, nor the Sunshine nor the Storm, which cannot be represented by any one of these, but which can be known only as that which transcends them all.

Now this tendency—the inward movement of the religious spirit impelling it to rise above material and visible objects, and to abstract, not merely from particular Nature-powers, but from Nature itself—reaches its full development in the Brahmanic conception of God. Here we find the religious consciousness, dissatisfied with the effort to reach God by the mediation either of the grander objects of Nature or of the finite world in its totality, attempting to pass *beyond* Nature to the idea of an invisible essence or reality transcending all finite and sensible things. 'When the eye has wearied itself with seeing and the ear with hearing and the imagination with the effort to gather up into one vision of material splendour all the scattered glories of the visible world, we feel, we know, that that after which we are seeking is something ineffably greater,'—such is the attitude of mind expressed by Brahmanic thought in utterances like these—"Not by words can we attain unto it, not by the heart, not by the eye. He alone attains to it who exclaims 'It is, It is.' Thus may it be perceived and apprehended in its essence."[1] "A wise man must anni-

[1] Kathaka-Upanishad, quoted by Bunsen, *Gott in der Geschichte*, ii., p. 136.

hilate all objects of sense in his mind, and contemplate continually only the One Existence which is like pure space. Brahma is without dimensions, quality, character or distinction."[1]

There is yet one other step which is needed to complete that movement of thought of which the Indian religions are the expression. The Brahmanic conception of God, like those which preceded it, contains imperfections which gradually disclose themselves, and so create the need for something higher and the impulse to reach it. It is not only a conception in which it is impossible for the spirit of man to find permanent satisfaction, but one which, carried out to its logical results, naturally gives rise to a reaction. It seems, at first sight, difficult to understand how a religion in which the idea of God is reached by rising above all that is finite and sensible, should be associated with a gross polytheistic worship and a fatalistic morality, such as we know to be the prevailing characteristic of Brahmanism. If God be conceived of as the Being which lies behind, and is simply the negation of, the phenomenal world, how shall we account for the seeming deification of almost every object in that world—the heavenly orbs, the material elements, plants, animals, mountains, rivers, the Indus, the Ganges, the Lotus flower, etc.; how shall we account for the unbridled license of a sensuous idolatry which, not content with

[1] Sankara, quoted *ibid.*, p. 138.

actual existences, invents a thousand monstrosities, incongruous and offensive shapes and symbols, as expressions of the Divine? Or again, how should a conception of God which would seem naturally to lead to an ascetic morality and a life of abstraction from the world and the gratifications of sense, have as its practical result a social system in which the grossest impurities are not only permitted, but perpetrated under the sanction of religion? The answer is, that a pantheistic, or rather acosmic, idea of God such as that of Brahmanism not only offers no hindrance to idolatry and immorality, but may be said even to lead to them by a logical necessity. A belief in the unity of God, as we understand that doctrine, is indeed incompatible with the belief in many Gods. A man cannot be a worshipper of the one living and true God of Christianity and at the same time a worshipper of the gods many and lords many of Paganism; nor, again, can he be a sincere believer in the pure and perfect object of Christian worship, and a practiser of gross licentiousness and cruelty. But that is because in Christianity the unity of God is not a pantheistic or abstract unity—the unity, *i.e.*, of a Being who is as closely related to any one finite existence and to any one class of actions as to another. It is true that to Christian thought and feeling the world is full of Deity. Christianity sees God in all things; and there is no object however insignificant, no evanescent aspect of nature, no meanest wayside flower, which does not possess for it a divine meaning and reveal to it a divine presence. Nay, to Christianity we owe also that deeper insight which can discern a soul of goodness even in things evil—a divine purpose and plan beneath the discord of man's passions and the strife and sin of the world. But the Christian deification of the world is not an apotheosis of the world as it is to the outward eye, but of the world as its hidden significance is revealed, of the world as it is seen *sub specie æternitatis;* and this is a world into which reason has infused its own order, in which spiritual intuition has distinguished the apparent from the true, the accidental from the essential, the surface forms and vanishing semblances from the eternal reality. On the other hand, a religion which regards God simply as the unknown and incomprehensible Being or Existence beyond the finite, can take no account of distinctions in the finite. In such a religion all finite things stand in one and the same relation to Him. For a God who is reached by the negation of all finite determination is simply the abstract notion of Being; and all existences, objects, actions, seeing they have this in common that *they are,* bear one and the same relation to Him. No one of them is nearer to Him, no one more remote from Him, than another. Being manifests itself alike in the mean and the great, in the vile, obscene, deformed, and the noble, the pure and the beautiful. It expresses itself equally in the lowest and highest forms of organic life, in reptiles, and beasts of prey, and in the human form divine. Moral distinctions disappear in such a conception of God. He is no nearer to the pure in heart than to the heart which is the haunt of selfish and sensual lusts. The lowest appetites and the loftiest moral aspirations, the grossest cruelties and impurities and the most heroic virtues, are alike consecrated by the presence of Deity. It is this view of the subject which accounts for that indiscriminating consecration of the finite world in its immediate multiplicity of forms and existences which is the characteristic of Brahmanic mythology. And it is this view also which accounts for its defective morality. In a social system based on such a notion of Deity, whatever is, simply *because* it is, is right and divine. We need not wonder therefore to find in it not only the tolerance or sanction of vices which spring from the natural desires, but also of institutions like the system of Caste, involving and perpetuating inequalities the most cruel and unnatural.

But Brahmanism, as we have said, is not the final step in that movement of the religious consciousness which is reflected in the Indian religions. It was only a one-sided expression of its own idea of God, and it led by a necessary impulse of reaction to that phase of religious thought and feeling which is known as Buddhism. Buddhism, in one point of view, is a revolt against the immoral and anti-social results of Brahmanism, the recoil of the aggrieved moral instincts from the cruel inequalities of Caste and the separation of religion from morality. But whatever other influences may have lent force to the new religious movement, it is in the inner logic of religion that we find the true secret of its origin. While both start from a common idea of God, Brahmanism may be described as the false or illegitimate consecration of the finite, Buddhism as the recall of the religious consciousness to that elevation above the finite from which it had fallen away. The idolatry and false morality of Brahmanism was, as we have seen, logically connected with one aspect of its idea of God; but though formally, it was not really true to that idea. When you have begun by saying that no outward material object can represent God, that neither in the heavens above, nor in the earth beneath, nor in all things they contain, even if you combined them in one conception of finite, sensuous greatness, can you find anything that truly expresses Him; when, in other words, you have risen beyond all that is finite in the search after God, and asserted that it is impossible to name or know Him, or to say aught but that He is that which the finite is not,—you cannot legitimately return to rehabilitate the world which you have already denied and renounced. It is not because of what the world is, but of what it is not, that we seek rest in the Infinite. God is not the being, but the non-being of all that is seen and temporal; nay, so little is there in this religion any trace of a positive movement, that we may even represent it as saying simply that God is not-being. So far from religion lending consecration to all finite things, to all natural desires and passions, it teaches us that only by looking on the world and the lust thereof as 'Maya,' as illusion, vanity, deceptive appearance, can we get near to God. So far from saying, 'Whatever is, is right,' and finding in this the sanction of our natural passions, our inhuman customs and traditions, it is truer to say, 'Whatever is, is wrong'; and it is only in emancipation from the thraldom of sense and habit, in ceasing from the thoughts, feelings, desires, that bind us to the finite, in the utter abnegation of ourselves and the world, that we rise into union with the Divine. Only in that emptiness is the Divine fulness hidden.—It is in some such movement of thought that we discern the explanation of that which is at first sight so inexplicable in Buddhism—its conception of God and its morality of negation and renunciation, culminating in that 'Nirvana'—that heaven of nothingness—in which the Buddhist finds the highest destiny and blessedness of man.

And now when we reached the final stage of the movement or process of development which we have traced in the early religions of India, it seems but a poor result we have travelled so far to gain. Has the long struggle of thought with the mystery of the world and human life issued only in the discovery that God is a negation, and blank annihilation the final destiny of man? We answer, that the result is not valueless viewed even in itself, but its real value is seen only when we regard it as a necessary step in the process towards higher things—'a light shining for man in a dark place, till the day dawn and the day star arise in his heart.' It is not valueless in itself, because the very discovery of the nothingness of the world and the illusoriness and inadequacy of its satisfactions is already the implicit revelation of that infinite standard by which we measure them and pronounce them vain. Though all that men seemed as yet to know is that this world can never satisfy, that to yield ourselves up to its passionate desires and hopes, is only to cheat and delude ourselves; yet to know this much implies the latent knowledge of much more. It implies the virtual presence of the idea of an infinite, all-satisfying Good, the prophetic sense of an eternal reality which mocks and throws contempt on the world's illusions, and with which in our deepest being we are really identified. And one who has got so far as this, though he know not what that reality is, is on the way to know it. The movement of thought which constitutes the religious life of man cannot be arrested here any more than at any prior stage of its course. How this implicit revelation became explicit; through what course of inward and outward discipline the human spirit had to pass till the God who revealed Himself within made Himself known in all the riches of His objective reality to the consciousness of man; how from a spiritual life, which was only the negation of self, man has risen to a life in which renunciation of the old self is the realisation of a new and better self, abnegation of the finite life participation in an infinite and eternal life—this is the problem which the scientific student of the history of religions must set himself to solve. The example we have given, however, may suffice for our present purpose—to show that it is only in the light of the idea of religion that the history of religions can be understood.

IV. To the foregoing view of the true function of a science of religions objection may be taken on various grounds. There are many who recoil from the notion of an organic development in religion as seeming to reduce religion to a natural growth, and so to throw doubt on its objective truth. To others there is something offensive in a theory which seems to include under the common designation of 'religion' the superstitions of heathendom and the spiritual faith of Christianity, and to assert an essential relation between the latter and the puerile and degrading conceptions and impure and sanguinary rites of barbarous races, or the fabulous mythologies and the sensuous idolatry of more civilized races. Above all, the idea of an organic development in religion seems to be inconsistent with the character of Christianity as a religion of divine or supernatural origin. If it does not reduce Christianity to the same level with other religions, it at least seems to imply that Christianity is to be regarded as their natural and necessary product —the last and highest, perhaps, of the ethnic religions, but not in its genesis and authority essentially distinct from them.

There are, however, some considerations which may serve to modify the aversion which, on these and similar grounds, many entertain towards the notion of a historic development in religion.

It is, no doubt, true that historic research into the origin of religious beliefs has sometimes been prosecuted in a sceptical or anti-religious spirit, and that in tracing the manifestation of the religious sentiment among primitive races, the covert intention of some writers has been to undermine the objective truth of religion and to reduce it to a mere subjective product of human feeling. By such writers the origin of religion has often been traced, not to what is highest but to what is lowest in human nature. Its ultimate source has been found in the sensuous needs, the timidity and terror, the ignorance and weakness, the craven fear of the supernatural, which are the natural characteristics of barbarous races.

But, in the first place, it is to be considered that much that has been ascribed to the province of religion is really foreign to it. Many facts have been included in the 'natural history of religion' and adduced as illustrating the rise of 'the religious sentiment,' which have really no relation to religion at all. Thus, as has been already pointed out, the phenomena of savage life have no more bearing on the origin of religion than on the origin of science or philosophy or art. But even if religion be so defined as to embrace some of these phenomena, it is to be considered that, in this as in other cases, the real value of a thing is determined, not by its empirical origin or by the accidents of its outward history, but by its own inherent nature. The criterion by which we judge of the worth of that which has grown from less to more is not, how it arose, but *what it is*—not what external conditions have contributed to its rise and progress, but what it has actually become. Reason and thought in man are what they are, even though it were proved that the rational has slowly emerged out of the animal nature; nor does mind or intelligence in man become other than it is, whether we think of him as made 'out of nothing,' or out of 'the dust of the earth,' or as developed by infinitesimal transitions out of 'the anthropoid ape.' So again, it is not by looking back to the origin of science or philosophy that we determine their value in the scale of human possessions. It may be possible to show that Astronomy grew out of Astrology, that modern Chemistry owes much to Alchemy; but the inherent worth of either of these sciences is not discredited by the fact that its history includes a stage when men believed in planetary influences, or expended their thought and toil on the transmutation of metals and the search for the philosopher's stone. In like manner, the essential character and worth of religion, the idea of God which Christianity reveals, the purity and elevation of its moral teaching, the exalted hopes and aspirations which it cherishes within us, remain the same, even if it could be shown that, historically, what is called 'the religious sentiment' can be traced back to a beginning much more ignoble than we believe its true beginning to have been. The real ground for humiliation is not in the fetishism out of which religion is said to have sprung, or in the childish superstitions and irrational observances that have been the accidents of its history, but rather in the element of fetishism and unreason that often still clings to it, in the admixture of vulgar magic which still deforms its worship and in the remains of meaningless and irrational dogma which still corrupt its faith.

Those writers who think to explain, or rather to explain away, religion, by tracing it back to its supposed empirical origin—who conceive themselves, for instance, to have proved, by historic evidence, that religion is ultimately a product of fear, or abject dependence, or kindred feelings—overlook the distinction between the historical beginning of a thing and its essential principle, or origin in thought. In all organic existence 'origin' has a double meaning. It may mean commencement in time, the immediate phenomenal fact of beginning or birth; or it may mean the ideal principle, the conception, or essential notion which is embodied in the phenomenal form. It is, however, not the former, but the latter, in which the true origin—the ultimate or final cause—of the thing is to be sought. The beginning of a piece of mechanism or a work of art is the first stroke of the chisel, or the first line which the pencil inscribes on the canvas. But the real origin is prior to that,—in the idea or conception of the whole, in the creative ideal of the perfect work, which determines its outward commencement, and regulates its whole subsequent progress. The true origin of the plant is not the first stirring of vital activity and interaction in the seed or germ; it is that which dominates and determines the outward phenomenal beginning, to wit, the essential idea or principle of the thing, by reason of which this particle of matter acts differently from all other particles—the potentiality in virtue of which one piece of matter developes into wheat or oats, another into fruit or flower, a third into oak or elm. In such cases, there is a sense in which the end is the real beginning; and if we are to seek anywhere for the true origin of the thing, it is not in the factual commencement, but in the final result—in that perfected development towards which, all through its course, it was tending, and which was silently dominating the beginning and every successive stage of its outward history. In like manner, whatever be the form of human experience from which we date the historical beginning of religion, it is not in it that we must look for the true origin and explanation of it. When naturalistic theorists go back to ransack the earliest traditions of primitive races, and having lighted on some obscure facts—such as the ascription of mysterious virtues to material objects, or the rude attempts to propitiate invisible powers by sacrifice—forthwith triumphantly point to these and similar phenomena as the real origin, the parent source of all religions, the discovery is only an imaginary one. In religion it is not to the beginning, but to the end that we must look for the true origin and explanation of its history. The earliest religious phenomena may contain in them the promise and potentiality of the religious future of the world; but it is so only because, and in so far as, the power of the highest or perfect religion is already working in them, shaping them for itself, and so showing itself to be their real source and origin.

Nor, finally, is there anything in the idea of organic development, rightly viewed, which derogates from the claim of Christianity to be a religion of divine or supernatural origin. It is not the interest of the apologist for Christianity to sever it from all connection with the religious thought and culture of the pre-Christian ages. That is only a narrow and unreflecting piety which makes light of those anticipations or presentiments of Christian truth which are to be found in the earlier religions, or which regards every recognition of a true spiritual element in these religions as obscuring the claim of Christianity to be regarded as a revelation from heaven. We do not pay any real homage to the supernatural by disconnecting it as much as possible from the natural and human; we render only a spurious tribute to the divine Author of revelation by supposing that all that through the long lapse of ages men had believed concerning Him was error and falsehood, and that the religious ideas of the past must be wiped clean out of the human spirit in order that a new message from heaven might be written upon it by the finger of God. On the contrary, if Christianity finds its highest evidence in the response which its truths awaken in the spiritual intelligence; if its divine power is shown, above all, in this, that it has moulded the spiritual life of the world, not mechanically and as by mere outward force, but by the inward transfusion of its ideas and principles into all the springs of human thought and action; then it is impossible that Christianity could have been out of essential relation to the spiritual consciousness of the world and to the discipline of ages which had made that consciousness what it was. So obvious is this that the Christian apologist in our day usually finds one of his strongest arguments for the divine origin of Christianity in the fact that it meets 'the unconscious longings of heathendom.' It is now one of the recognised lines of apologetic thought to trace anticipations of Christian doctrine in the pre-Christian religions, and to point out the guesses at truth, the foreshadowings of moral and spiritual ideas, which, under many errors and superstitions, can be detected in the sacred books of India and China and Persia, and in general, in the religious notions, rites, observances, institutions, of the heathen world. Writers on this subject urge with much force that, pure, unmixed error is incapable of exerting any permanent influence over the mind of man, that religions which contained in them nothing but falsehood or which appealed only to the baser tendencies of human nature, would have been destitute of vitality; and therefore that that to which the great religions of antiquity owed their wide and lasting success must have been the element of truth that was in them. As even base money, to pass current, must have some resemblance to genuine coin or some admixture of good metal in it, so in religions which have spread far and wide and held their place for ages in the world's belief, we must be able to detect, as the secret of their power, some element common to them with that which we regard as the true religion. Further, all Christian apologists recognise in Judaism the prophecy and anticipation of Christian truth, and draw from the historical relations of the two religions one of the strongest arguments for the divine origin of Christianity. But the argument does not suffer, but only gains fresh force, if it can be shown that the highest thought and life, not simply of one isolated and outwardly insignificant nation, but of all the races and nations of the ancient world, constituted a preparation for it, that the whole order of human history in the pre-Christian ages pointed to Christ, and that He was, in this sense, 'the desire of all nations.'

The same argument is sometimes presented, in a slightly modified form, by writers who find an evidence for the divine origin of Christianity in the fact that Christ appeared "in the fulness of the times." A divine design, it is held, can be traced in the selection of the period at which the Christian revelation was given to the world.

There was then a remarkable coincidence of conditions favourable to the reception and rapid diffusion of the new religion; and amongst these, special stress is laid on the fact that the nations of the world had then become united under the universal dominion ot Rome, and that the facilities afforded by a universal external polity for the introduction of a universal religion were greatly increased by the general diffusion of Greek language and culture.

The principle upon which such arguments are based is, it must be admitted, a somewhat superficial one. It is not a very elevated idea of Providence which represents it as busying itself in providing facilities of travel and of rapid and safe intercommunication for the messengers of the Gospel. At any rate, if a divine interposition is to be inferred from such external arrangements, as a preparation for Christianity, it is surely a not less reverential view of the subject which leads us to trace a deeper preparation in the movements of men's minds, in the convergence of manifold spiritual tendencies, and in the gradual discipline of the human consciousness for the reception of the universal religion. If external facilities of communication infer divine intervention, is the inference less cogent when we see in the moulding of men's minds, in the progressive religious experience of mankind, in the gradual formation of their ideas and the awakening and development of their aspirations, a divinely-prepared way of access for the teachers of Christianity to the spirit of the waiting world?

The class of writers to whom we have referred do not, indeed, altogether ignore conditions of a somewhat less external character, in the providential preparation of the world for Christianity. The time, they argue, was propitious to Christianity in this respect also, that the old religions had become effete, and that mankind were yearning for something better. These religions had proved themselves abortive attempts to solve the problem of man's spiritual needs, and so had cleared the way for the announcement of the true solution. There had been a time when the Pagan mythologies were the expression of a real belief, instinct with the warmth and vitality of genuine, though mistaken spiritual convictions. But the mind of man had outgrown them. The intellectual and spiritual life of the civilised world had passed away from the popular religions, and whatever vitality it still manifested lay not in the sphere of religion but of philosophy. Even amongst the uneducated mass the worship of the old gods had dried up into a superstitious form from which the life had vanished. Amongst the Hebrew race only, there still survived a passionate devotion to that ancient faith which, both in its origin and content, far transcended the highest of the ethnic religions; but even the religion of the Hebrew was affected by the universal blight which had fallen on the spiritual life of man. Of its lofty monotheism little more remained than the husk of elaborate ceremonial in which it had been enshrined; its essential opposition to the beliefs of the heathen world survived only in the form of a fierce and fanatical exclusiveness, fed by wild hopes of national conquest and dominion. Hence Christianity appeared, it is said, at the moment when the old religions were played out, and the stage was cleared for the entrance of a new faith.

But it needs little reflection to see that in this representation of the relation of Christianity to the pre-Christian religions there is, at best, only half of the truth. It is a conception of the divine order of the world not less shallow than irreverent, which regards the religious experience of the pre-Christian ages only in the light of an abortive experiment, and represents uncounted generations of the human race as having been utilised by Providence merely to prove man's spiritual incapacity and ineptitude. A less ruthless method might surely have sufficed to bring out the proof that man can do nought but err till a *deus ex machinâ* comes down to set him right. Moreover the negative preparation which is all that this argument asserts, cannot be conceived of as *merely* negative. The very negation of the old involves an implicit affirmation of the new element which is to supplant it. When the former heavens and earth are 'ready to vanish away,' it can only be because there is already hovering before men's minds at least a dream of a 'new heavens and earth wherein dwelleth righteousness.' Forms and institutions in which the spiritual life of man had once clothed itself never die from mere exhaustion. If they betray signs of dissolution, it is because the thought and life they embodied have begun to pass beyond them, and are already feeling their way, with a certain prophetic consciousness of its nature, after something higher that is near at hand. The decaying and dying institutions have themselves educated the spirit of man up to the discovery of their own imperfection. It is the new wine which has burst the old bottles. Thus the decay of the old religions was not a mere process of negation, but one wrought by the hidden, implicit energy of the higher truth that was yet to be. The cheerless scepticism which had crept over men's minds and loosened the hold of former beliefs on their hearts, was already, in some measure, the unconscious expression of that higher unborn faith for which these old beliefs had prepared them, and a proof of their organic relation to it. On the other hand, in superseding the old religions, the new religion proved its relation to them. In destroying them it showed that it comprehended them — that its own profounder truth satisfied the spiritual needs which they had awakened, and reproduced in a higher form all the elements of truth which had been imperfectly expressed in them.

What, however, we are here specially concerned to notice is that the idea of organic development is in no way inconsistent with the claim of Christianity to be regarded as a religion of supernatural or divine origin. There would be some reason for the recoil of Christian feeling from this idea if it implied that there is nothing more in Christianity than a combination of pre-existing elements, or that its originality consists simply in the reproduction, in a collective form, of ideas contained in the religions and in the philosophical and ethical systems of the ancient world. No divine revelation would be needed to communicate to the world truths of which its higher minds were already in possession; and those who regard Christianity as a divine revelation are naturally alarmed at any theory which seems to represent the teaching of Christ and his apostles, if not as a plagiarism from other sources, as, at most, the natural outgrowth of heathen and Jewish thought.

But such a view of the origin of Christianity is not more historically improbable than it is inconsistent with a true idea of organic development. In whatever way we conceive of the revelation to the human consciousness of the new and original element in Christianity, the principle of development, so far from excluding such an element, would have no meaning without it. It is absolutely antagonistic to any such notion as that Christian doctrine is a mere compound of Greek, Oriental, and Jewish ingredients. However externally originated or conditioned, the appearance of Christianity in the world implies a new spiritual movement, an advance or elevation of the human spirit, which, though it does not obliterate, transcends all the results of its past history. To apply the idea of development to human history is by no means to find in the old the mechanical or efficient cause of the new. For in organic development the new, though presupposing the old, involves the introduction of a wholly original element, not given in the old. Hence we are not to conceive that Christianity could be elaborated out of pre-Christian religions and philosophies, any more than that life could be elaborated out of inorganic matter. To apply this principle to religion is to assert a relation between Christianity and the earlier stages of man's spiritual history; indeed, unless we suppose the human race to have been annihilated and a new race, out of all connection or continuity with the former, to have been created as the receptacle of the new religion —without some such monstrous supposition, we must think of Christianity as essentially related to the antecedent course of man's spiritual life, and related to it in the way which rational spiritual life, by its very nature, involves. But the connection of Christianity with the past, which we here assert, is a connection which at the same time involves the annulling and transmuting of the past by a new creative spiritual force. To assert it, therefore, is to hold that Christianity neither borrows nor reproduces the imperfect notions of God, be they what they may—pantheistic, dualistic, anthropomorphic, monotheistic—in which the religious aspirations of the old world had embodied themselves. In the light of this idea we can perceive these imperfect notions yielding up, under the transforming influence of Christianity, whatever element of truth lay hid in them, whilst that which was arbitrary and false falls away and dies. If, for example, the old Pantheistic idea that 'the things that are seen are temporal,' and that beneath all the passing shadows and semblances of things there is an enduring substance, a reality that is 'without variableness or shadow of turning'—if this idea comes to life again in the Christian consciousness, yet the new Pantheism does not, like the old, suppress, but rather elicits and quickens the individuality, the freedom, the moral life of man. If it says, 'The world passeth away and the lust thereof,' it says also, 'He that doeth the will of God abideth for ever.' If the antagonism between good and evil which gave Dualism its meaning and power survives in the Christian view of the world, yet the new Dualism, unlike that of the old religion, is consistent with the belief, not only in the ultimate triumph, but in the sole and absolute reality of good. If it asserts that 'sin hath entered into the world, and death by sin,' yet it declares that 'all things are of God,' that 'all things work together for good to them that love Him,' and that a time is coming when 'God shall be all in all.' If Christianity claims as its own that idea which Anthropomorphic religions foreshadowed—that man is the image of God, and that he is capable of rising into a Divine fellowship and of being made 'partaker of a Divine nature,' yet, in contrast with the old religions, it raises the human without limiting or lowering the Divine, and sees in all earthly goodness a reflexion of the nature of God without making the nature of God a reflexion of the weakness and imperfections of man. Lastly, if Christianity contains, in common with Monotheistic religions, the idea of a God elevated in His absolute being above the world, unaffected by its limits, incapable of being implicated in its imperfections, it yet enables us at the same time to think of God, not merely as an Omnipotent Power and Will above us, but as an Infinite Love within us. It sees in our purest thoughts and holiest actions God Himself 'working in us to will and to do of His good pleasure.' It tells us that 'our bodies are the temples of His Holy Spirit;' and it sets before us a human life as the fullest expression and revelation of the nature and life of God. Thus, whatever elements of truth, whatever broken and scattered rays of light the old religions contained, Christianity takes up into itself, explaining all, harmonising all, by a divine alchemy transmuting all, yet immeasurably transcending all—'gathering together in one all things in heaven and earth' in its 'revelation of the mystery hid from ages,' the revelation of One who is at one and the same time Father, Son and Spirit; above all, through all, and in all.

THE END.